The Passion of the Keef

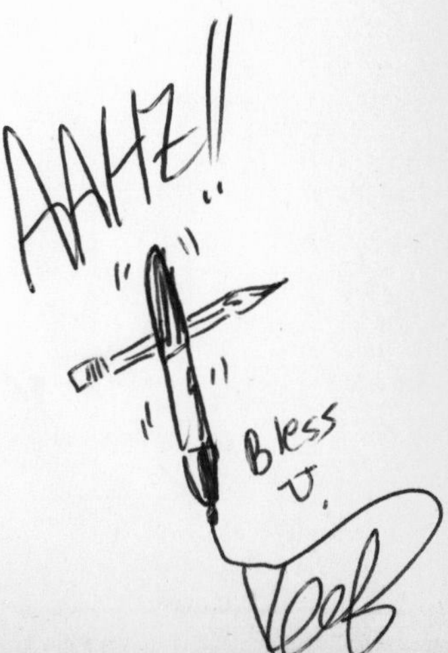
AAHZ!!
Bless U.
Keef

The Fourth **K** Chronicles compendium

The Passion

cartoons by

Keith Knight

foreword by Aaron McGruder

of the Keef

Manic D Press
San Francisco

Dedicated:

To the woman who dared to
tame these wild loins.
Kerstin Konietzka-Knight...
Oh how I love thee...

Acknowledgments:

Thanks to Jennifer, Pete, & Lisa for coming back again & again & again; Mr. McGruder for the spiffy foreword; all the publications that continue to run the strip; to all my faithful readers (keep sending those tips and little victories!!); Mr. Gidley, my "official fanboy"; my friends and former roommates for not suing; and most of all, thanks to my incredibly diverse and continually expanding family, now reaching as far as the Black Forest in Germany...I love you all!!

The Passion of the Keef: the fourth K Chronicles Compendium ©2005 by Keith Knight. All rights reserved. Published by Manic D Press. No part of this book maybe used or reproduced in any manner whatsoever without written permission from author or publisher except in the case of brief quotations embodied in critical articles or reviews. For information, address Manic D Press, Box 410804, San Francisco, California 94141. **www.manicdpress.com**

ISBN 0-916397-67-X

Book design: Lisa Beres

Printed in the United States of America

Send cheers and little victories to:
Keith Knight P.O. Box 591794 San Francisco, Ca. 94159-1794
keef@kchronicles.com
www.kchronicles.com

the foreword courtesy of aaron mcgruder.

Also by Keith Knight:
Dances with Sheep: A K Chronicles Compendium
Fear of A Black Marker: Another K Chronicles Compendium
What a Long, Strange Strip It?s Been: Yet Another K Chronicles Compendium
Red, White, Black and Blue: A (th)ink Anthology

AND NOW... A MESSAGE FROM GOD

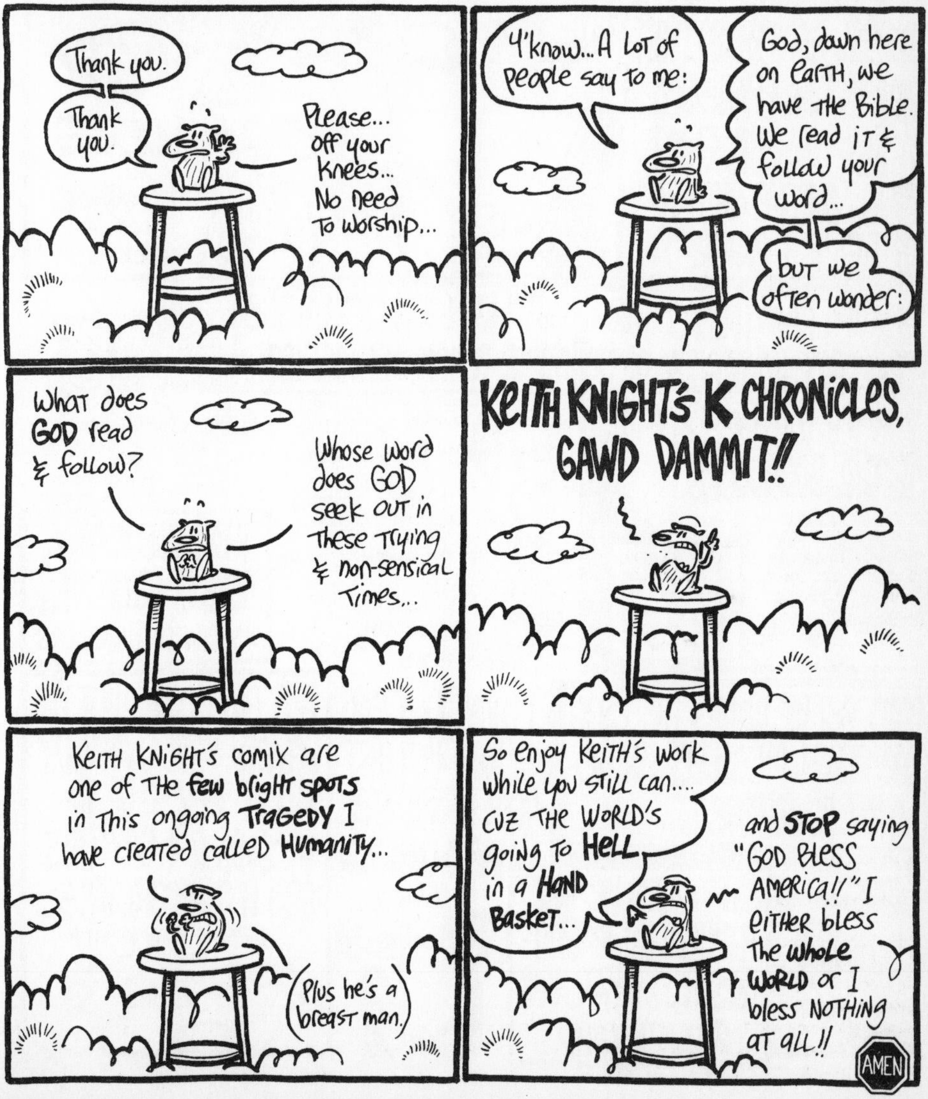
Thank you.
Thank you.
Please... off your knees... No need to worship...
Y'know... A lot of people say to me:
God, down here on Earth, we have the Bible. We read it & follow your word...
but we often wonder:
What does GOD read & follow?
Whose word does GOD seek out in these trying & non-sensical times...
KEITH KNIGHT'S K CHRONICLES, GAWD DAMMIT!!
Keith Knight's comix are one of the few bright spots in this ongoing tragedy I have created called Humanity...
(Plus he's a breast man.)
So enjoy Keith's work while you still can.... Cuz the world's going to HELL in a HAND BASKET...
and STOP saying "GOD BLESS AMERICA!!" I either bless the WHOLE WORLD or I bless NOTHING at all!!
AMEN

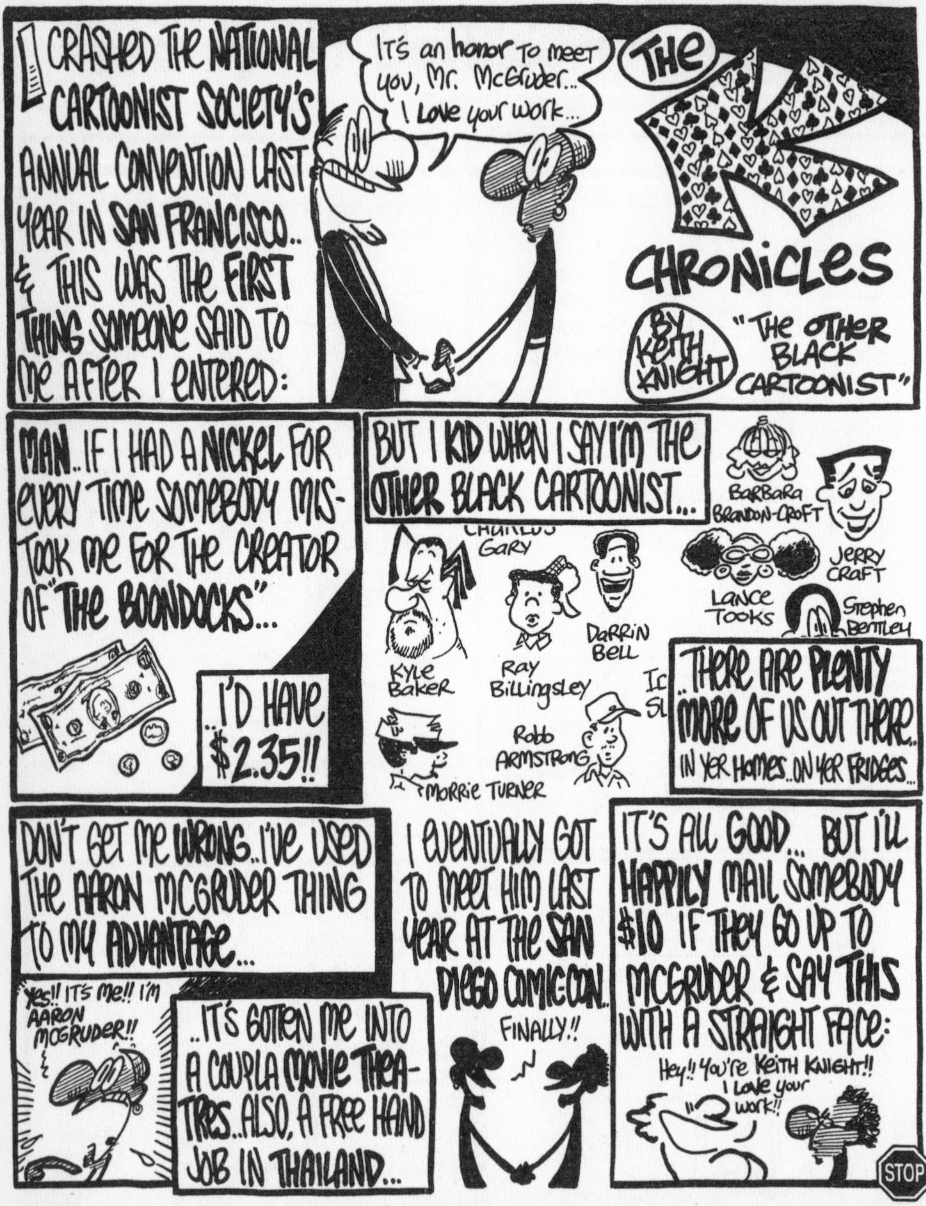
I CRASHED THE NATIONAL CARTOONIST SOCIETY'S ANNUAL CONVENTION LAST YEAR IN SAN FRANCISCO.. & THIS WAS THE FIRST THING SOMEONE SAID TO ME AFTER I ENTERED:
It's an honor to meet you, Mr. McGruder... I love your work...
THE K CHRONICLES
BY KEITH KNIGHT
"THE OTHER BLACK CARTOONIST"
MAN.. IF I HAD A NICKEL FOR EVERY TIME SOMEBODY MIS-TOOK ME FOR THE CREATOR OF "THE BOONDOCKS"...
..I'D HAVE $2.35!!
BUT I KID WHEN I SAY I'M THE OTHER BLACK CARTOONIST...
BARBARA BRANDON-CROFT
Gary
JERRY CRAFT
LANCE TOOKS
STEPHEN BENTLEY
DARRIN BELL
KYLE BAKER
RAY BILLINGSLEY
ROBB ARMSTRONG
MORRIE TURNER
..THERE ARE PLENTY MORE OF US OUT THERE..
IN YER HOMES..ON YER FRIDGES...
DON'T GET ME WRONG..I'VE USED THE AARON MCGRUDER THING TO MY ADVANTAGE...
YES!! IT'S ME!! I'M AARON MCGRUDER!!
..IT'S GOTTEN ME INTO A COUPLA MOVIE THEATRES..ALSO, A FREE HAND JOB IN THAILAND...
I EVENTUALLY GOT TO MEET HIM LAST YEAR AT THE SAN DIEGO COMIC-CON..
FINALLY!!
IT'S ALL GOOD... BUT I'LL HAPPILY MAIL SOMEBODY $10 IF THEY GO UP TO MCGRUDER & SAY THIS WITH A STRAIGHT FACE:
Hey!! You're KEITH KNIGHT!! I Love your work!!
STOP

I'm happily hatin' on Keith Knight.

I first discovered Keith years ago — I think it was in that limbo period between when The Boondocks got signed but before it came out, when I would just hang around in Borders and think how cool it was going to be to be the smartest, hippest, coolest black cartoonist out. Then I wandered over to the comics section and saw "Fear of a Black Marker". Keith was already cooler than me for three reasons: **1) He had a book. 2) There was some gushing comments in the book by Garry Trudeau. 3) He had successfully flipped a Public Enemy song title.** Damn, and I almost had this "cool young black cartoonist thing" all to myself.

It was time to hate.

When I actually opened the book, I was amazed not only how funny the strip was, but how different it was. Different than anything I had ever seen. It was so dense, but fluid and energetic and wild. And it was very, very smart, and very, very funny.

I still hate on Keith. But it's a **good** hate. It's the "Damn I wish I had thought of that joke but I'm not as crazy as that nigga so oh well" kinda hate. It's the kind of petty, small, jealous hate that let's you know the person your hating is doing something right, and that you're doing something very wrong. Hating, for me, is like a coping mechanism. **It's crutch, yes ... but a dependable one.**

And let's hope he decides to do a daily strip, 'cause it would be fun to hate on Keith every single day, wouldn't it?

And so, in closing, I say this to Keith,
Keith, I hope this all comes crashing down around you. **Bastard.**

Hatefully yours,

Aaron McGruder
(The Other Black Cartoonist)

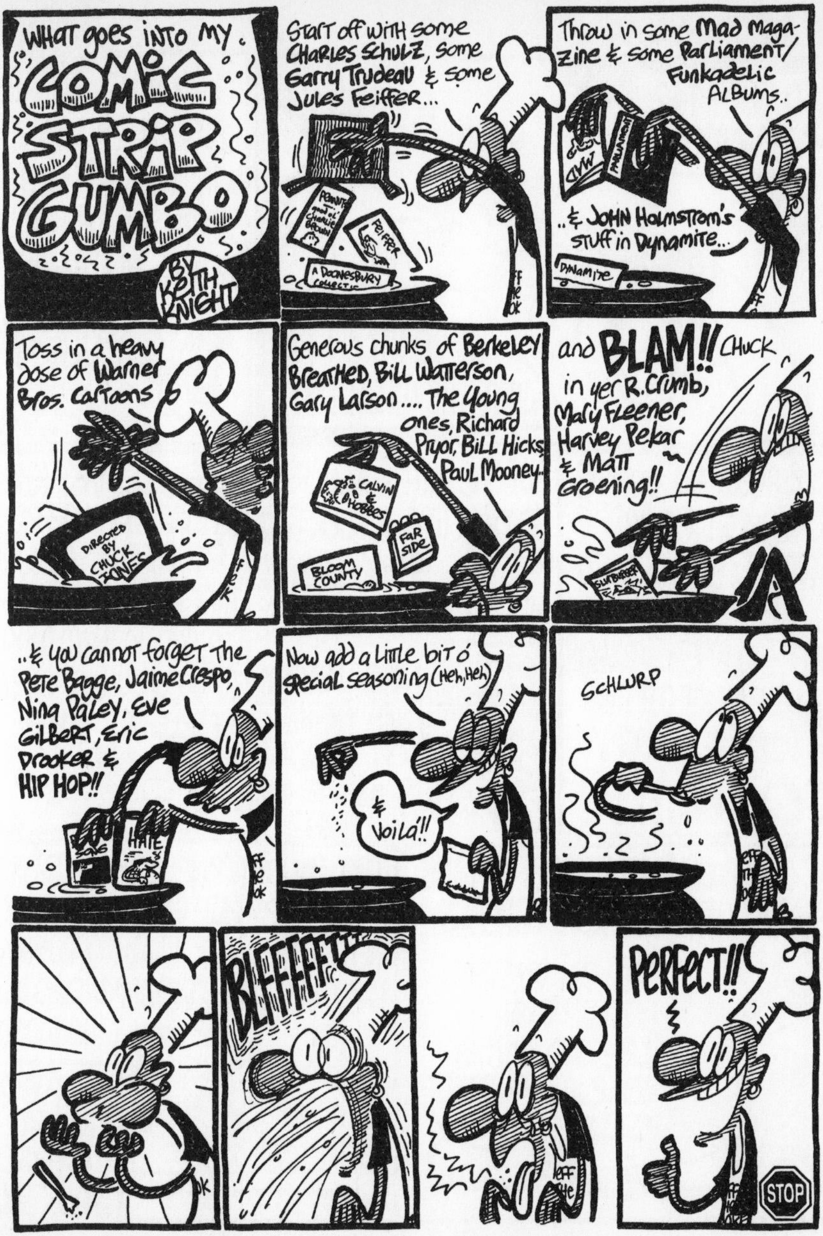

WHAT goes INTO MY
COMIC STRIP GUMBO
BY KEITH KNIGHT
Start off with some CHARLES SCHULZ, some Garry Trudeau & some Jules Feiffer...
PEANUTS good ol' Charlie Brown
FEIFFER
A DOONESBURY COLLECTIC
Throw in some Mad Magazine & some Parliament/Funkadelic ALBUMS..
MAD
PARLIAMENT
..& JOHN Holmstrom's stuff in Dynamite...
DYNAMITE
Toss in a heavy dose of Warner Bros. Cartoons
DIRECTED BY CHUCK JONES
Generous chunks of Berkeley Breathed, Bill Watterson, Gary Larson.... The Young ones, Richard Pryor, Bill Hicks, Paul Mooney..
CALVIN & HOBBES
FAR SIDE
BLOOM COUNTY
and BLAM!! CHUCK in yer R. Crumb, Mary Fleener, Harvey Pekar & Matt Groening!!
..& you cannot forget the Pete Bagge, Jaime Crespo, Nina Paley, Eve Gilbert, Eric Drooker & HIP HOP!!
HATE
Now add a little bit o' special seasoning (Heh, Heh)
& Voilà!!
SCHLURP
BLFFFFFT
PERFECT!!
STOP

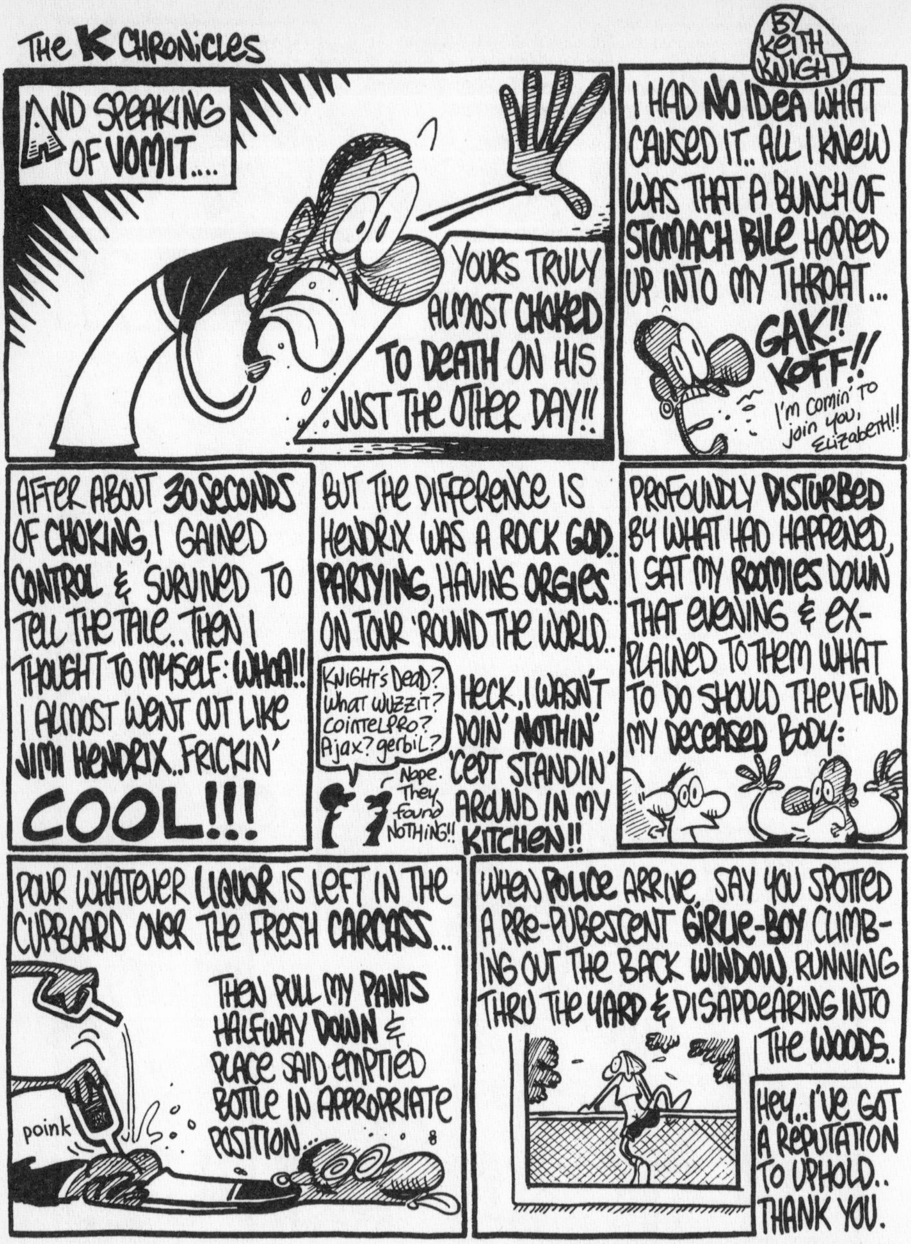
THE K CHRONICLES
BY KEITH KNIGHT
AND SPEAKING OF VOMIT....
YOURS TRULY ALMOST CHOKED TO DEATH ON HIS JUST THE OTHER DAY!!
I HAD NO IDEA WHAT CAUSED IT.. ALL I KNEW WAS THAT A BUNCH OF STOMACH BILE HOPPED UP INTO MY THROAT...
GAK!! KOFF!!
I'm comin' to join you, Elizabeth!!
AFTER ABOUT 30 SECONDS OF CHOKING, I GAINED CONTROL & SURVIVED TO TELL THE TALE.. THEN I THOUGHT TO MYSELF: WHOA!! I ALMOST WENT OUT LIKE JIMI HENDRIX.. FRICKIN' COOL!!!
BUT THE DIFFERENCE IS HENDRIX WAS A ROCK GOD.. PARTYING, HAVING ORGIES.. ON TOUR 'ROUND THE WORLD..
KNIGHT'S DEAD? WHAT WUZZIT? COINTELPRO? AJAX? GERBIL?
Nope. They found NOTHING!!
HECK, I WASN'T DOIN' NOTHIN' 'CEPT STANDIN' AROUND IN MY KITCHEN!!
PROFOUNDLY DISTURBED BY WHAT HAD HAPPENED, I SAT MY ROOMIES DOWN THAT EVENING & EXPLAINED TO THEM WHAT TO DO SHOULD THEY FIND MY DECEASED BODY:
POUR WHATEVER LIQUOR IS LEFT IN THE CUPBOARD OVER THE FRESH CARCASS...
THEN PULL MY PANTS HALFWAY DOWN & PLACE SAID EMPTIED BOTTLE IN APPROPRIATE POSITION...
poink
WHEN POLICE ARRIVE, SAY YOU SPOTTED A PRE-PUBESCENT GIRLIE-BOY CLIMBING OUT THE BACK WINDOW, RUNNING THRU THE YARD & DISAPPEARING INTO THE WOODS..
HEY.. I'VE GOT A REPUTATION TO UPHOLD.. THANK YOU.

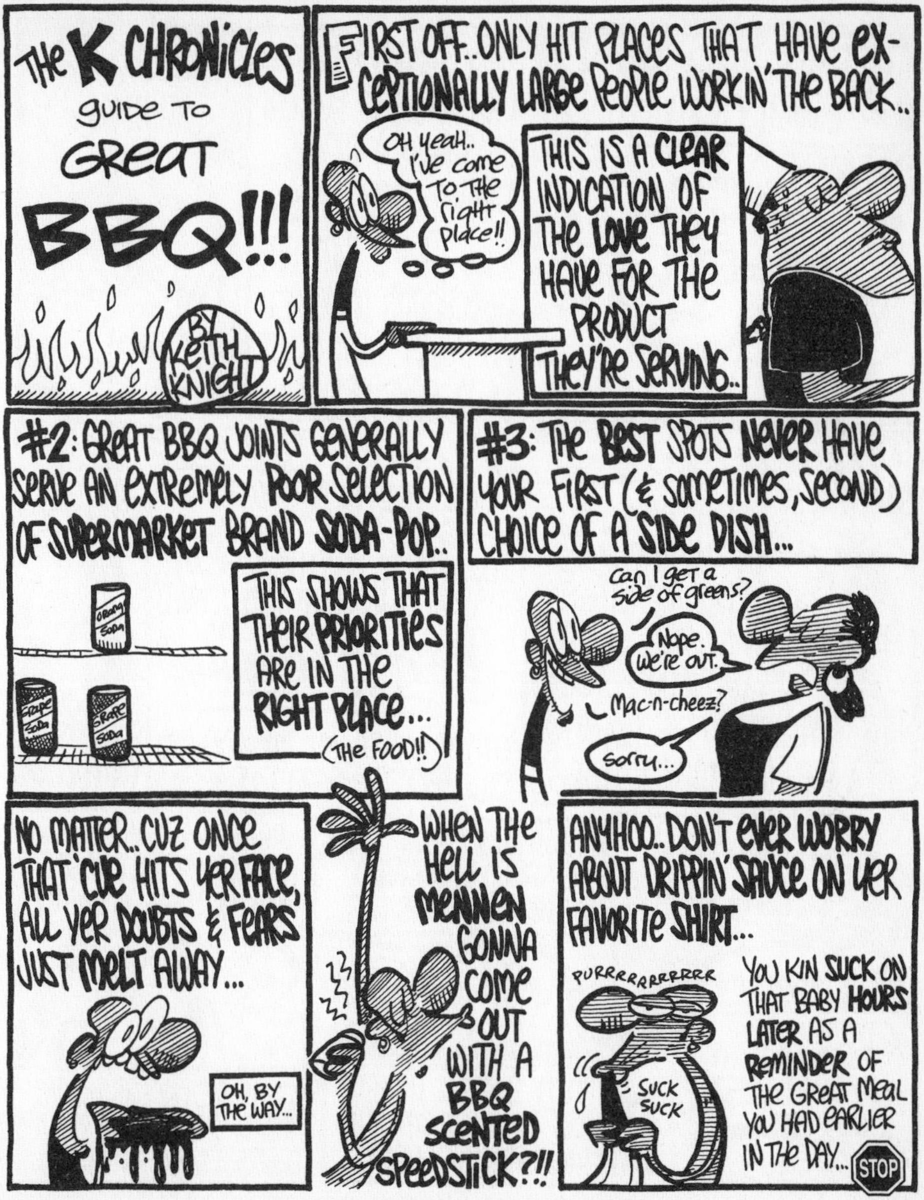
THE K CHRONICLES guide to GREAT BBQ!!!
BY KEITH KNIGHT
FIRST OFF.. ONLY HIT PLACES THAT HAVE EXCEPTIONALLY LARGE PEOPLE WORKIN' THE BACK..
OH YEAH.. I've come to the right place!!
THIS IS A CLEAR INDICATION OF THE LOVE THEY HAVE FOR THE PRODUCT THEY'RE SERVING..
#2: GREAT BBQ JOINTS GENERALLY SERVE AN EXTREMELY POOR SELECTION OF SUPERMARKET BRAND SODA-POP..
Orange Soda
Grape Soda
Grape Soda
THIS SHOWS THAT THEIR PRIORITIES ARE IN THE RIGHT PLACE...
(THE FOOD!!)
#3: THE BEST SPOTS NEVER HAVE YOUR FIRST (& SOMETIMES, SECOND) CHOICE OF A SIDE DISH...
Can I get a side of greens?
Nope. We're out.
Mac-n-cheez?
Sorry...
NO MATTER.. CUZ ONCE THAT 'CUE HITS YER FACE, ALL YER DOUBTS & FEARS JUST MELT AWAY...
OH, BY THE WAY...
WHEN THE HELL IS MENNEN GONNA COME OUT WITH A BBQ SCENTED SPEEDSTICK?!!
ANYHOO.. DON'T EVER WORRY ABOUT DRIPPIN' SAUCE ON YER FAVORITE SHIRT...
PURRRRRRRRRRR
SUCK SUCK
YOU KIN SUCK ON THAT BABY HOURS LATER AS A REMINDER OF THE GREAT MEAL YOU HAD EARLIER IN THE DAY...
STOP

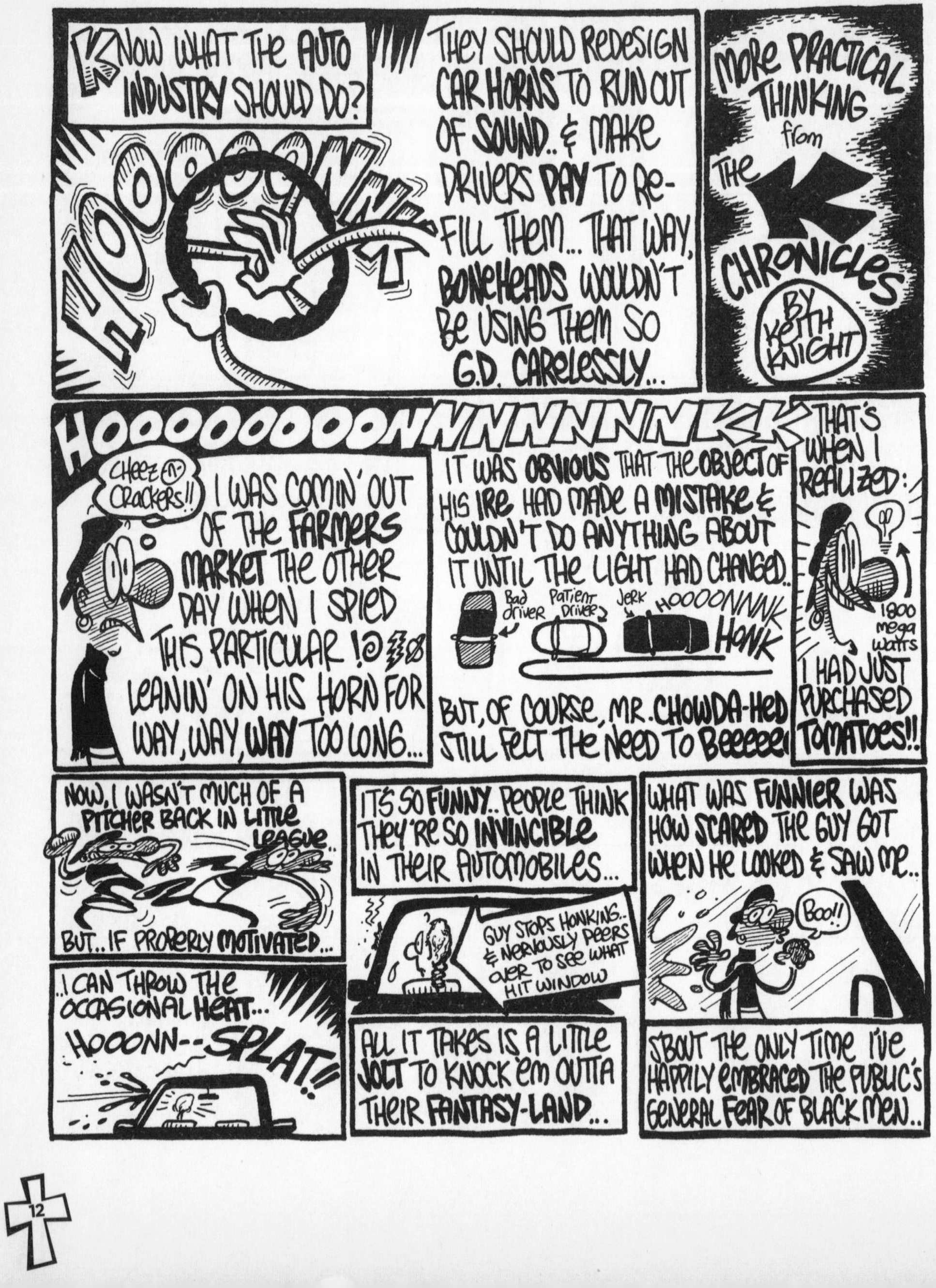
KNOW WHAT THE AUTO INDUSTRY SHOULD DO?
HOOOOOONNK
THEY SHOULD REDESIGN CAR HORNS TO RUN OUT OF SOUND.. & MAKE DRIVERS PAY TO RE-FILL THEM... THAT WAY, BONEHEADS WOULDN'T BE USING THEM SO G.D. CARELESSLY...
MORE PRACTICAL THINKING from THE K CHRONICLES
BY KEITH KNIGHT
HOOOOOOOOONNNNNNNKK
CHEEZ-N-CRACKERS!!
I WAS COMIN' OUT OF THE FARMERS MARKET THE OTHER DAY WHEN I SPIED THIS PARTICULAR !@#Ø LEANIN' ON HIS HORN FOR WAY, WAY, WAY TOO LONG...
IT WAS OBVIOUS THAT THE OBJECT OF HIS IRE HAD MADE A MISTAKE & COULDN'T DO ANYTHING ABOUT IT UNTIL THE LIGHT HAD CHANGED..
Bad driver
Patient Driver
Jerk
HOOOONNNK
HONK
BUT, OF COURSE, MR. CHOWDA-HED STILL FELT THE NEED TO BEEEEEE
THAT'S WHEN I REALIZED:
1800 mega watts
I HAD JUST PURCHASED TOMATOES!!
NOW, I WASN'T MUCH OF A PITCHER BACK IN LITTLE LEAGUE...
BUT.. IF PROPERLY MOTIVATED...
..I CAN THROW THE OCCASIONAL HEAT...
HOOONN--SPLAT!!
IT'S SO FUNNY.. PEOPLE THINK THEY'RE SO INVINCIBLE IN THEIR AUTOMOBILES...
GUY STOPS HONKING.. & NERVOUSLY PEERS OVER TO SEE WHAT HIT WINDOW
ALL IT TAKES IS A LITTLE JOLT TO KNOCK 'EM OUTTA THEIR FANTASY-LAND...
WHAT WAS FUNNIER WAS HOW SCARED THE GUY GOT WHEN HE LOOKED & SAW ME...
BOO!!
'BOUT THE ONLY TIME I'VE HAPPILY EMBRACED THE PUBLIC'S GENERAL FEAR OF BLACK MEN..

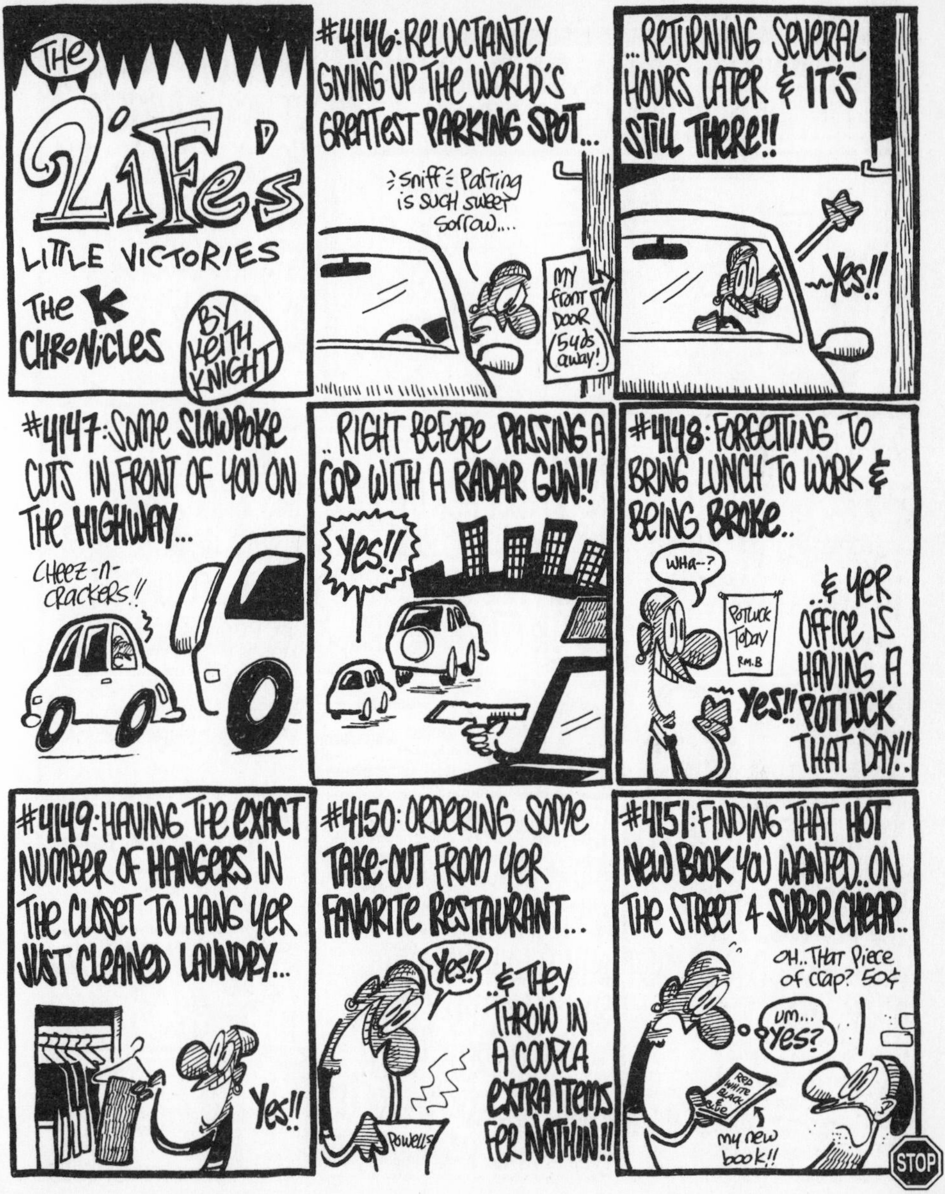
THE
Life's
LITTLE VICTORIES
THE K CHRONICLES
BY KEITH KNIGHT
#4146: RELUCTANTLY GIVING UP THE WORLD'S GREATEST PARKING SPOT...
SNIFF PARTING IS SUCH SWEET SORROW....
MY FRONT DOOR (5 YDS AWAY!)
...RETURNING SEVERAL HOURS LATER & IT'S STILL THERE!!
YES!!
#4147: SOME SLOWPOKE CUTS IN FRONT OF YOU ON THE HIGHWAY...
CHEEZ-N-CRACKERS!!
..RIGHT BEFORE PASSING A COP WITH A RADAR GUN!!
YES!!
#4148: FORGETTING TO BRING LUNCH TO WORK & BEING BROKE..
WHA--?
POTLUCK TODAY RM. B
..& YER OFFICE IS HAVING A POTLUCK THAT DAY!!
YES!!
#4149: HAVING THE EXACT NUMBER OF HANGERS IN THE CLOSET TO HANG YER JUST CLEANED LAUNDRY...
YES!!
#4150: ORDERING SOME TAKE-OUT FROM YER FAVORITE RESTAURANT...
YES!!
..& THEY THROW IN A COUPLA EXTRA ITEMS FER NOTHIN!!
POWELL'S
#4151: FINDING THAT HOT NEW BOOK YOU WANTED..ON THE STREET 4 SUPER CHEAP..
OH..THAT PIECE OF CRAP? 50¢
UM... YES?
RED WHITE BLACK & BLUE
MY NEW BOOK!!
STOP

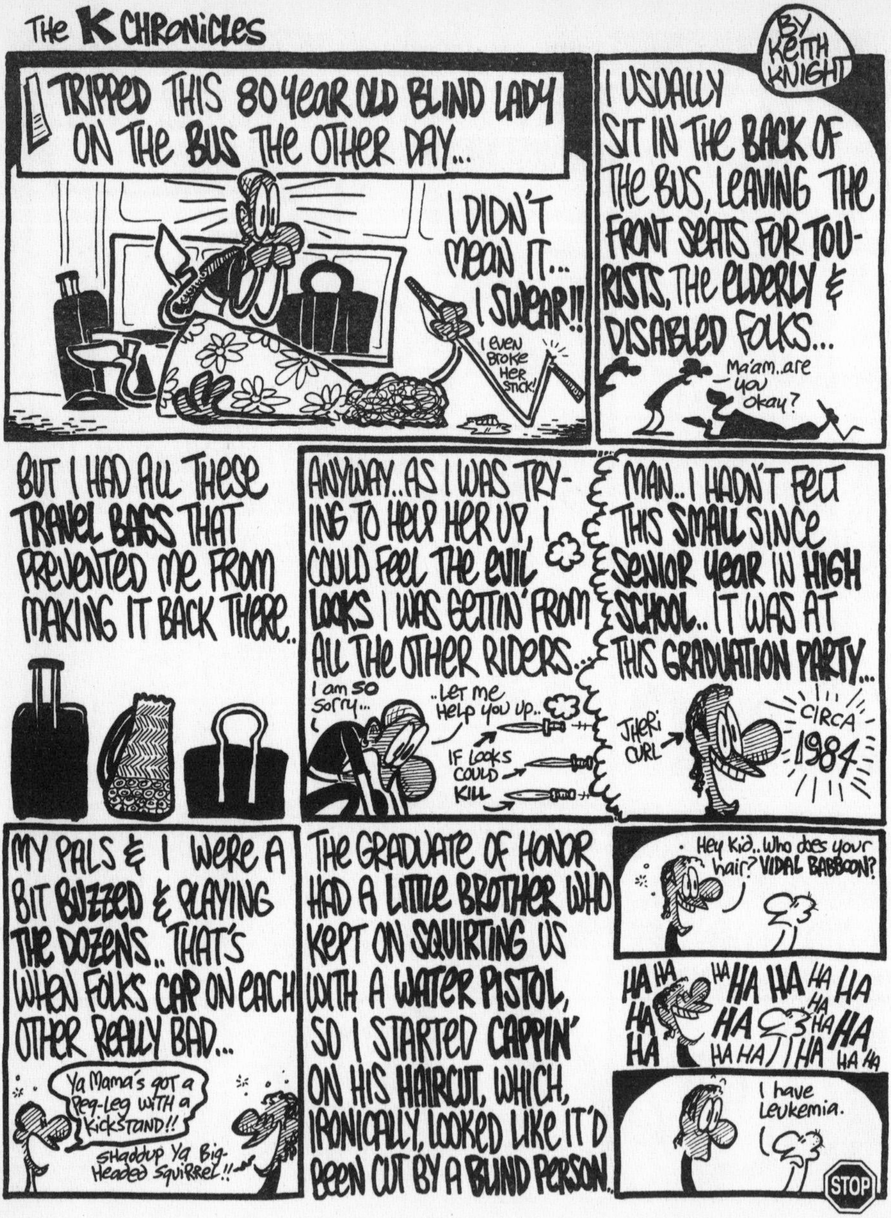
The K Chronicles
By Keith Knight
I tripped this 80 year old blind lady on the bus the other day...
I didn't mean it... I swear!!
I even broke her stick!
I usually sit in the back of the bus, leaving the front seats for tourists, the elderly & disabled folks...
Ma'am..are you okay?
But I had all these travel bags that prevented me from making it back there..
Anyway.. as I was trying to help her up, I could feel the evil looks I was gettin' from all the other riders...
I am so sorry...
..Let me help you up..
If looks could kill
Man.. I hadn't felt this small since senior year in high school.. It was at this graduation party...
Jheri curl
Circa 1984
My pals & I were a bit buzzed & playing the dozens.. That's when folks cap on each other really bad...
Ya Mama's got a peg-leg with a kickstand!!
Shaddup ya big-headed squirrel!!
The graduate of honor had a little brother who kept on squirting us with a water pistol, so I started cappin' on his haircut, which, ironically, looked like it'd been cut by a blind person..
Hey kid.. Who does your hair? Vidal Babboon?
HA HA HA HA HA HA HA HA HA HA HA HA HA HA HA HA HA HA HA
I have leukemia.
STOP

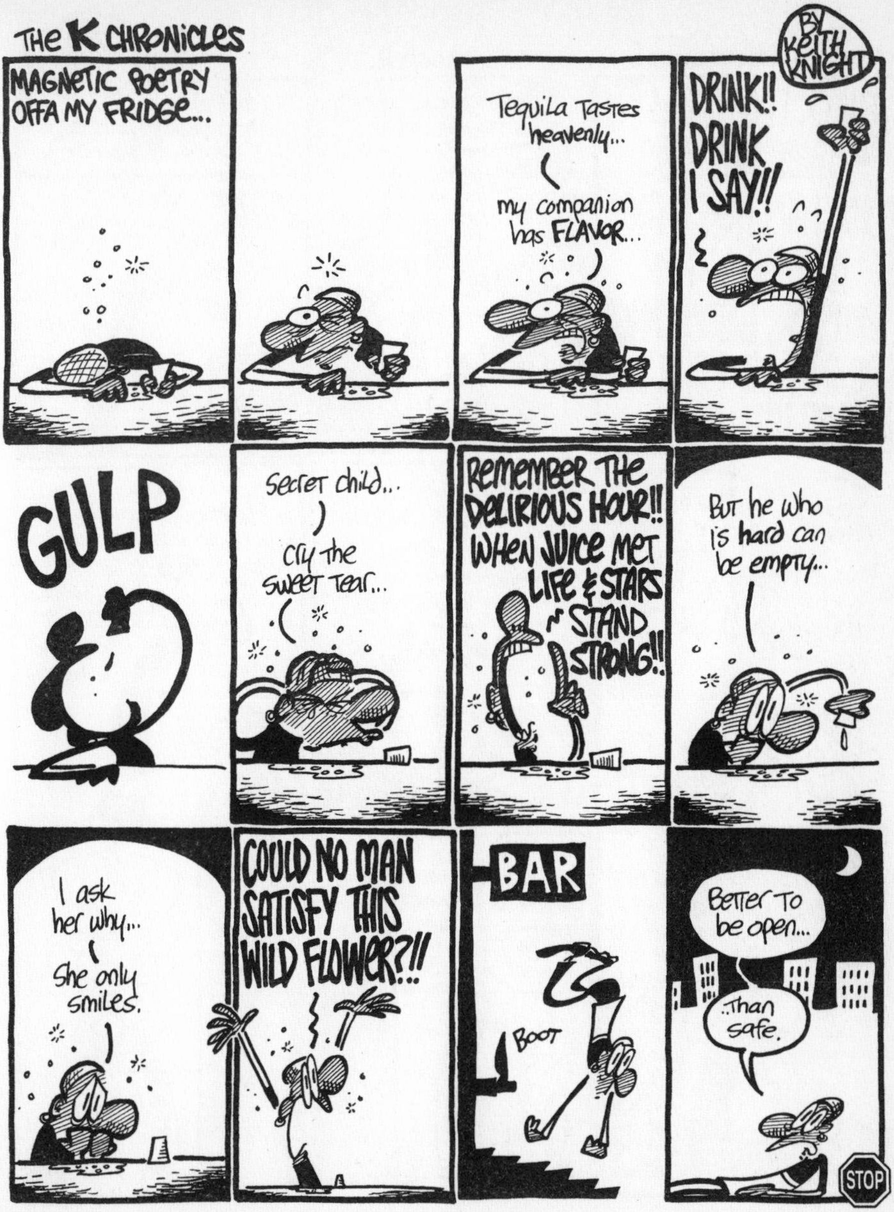
THE K CHRONICLES
BY KEITH KNIGHT
MAGNETIC POETRY OFFA MY FRIDGE...
Tequila Tastes heavenly...
my companion has FLAVOR...
DRINK!! DRINK I SAY!!
GULP
Secret child...
cry the sweet tear...
REMEMBER THE DELIRIOUS HOUR!! WHEN JUICE MET LIFE & STARS ~ STAND STRONG!!
But he who is hard can be empty...
I ask her why...
She only smiles.
COULD NO MAN SATISFY THIS WILD FLOWER?!!
BAR
BOOT
Better to be open...
...Than safe.
STOP

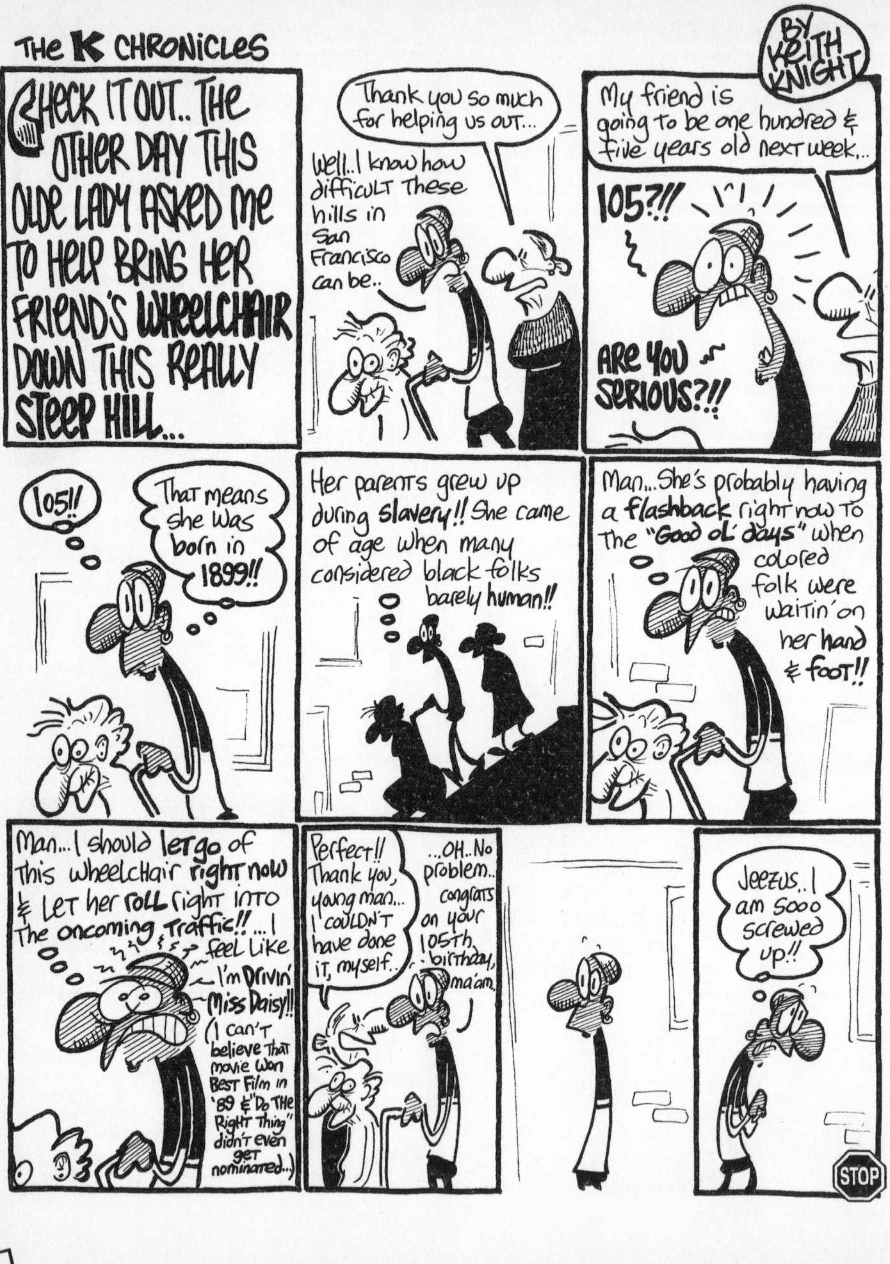
THE K CHRONICLES
BY KEITH KNIGHT
CHECK IT OUT.. THE OTHER DAY THIS OLDE LADY ASKED ME TO HELP BRING HER FRIEND'S WHEELCHAIR DOWN THIS REALLY STEEP HILL...
Thank you so much for helping us out...
Well.. I know how difficult these hills in San Francisco can be..
My friend is going to be one hundred & five years old next week...
105?!!
ARE YOU SERIOUS?!!
105!!
That means she was born in 1899!!
Her parents grew up during slavery!! She came of age when many considered black folks barely human!!
Man... She's probably having a flashback right now to the "Good ol' days" when colored folk were waitin' on her hand & foot!!
Man... I should let go of this wheelchair right now & let her roll right into the oncoming traffic!! ...I feel like I'm Drivin' Miss Daisy!!
(I can't believe that movie won Best Film in '89 & "Do the Right Thing" didn't even get nominated...)
Perfect!! Thank you, young man... I couldn't have done it, myself..
...OH.. No problem.. congrats on your 105th birthday, ma'am..
Jeezus.. I am sooo screwed up!!
STOP

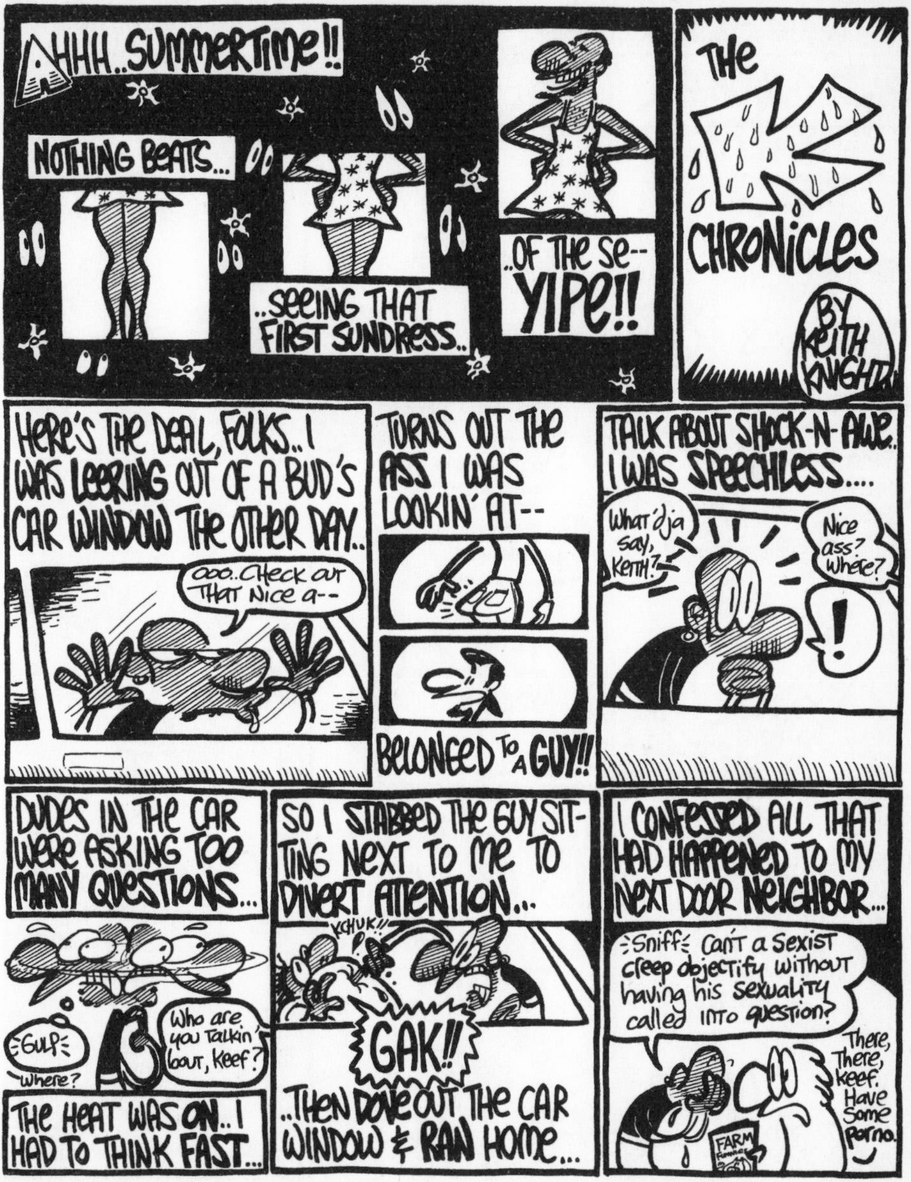
AHHH..SUMMERTIME!!
NOTHING BEATS...
..SEEING THAT FIRST SUNDRESS..
..OF THE SE--
YIPE!!
THE K CHRONICLES
BY KEITH KNIGHT
HERE'S THE DEAL, FOLKS..I WAS LEERING OUT OF A BUD'S CAR WINDOW THE OTHER DAY..
OOO..CHECK OUT THAT NICE A--
TURNS OUT THE ASS I WAS LOOKIN' AT--
BELONGED TO A GUY!!
TALK ABOUT SHOCK-N-AWE.. I WAS SPEECHLESS....
WHAT'DJA SAY, KEITH?
NICE ASS? WHERE?
!
DUDES IN THE CAR WERE ASKING TOO MANY QUESTIONS...
GULP
WHERE?
WHO ARE YOU TALKIN' BOUT, KEEF?
THE HEAT WAS ON..I HAD TO THINK FAST...
SO I STABBED THE GUY SITTING NEXT TO ME TO DIVERT ATTENTION...
KCHUK!!
GAK!!
..THEN DOVE OUT THE CAR WINDOW & RAN HOME...
I CONFESSED ALL THAT HAD HAPPENED TO MY NEXT DOOR NEIGHBOR...
SNIFF CAN'T A SEXIST CREEP OBJECTIFY WITHOUT HAVING HIS SEXUALITY CALLED INTO QUESTION?
THERE, THERE, KEEF. HAVE SOME PORNO.
FARM

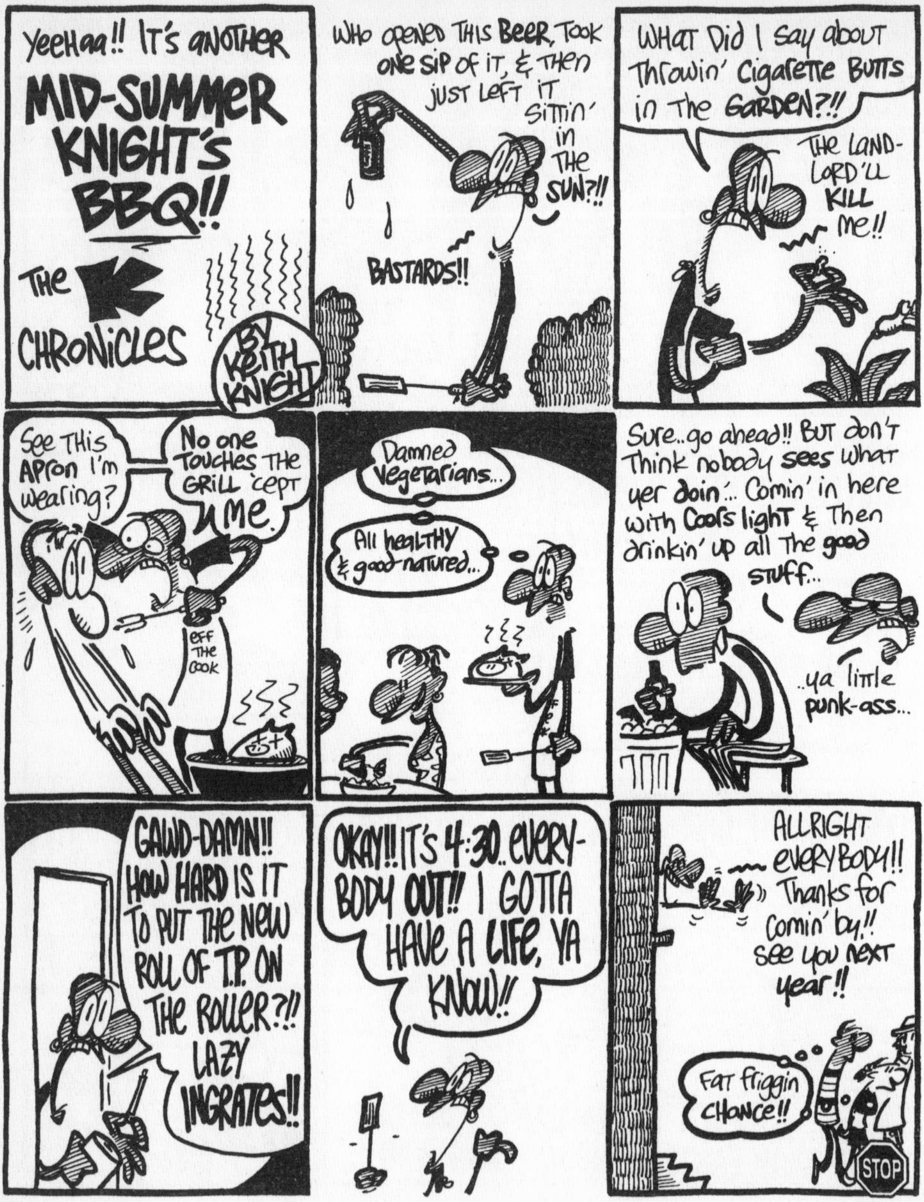
YeeHaa!! IT'S anOTHER
MID-SUMMER KNIGHT'S BBQ!!
THE K CHRONICLES
BY KEITH KNIGHT
WHO OPENED THIS BEER, TOOK ONE SIP OF IT, & THEN JUST LEFT IT SITTIN' IN THE SUN?!!
BASTARDS!!
WHAT DID I say about Throwin' Cigarette BUTTS in The GARDEN?!!
THE LAND-LORD'LL KILL me!!
See THIS APron I'm wearing?
No one TOUCHES THE GRILL 'cept me.
EFF THE COOK
Damned Vegetarians...
All healTHY & good-natured...
Sure..go ahead!! BUT don't Think nobody sees What yer doin'... Comin' in here with Coors light & Then drinkin' up all The good STUFF...
..ya little punk-ass...
GAWD-DAMN!! HOW HARD IS IT TO PUT THE NEW ROLL OF T.P. ON THE ROLLER?!! LAZY INGRATES!!
OKAY!! IT'S 4:30.. EVERY-BODY OUT!! I GOTTA HAVE A LIFE, YA KNOW!!
ALLRIGHT EVERYBODY!! Thanks for Comin' by!! see you NEXT year!!
Fat friggin CHANCE!!
STOP

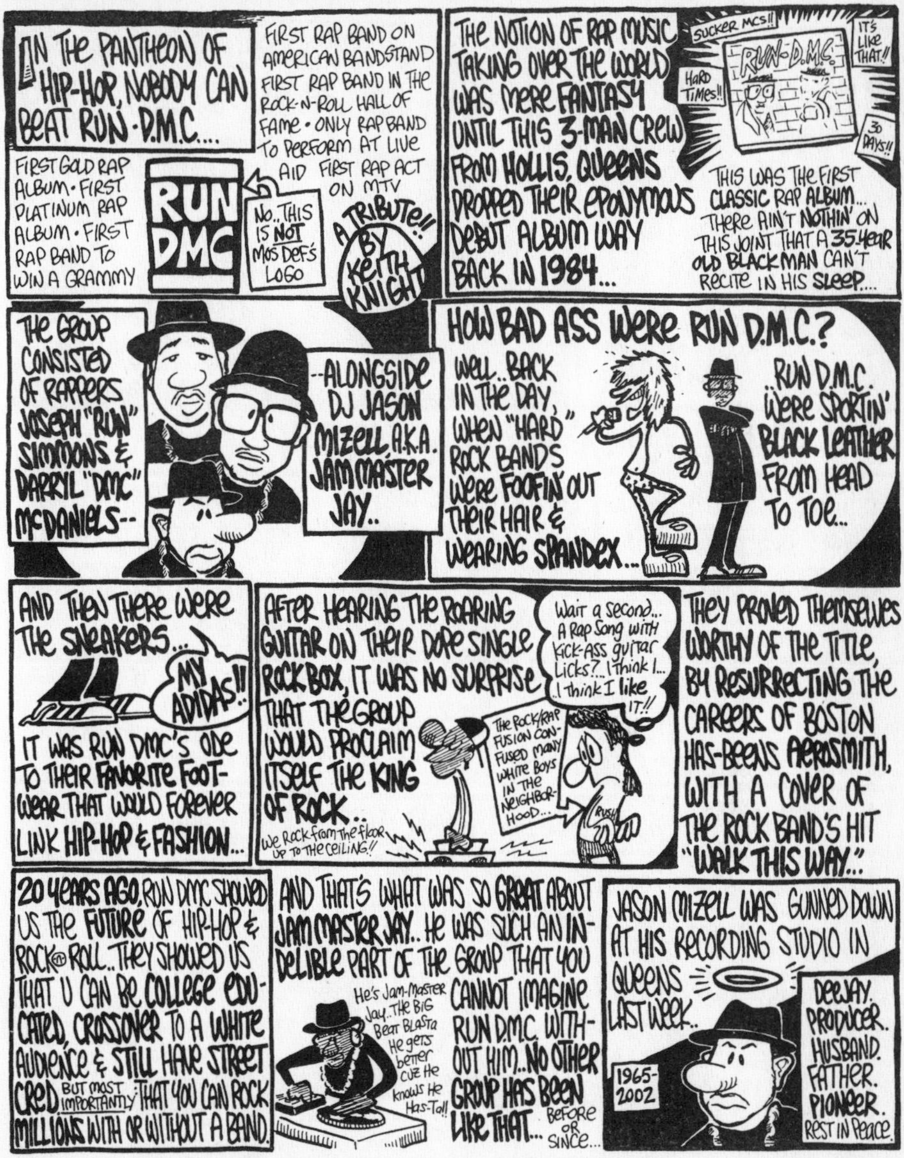

IN THE PANTHEON OF HIP-HOP, NOBODY CAN BEAT RUN-D.M.C....
FIRST RAP BAND ON AMERICAN BANDSTAND • FIRST RAP BAND IN THE ROCK-N-ROLL HALL OF FAME • ONLY RAP BAND TO PERFORM AT LIVE AID • FIRST RAP ACT ON MTV
FIRST GOLD RAP ALBUM • FIRST PLATINUM RAP ALBUM • FIRST RAP BAND TO WIN A GRAMMY
RUN DMC
NO.. THIS IS NOT MOS DEF'S LOGO
A TRIBUTE!! BY KEITH KNIGHT
THE NOTION OF RAP MUSIC TAKING OVER THE WORLD WAS MERE FANTASY UNTIL THIS 3-MAN CREW FROM HOLLIS, QUEENS DROPPED THEIR EPONYMOUS DEBUT ALBUM WAY BACK IN 1984...
SUCKER MCS!!
IT'S LIKE THAT!!
RUN-D.M.C.
HARD TIMES!!
30 DAYS!!
THIS WAS THE FIRST CLASSIC RAP ALBUM... THERE AIN'T NOTHIN' ON THIS JOINT THAT A 35-YEAR OLD BLACK MAN CAN'T RECITE IN HIS SLEEP....
THE GROUP CONSISTED OF RAPPERS JOSEPH "RUN" SIMMONS & DARRYL "DMC" McDANIELS--
--ALONGSIDE DJ JASON MIZELL A.K.A. JAM MASTER JAY..
HOW BAD ASS WERE RUN D.M.C.?
WELL.. BACK IN THE DAY, WHEN "HARD" ROCK BANDS WERE FOOFIN' OUT THEIR HAIR & WEARING SPANDEX...
..RUN D.M.C. WERE SPORTIN' BLACK LEATHER FROM HEAD TO TOE...
AND THEN THERE WERE THE SNEAKERS...
MY ADIDAS!!
IT WAS RUN DMC'S ODE TO THEIR FAVORITE FOOT-WEAR THAT WOULD FOREVER LINK HIP-HOP & FASHION...
AFTER HEARING THE ROARING GUITAR ON THEIR DOPE SINGLE ROCK BOX, IT WAS NO SURPRISE THAT THE GROUP WOULD PROCLAIM ITSELF THE KING OF ROCK..
We Rock from the floor up to the ceiling!!
Wait a second... A Rap Song with Kick-Ass guitar Licks?.. I think I... ..I think I like IT!!
THE ROCK/RAP FUSION CONFUSED MANY WHITE BOYS IN THE NEIGHBORHOOD...
RUSH
THEY PROVED THEMSELVES WORTHY OF THE TITLE, BY RESURRECTING THE CAREERS OF BOSTON HAS-BEENS AEROSMITH, WITH A COVER OF THE ROCK BAND'S HIT "WALK THIS WAY."
20 YEARS AGO, RUN DMC SHOWED US THE FUTURE OF HIP-HOP & ROCK-N-ROLL.. THEY SHOWED US THAT U CAN BE COLLEGE EDUCATED, CROSSOVER TO A WHITE AUDIENCE & STILL HAVE STREET CRED BUT MOST IMPORTANTLY: THAT YOU CAN ROCK MILLIONS WITH OR WITHOUT A BAND.
AND THAT'S WHAT WAS SO GREAT ABOUT JAM MASTER JAY.. HE WAS SUCH AN INDELIBLE PART OF THE GROUP THAT YOU CANNOT IMAGINE RUN D.M.C. WITHOUT HIM.. NO OTHER GROUP HAS BEEN LIKE THAT... BEFORE OR SINCE...
He's Jam-Master Jay.. The Big Beat Blasta He gets better cuz He knows He Has-To!!
JASON MIZELL WAS GUNNED DOWN AT HIS RECORDING STUDIO IN QUEENS LAST WEEK..
1965-2002
DEEJAY. PRODUCER. HUSBAND. FATHER. PIONEER. REST IN PEACE.

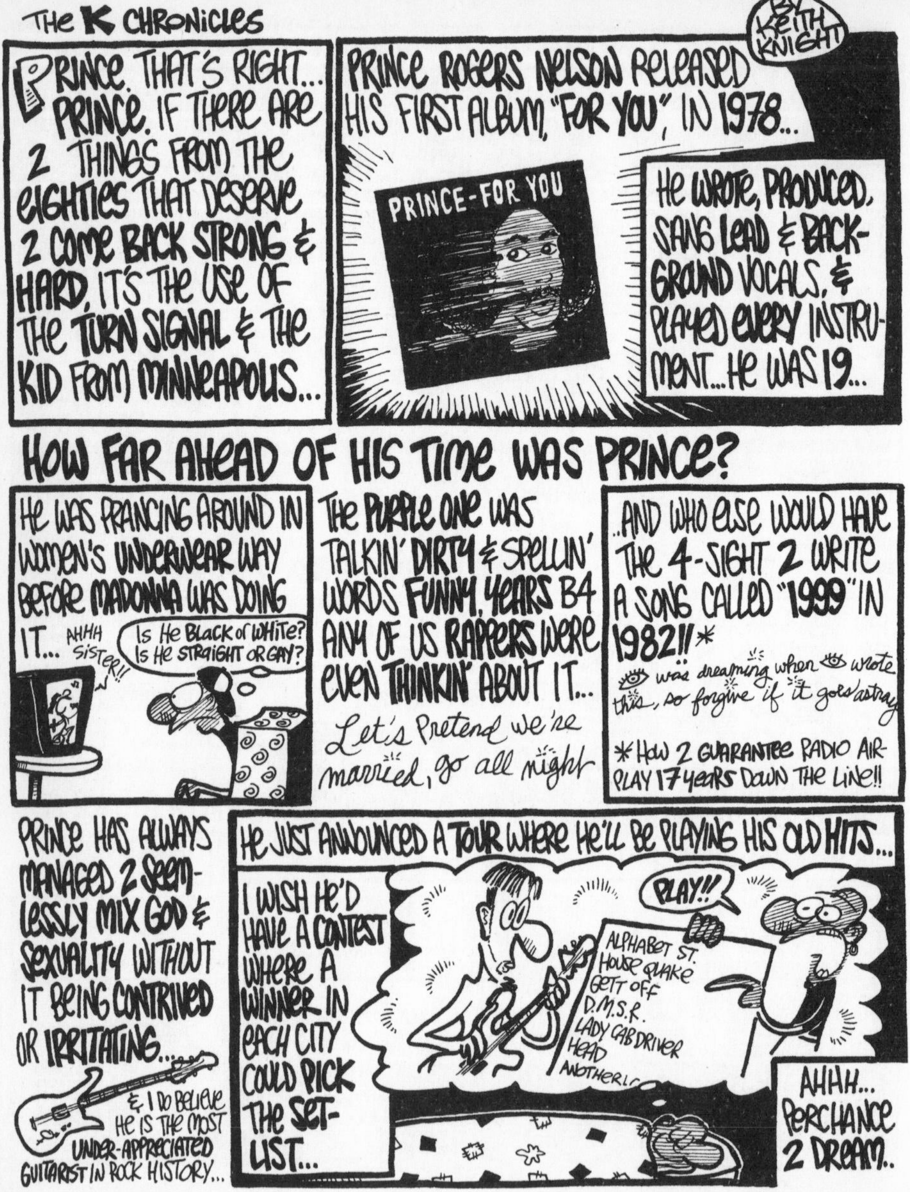
THE K CHRONICLES
BY KEITH KNIGHT
PRINCE. THAT'S RIGHT... PRINCE. IF THERE ARE 2 THINGS FROM THE EIGHTIES THAT DESERVE 2 COME BACK STRONG & HARD, IT'S THE USE OF THE TURN SIGNAL & THE KID FROM MINNEAPOLIS...
PRINCE ROGERS NELSON RELEASED HIS FIRST ALBUM, "FOR YOU", IN 1978...
PRINCE - FOR YOU
HE WROTE, PRODUCED, SANG LEAD & BACK-GROUND VOCALS, & PLAYED EVERY INSTRU-MENT... HE WAS 19...
HOW FAR AHEAD OF HIS TIME WAS PRINCE?
HE WAS PRANCING AROUND IN WOMEN'S UNDERWEAR WAY BEFORE MADONNA WAS DOING IT...
AHHH SISTER!!
IS HE BLACK OR WHITE? IS HE STRAIGHT OR GAY?
THE PURPLE ONE WAS TALKIN' DIRTY & SPELLIN' WORDS FUNNY, YEARS B4 ANY OF US RAPPERS WERE EVEN THINKIN' ABOUT IT...
Let's Pretend we're married, go all night
...AND WHO ELSE WOULD HAVE THE 4-SIGHT 2 WRITE A SONG CALLED "1999" IN 1982!! *
was dreaming when wrote this, so forgive if it goes astray
* HOW 2 GUARANTEE RADIO AIR-PLAY 17 YEARS DOWN THE LINE!!
PRINCE HAS ALWAYS MANAGED 2 SEEM-LESSLY MIX GOD & SEXUALITY WITHOUT IT BEING CONTRIVED OR IRRITATING...
& I DO BELIEVE HE IS THE MOST UNDER-APPRECIATED GUITARIST IN ROCK HISTORY...
HE JUST ANNOUNCED A TOUR WHERE HE'LL BE PLAYING HIS OLD HITS...
I WISH HE'D HAVE A CONTEST WHERE A WINNER IN EACH CITY COULD PICK THE SET-LIST...
PLAY!!
ALPHABET ST.
HOUSE QUAKE
GETT OFF
D.M.S.R.
LADY CAB DRIVER
HEAD
ANOTHER!
AHHH... PERCHANCE 2 DREAM..

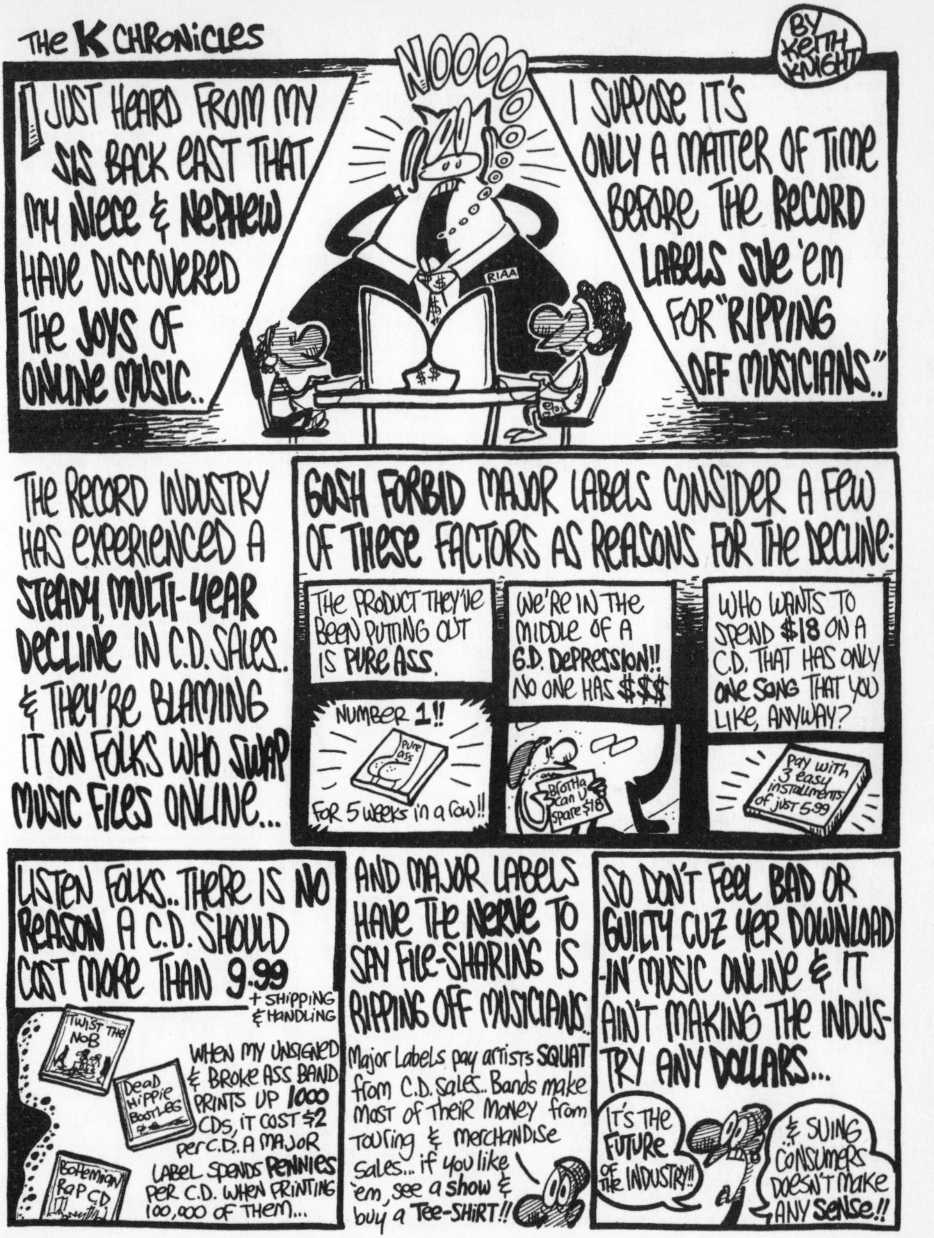

THE K CHRONICLES
BY KEITH KNIGHT
I JUST HEARD FROM MY SIS BACK EAST THAT MY NIECE & NEPHEW HAVE DISCOVERED THE JOYS OF ONLINE MUSIC..
NOOOOOOOOOO
RIAA
I SUPPOSE IT'S ONLY A MATTER OF TIME BEFORE THE RECORD LABELS SUE 'EM FOR "RIPPING OFF MUSICIANS."..
THE RECORD INDUSTRY HAS EXPERIENCED A STEADY, MULTI-YEAR DECLINE IN C.D. SALES.. & THEY'RE BLAMING IT ON FOLKS WHO SWAP MUSIC FILES ONLINE...
GOSH FORBID MAJOR LABELS CONSIDER A FEW OF THESE FACTORS AS REASONS FOR THE DECLINE:
THE PRODUCT THEY'VE BEEN PUTTING OUT IS PURE ASS.
WE'RE IN THE MIDDLE OF A G.D. DEPRESSION!! NO ONE HAS $$$
WHO WANTS TO SPEND $18 ON A C.D. THAT HAS ONLY ONE SONG THAT YOU LIKE, ANYWAY?
NUMBER 1!!
PURE ASS
FOR 5 WEEKS IN A ROW!!
BROTHA CAN U SPARE $18
PAY WITH 3 EASY INSTALLMENTS OF JUST 5.99
LISTEN FOLKS.. THERE IS NO REASON A C.D. SHOULD COST MORE THAN 9.99
+ SHIPPING & HANDLING
TWIST THE NOB
DEAD HIPPIE BOOTLEGS
BOHEMIAN RAP CD
WHEN MY UNSIGNED & BROKE ASS BAND PRINTS UP 1000 CDS, IT COST $2 PER C.D. A MAJOR LABEL SPENDS PENNIES PER C.D. WHEN PRINTING 100,000 OF THEM...
AND MAJOR LABELS HAVE THE NERVE TO SAY FILE-SHARING IS RIPPING OFF MUSICIANS..
Major Labels pay artists SQUAT from C.D. sales.. Bands make most of their money from touring & merchandise sales... if you like 'em, see a show & buy a TEE-SHIRT!!
SO DON'T FEEL BAD OR GUILTY CUZ YER DOWNLOAD-IN' MUSIC ONLINE & IT AIN'T MAKING THE INDUS-TRY ANY DOLLARS...
IT'S THE FUTURE OF THE INDUSTRY!!
..& SUING CONSUMERS DOESN'T MAKE ANY SENSE!!

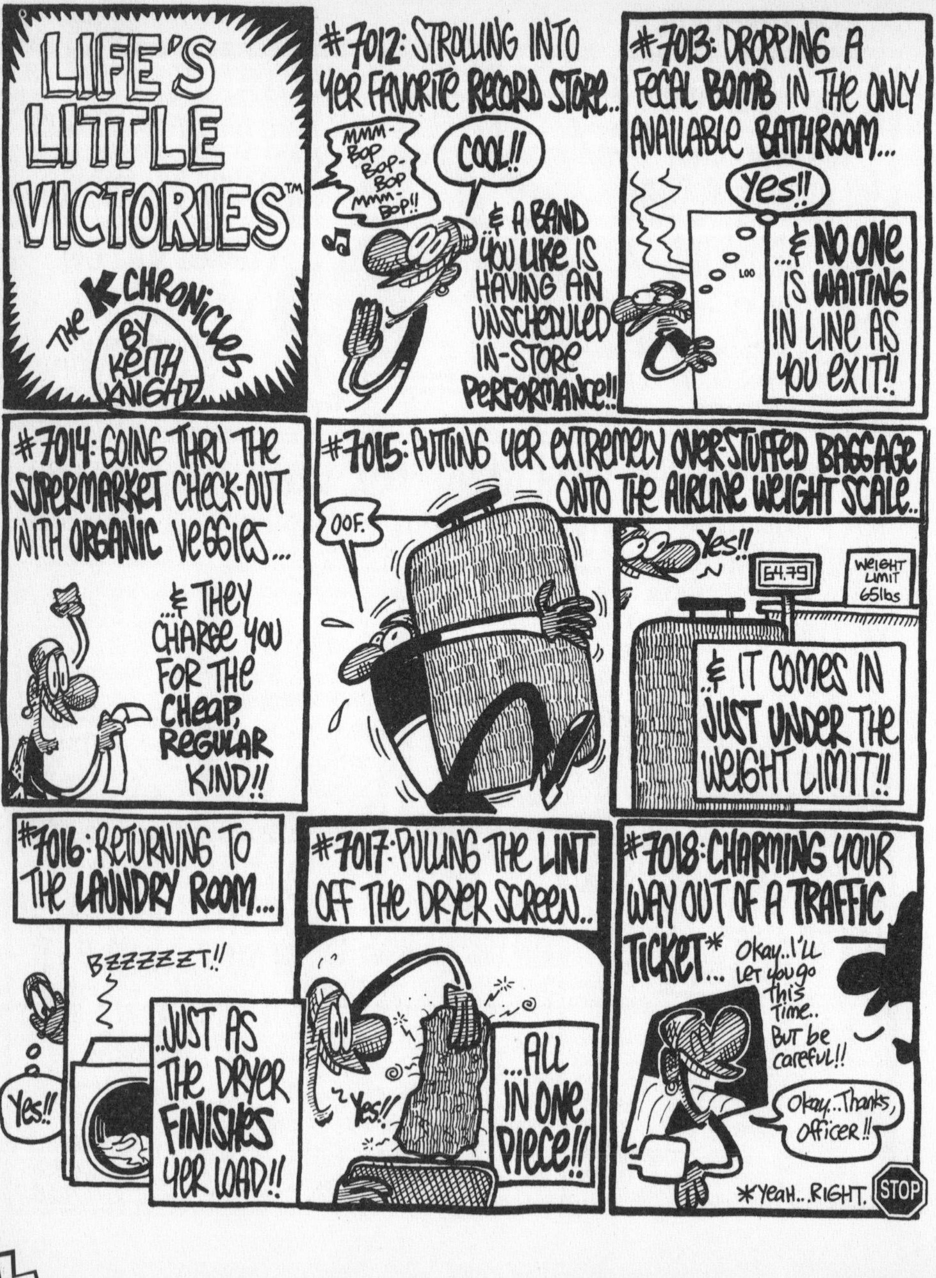
LIFE'S LITTLE VICTORIES™
THE K CHRONICLES
BY KEITH KNIGHT
#7012: STROLLING INTO YER FAVORITE RECORD STORE...
MMM-BOP BOP-BOP MMM-BOP!!
COOL!!
...& A BAND YOU LIKE IS HAVING AN UNSCHEDULED IN-STORE PERFORMANCE!!
#7013: DROPPING A FECAL BOMB IN THE ONLY AVAILABLE BATHROOM...
YES!!
LOO
...& NO ONE IS WAITING IN LINE AS YOU EXIT!!
#7014: GOING THRU THE SUPERMARKET CHECK-OUT WITH ORGANIC VEGGIES...
...& THEY CHARGE YOU FOR THE CHEAP, REGULAR KIND!!
#7015: PUTTING YER EXTREMELY OVER-STUFFED BAGGAGE ONTO THE AIRLINE WEIGHT SCALE..
OOF.
YES!!
64.79
WEIGHT LIMIT 65lbs
...& IT COMES IN JUST UNDER THE WEIGHT LIMIT!!
#7016: RETURNING TO THE LAUNDRY ROOM...
BZZZZZT!!
YES!!
..JUST AS THE DRYER FINISHES YER LOAD!!
#7017: PULLING THE LINT OFF THE DRYER SCREEN..
YES!!
...ALL IN ONE PIECE!!
#7018: CHARMING YOUR WAY OUT OF A TRAFFIC TICKET*...
Okay..I'll let you go this time.. But be careful!!
Okay...Thanks, officer!!
*YEAH...RIGHT.
STOP

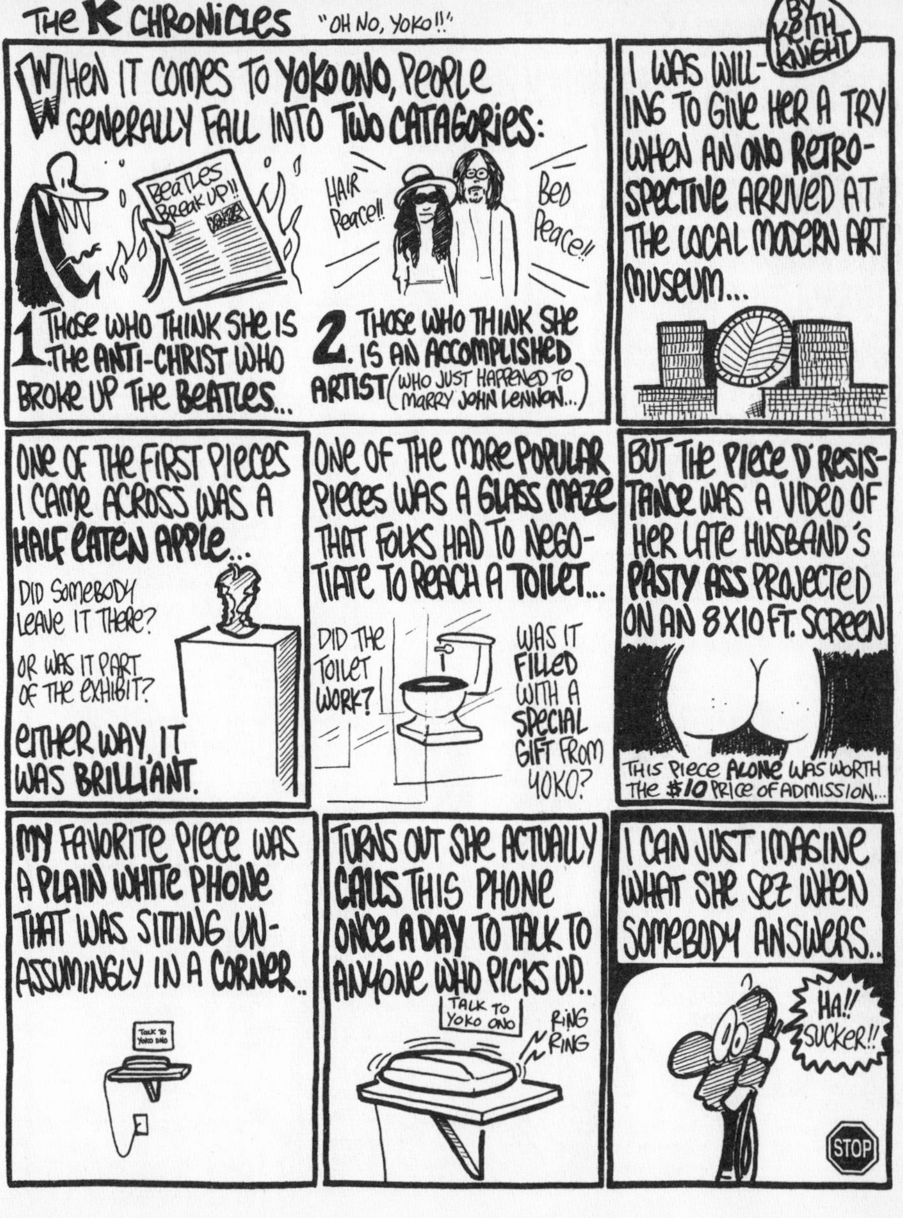
THE K CHRONICLES "OH NO, YOKO!!"
BY KEITH KNIGHT
WHEN IT COMES TO YOKO ONO, PEOPLE GENERALLY FALL INTO TWO CATAGORIES:
BEATLES BREAK UP!!
HAIR PEACE!!
BED PEACE!!
1. THOSE WHO THINK SHE IS THE ANTI-CHRIST WHO BROKE UP THE BEATLES...
2. THOSE WHO THINK SHE IS AN ACCOMPLISHED ARTIST (WHO JUST HAPPENED TO MARRY JOHN LENNON...)
I WAS WILLING TO GIVE HER A TRY WHEN AN ONO RETROSPECTIVE ARRIVED AT THE LOCAL MODERN ART MUSEUM...
ONE OF THE FIRST PIECES I CAME ACROSS WAS A HALF EATEN APPLE...
DID SOMEBODY LEAVE IT THERE?
OR WAS IT PART OF THE EXHIBIT?
EITHER WAY, IT WAS BRILLIANT.
ONE OF THE MORE POPULAR PIECES WAS A GLASS MAZE THAT FOLKS HAD TO NEGOTIATE TO REACH A TOILET...
DID THE TOILET WORK?
WAS IT FILLED WITH A SPECIAL GIFT FROM YOKO?
BUT THE PIECE D' RESISTANCE WAS A VIDEO OF HER LATE HUSBAND'S PASTY ASS PROJECTED ON AN 8X10 FT. SCREEN
THIS PIECE ALONE WAS WORTH THE $10 PRICE OF ADMISSION...
MY FAVORITE PIECE WAS A PLAIN WHITE PHONE THAT WAS SITTING UNASSUMINGLY IN A CORNER..
TALK TO YOKO ONO
TURNS OUT SHE ACTUALLY CALLS THIS PHONE ONCE A DAY TO TALK TO ANYONE WHO PICKS UP..
TALK TO YOKO ONO
RING RING
I CAN JUST IMAGINE WHAT SHE SEZ WHEN SOMEBODY ANSWERS...
HA!! SUCKER!!
STOP

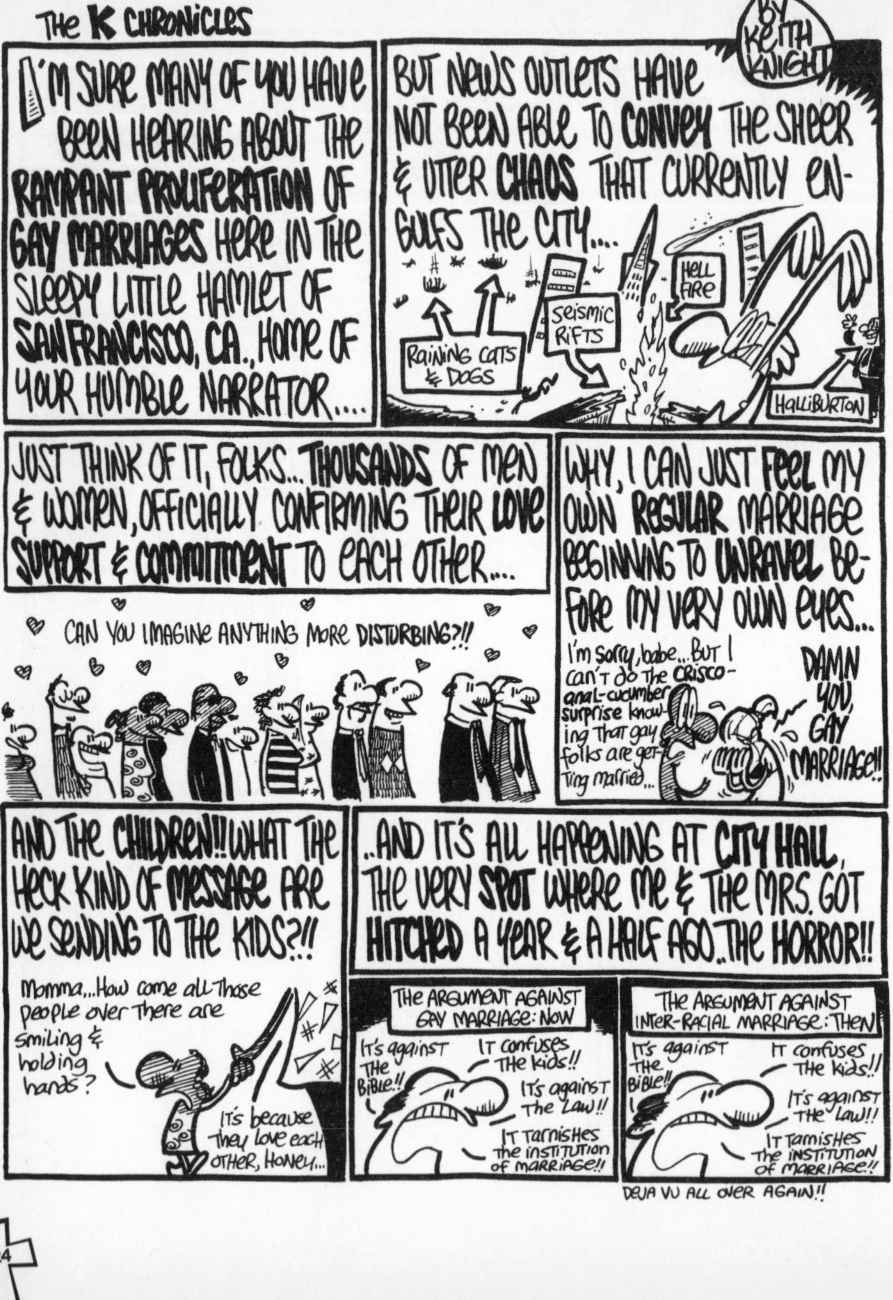
The K Chronicles
By Keith Knight
I'm sure many of you have been hearing about the rampant proliferation of gay marriages here in the sleepy little hamlet of San Francisco, CA., home of your humble narrator....
But news outlets have not been able to convey the sheer & utter chaos that currently engulfs the city....
Raining cats & dogs
Seismic rifts
Hell fire
Halliburton
Just think of it, folks... thousands of men & women, officially confirming their love support & commitment to each other....
Can you imagine anything more disturbing?!!
Why, I can just feel my own regular marriage beginning to unravel before my very own eyes...
I'm sorry, babe... But I can't do the Crisco-anal-cucumber surprise knowing that gay folks are getting married...
Damn you, gay marriage!!
And the children!! What the heck kind of message are we sending to the kids?!!
Momma... How come all those people over there are smiling & holding hands?
It's because they love each other, honey...
..And it's all happening at City Hall, the very spot where me & the Mrs. got hitched a year & a half ago.. The horror!!
The argument against gay marriage: Now
It's against the Bible!!
It confuses the kids!!
It's against the law!!
It tarnishes the institution of marriage!!
The argument against inter-racial marriage: Then
It's against the Bible!!
It confuses the kids!!
It's against the law!!
It tarnishes the institution of marriage!!
Deja vu all over again!!

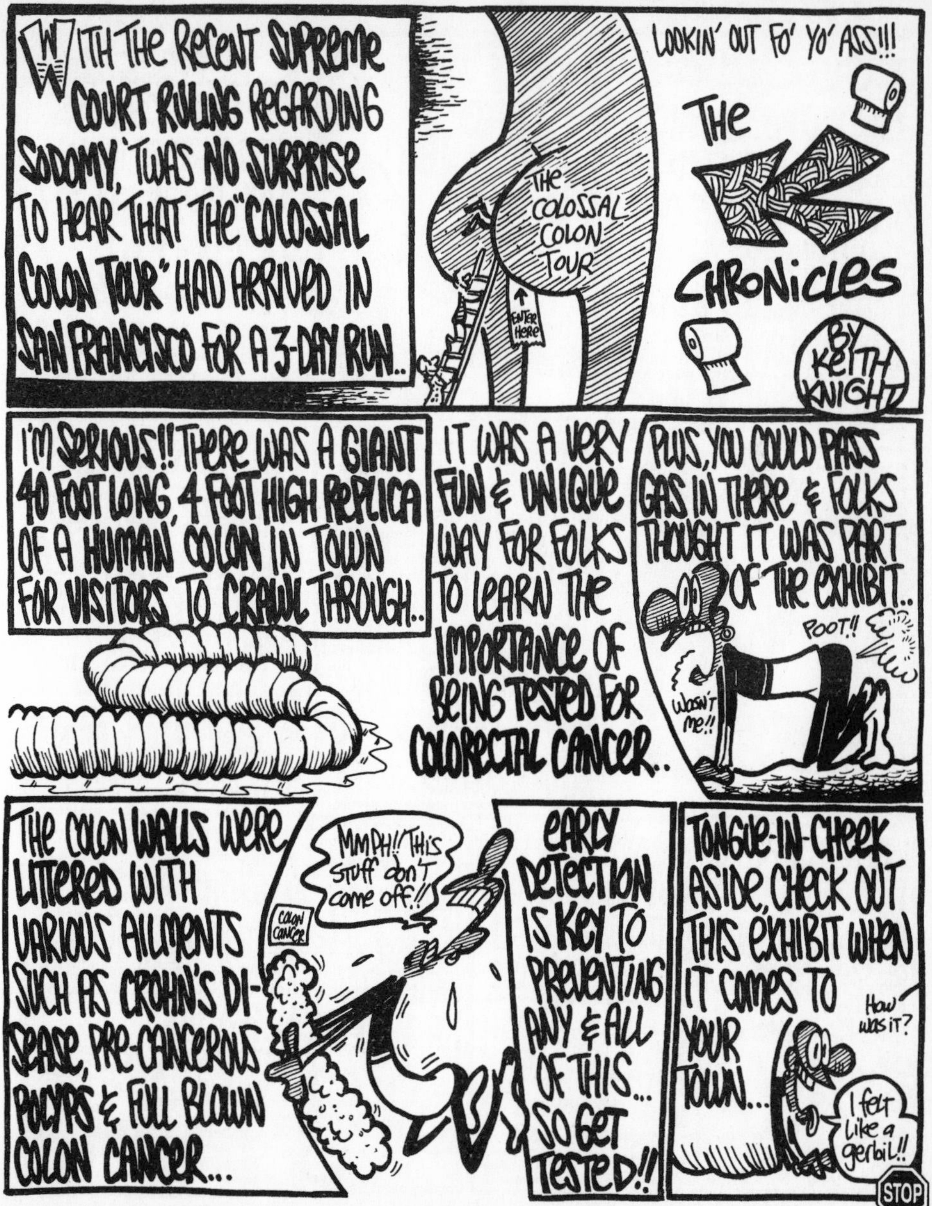
WITH THE RECENT SUPREME COURT RULING REGARDING SODOMY, 'TWAS NO SURPRISE TO HEAR THAT THE "COLOSSAL COLON TOUR" HAD ARRIVED IN SAN FRANCISCO FOR A 3-DAY RUN..
THE COLOSSAL COLON TOUR
ENTER HERE
LOOKIN' OUT FO' YO' ASS!!!
THE K CHRONICLES
BY KEITH KNIGHT
I'M SERIOUS!! THERE WAS A GIANT 40 FOOT LONG, 4 FOOT HIGH REPLICA OF A HUMAN COLON IN TOWN FOR VISITORS TO CRAWL THROUGH..
IT WAS A VERY FUN & UNIQUE WAY FOR FOLKS TO LEARN THE IMPORTANCE OF BEING TESTED FOR COLORECTAL CANCER..
PLUS, YOU COULD PASS GAS IN THERE & FOLKS THOUGHT IT WAS PART OF THE EXHIBIT..
POOT!!
WASN'T ME!!
THE COLON WALLS WERE LITTERED WITH VARIOUS AILMENTS SUCH AS CROHN'S DISEASE, PRE-CANCEROUS POLYPS & FULL BLOWN COLON CANCER...
MMPH!! THIS STUFF DON'T COME OFF!!
COLON CANCER
EARLY DETECTION IS KEY TO PREVENTING ANY & ALL OF THIS... SO GET TESTED!!
TONGUE-IN-CHEEK ASIDE, CHECK OUT THIS EXHIBIT WHEN IT COMES TO YOUR TOWN...
HOW WAS IT?
I FELT LIKE A GERBIL!!
STOP

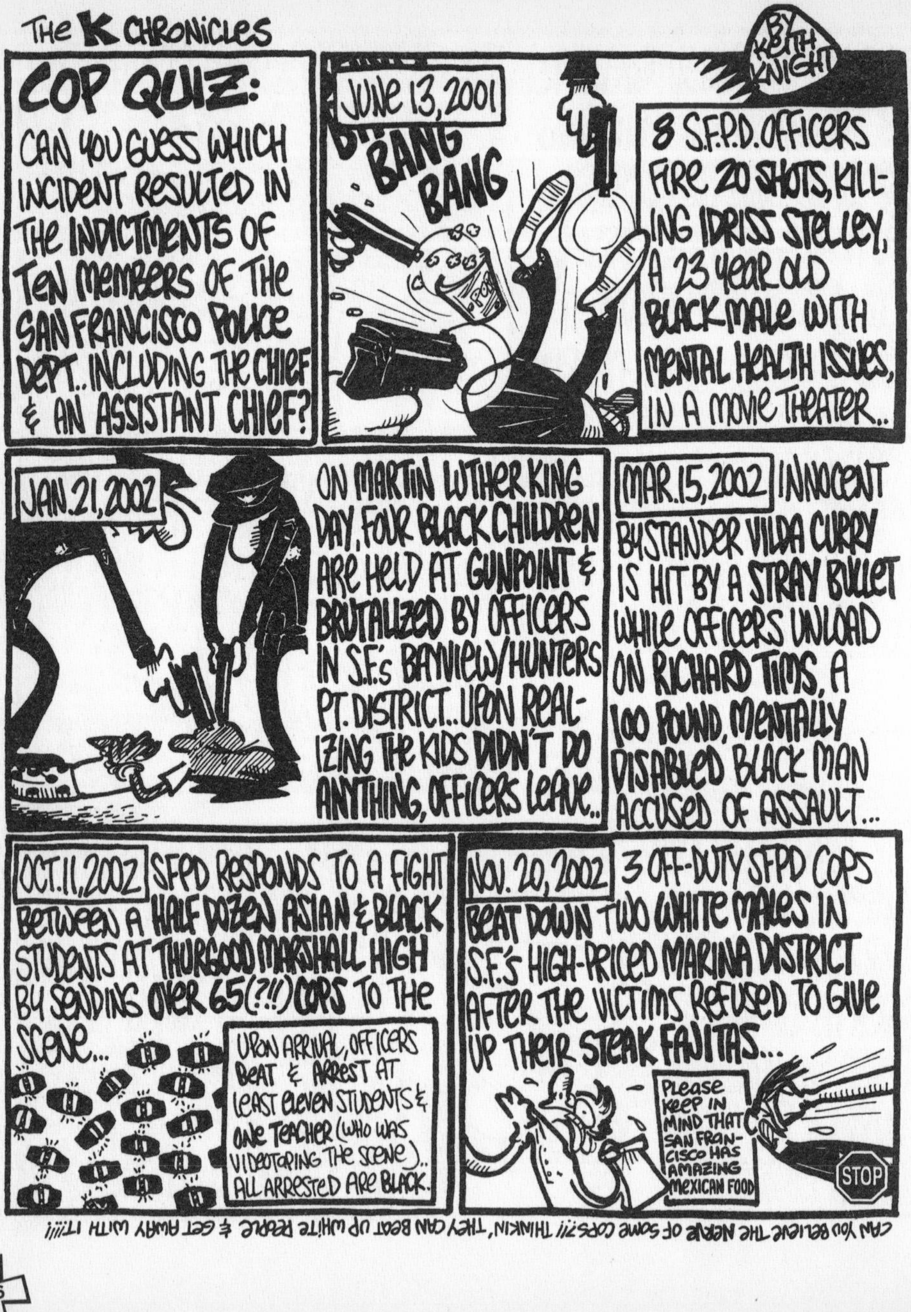

THE K CHRONICLES
BY KEITH KNIGHT
COP QUIZ:
CAN YOU GUESS WHICH INCIDENT RESULTED IN THE INDICTMENTS OF TEN MEMBERS OF THE SAN FRANCISCO POLICE DEPT.. INCLUDING THE CHIEF & AN ASSISTANT CHIEF?
JUNE 13, 2001
BANG
BANG
8 S.F.P.D. OFFICERS FIRE 20 SHOTS, KILLING IDRISS STELLEY, A 23 YEAR OLD BLACK MALE WITH MENTAL HEALTH ISSUES, IN A MOVIE THEATER..
JAN. 21, 2002
ON MARTIN LUTHER KING DAY, FOUR BLACK CHILDREN ARE HELD AT GUNPOINT & BRUTALIZED BY OFFICERS IN S.F.'s BAYVIEW/HUNTERS PT. DISTRICT.. UPON REALIZING THE KIDS DIDN'T DO ANYTHING, OFFICERS LEAVE..
MAR. 15, 2002
INNOCENT BYSTANDER VILDA CURRY IS HIT BY A STRAY BULLET WHILE OFFICERS UNLOAD ON RICHARD TIMS, A 100 POUND, MENTALLY DISABLED BLACK MAN ACCUSED OF ASSAULT...
OCT. 11, 2002
SFPD RESPONDS TO A FIGHT BETWEEN A HALF DOZEN ASIAN & BLACK STUDENTS AT THURGOOD MARSHALL HIGH BY SENDING OVER 65 (?!!) COPS TO THE SCENE...
UPON ARRIVAL, OFFICERS BEAT & ARREST AT LEAST ELEVEN STUDENTS & ONE TEACHER (WHO WAS VIDEOTAPING THE SCENE).. ALL ARRESTED ARE BLACK.
NOV. 20, 2002
3 OFF-DUTY SFPD COPS BEAT DOWN TWO WHITE MALES IN S.F.'S HIGH-PRICED MARINA DISTRICT AFTER THE VICTIMS REFUSED TO GIVE UP THEIR STEAK FAJITAS...
PLEASE KEEP IN MIND THAT SAN FRANCISCO HAS AMAZING MEXICAN FOOD
STOP
CAN YOU BELIEVE THE NERVE OF SOME COPS?!! THINKIN' THEY CAN BEAT UP WHITE PEOPLE & GET AWAY WITH IT?!!!

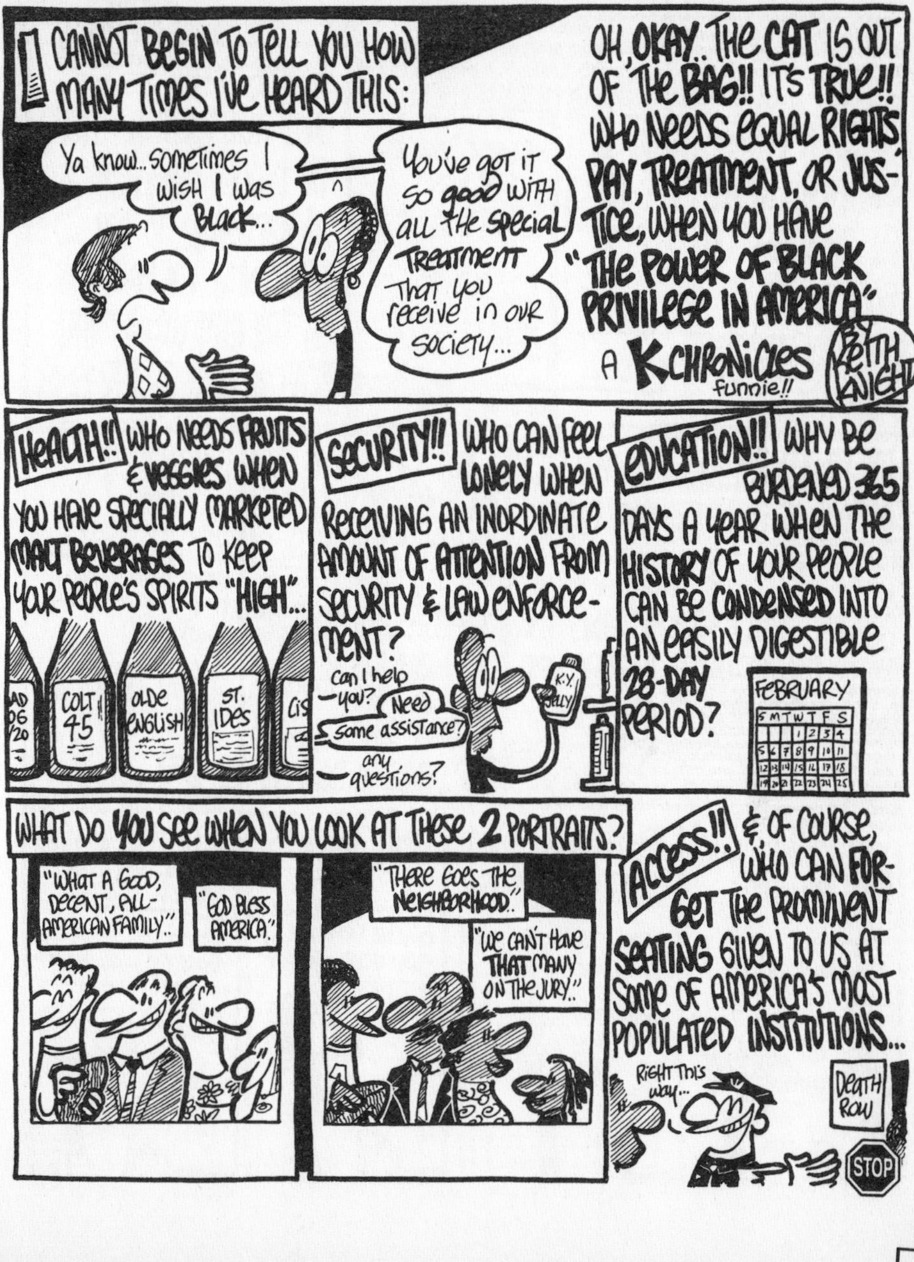

I CANNOT BEGIN TO TELL YOU HOW MANY TIMES I'VE HEARD THIS:
Ya know... sometimes I wish I was Black...
You've got it so good with all the special treatment that you receive in our society...
OH, OKAY.. THE CAT IS OUT OF THE BAG!! IT'S TRUE!! WHO NEEDS EQUAL RIGHTS, PAY, TREATMENT, OR JUSTICE, WHEN YOU HAVE "THE POWER OF BLACK PRIVILEGE IN AMERICA"
A K CHRONICLES funnie!!
BY KEITH KNIGHT
HEALTH!! WHO NEEDS FRUITS & VEGGIES WHEN YOU HAVE SPECIALLY MARKETED MALT BEVERAGES TO KEEP YOUR PEOPLE'S SPIRITS "HIGH"...
COLT 45
OLDE ENGLISH
ST. IDES
SECURITY!! WHO CAN FEEL LONELY WHEN RECEIVING AN INORDINATE AMOUNT OF ATTENTION FROM SECURITY & LAW ENFORCEMENT?
Can I help you?
Need some assistance?
any questions?
K.Y. JELLY
EDUCATION!! WHY BE BURDENED 365 DAYS A YEAR WHEN THE HISTORY OF YOUR PEOPLE CAN BE CONDENSED INTO AN EASILY DIGESTIBLE 28-DAY PERIOD?
FEBRUARY
WHAT DO YOU SEE WHEN YOU LOOK AT THESE 2 PORTRAITS?
"WHAT A GOOD, DECENT, ALL-AMERICAN FAMILY.."
"GOD BLESS AMERICA."
"THERE GOES THE NEIGHBORHOOD."
"WE CAN'T HAVE THAT MANY ON THE JURY.."
ACCESS!! & OF COURSE, WHO CAN FORGET THE PROMINENT SEATING GIVEN TO US AT SOME OF AMERICA'S MOST POPULATED INSTITUTIONS...
RIGHT THIS WAY...
DEATH ROW
STOP

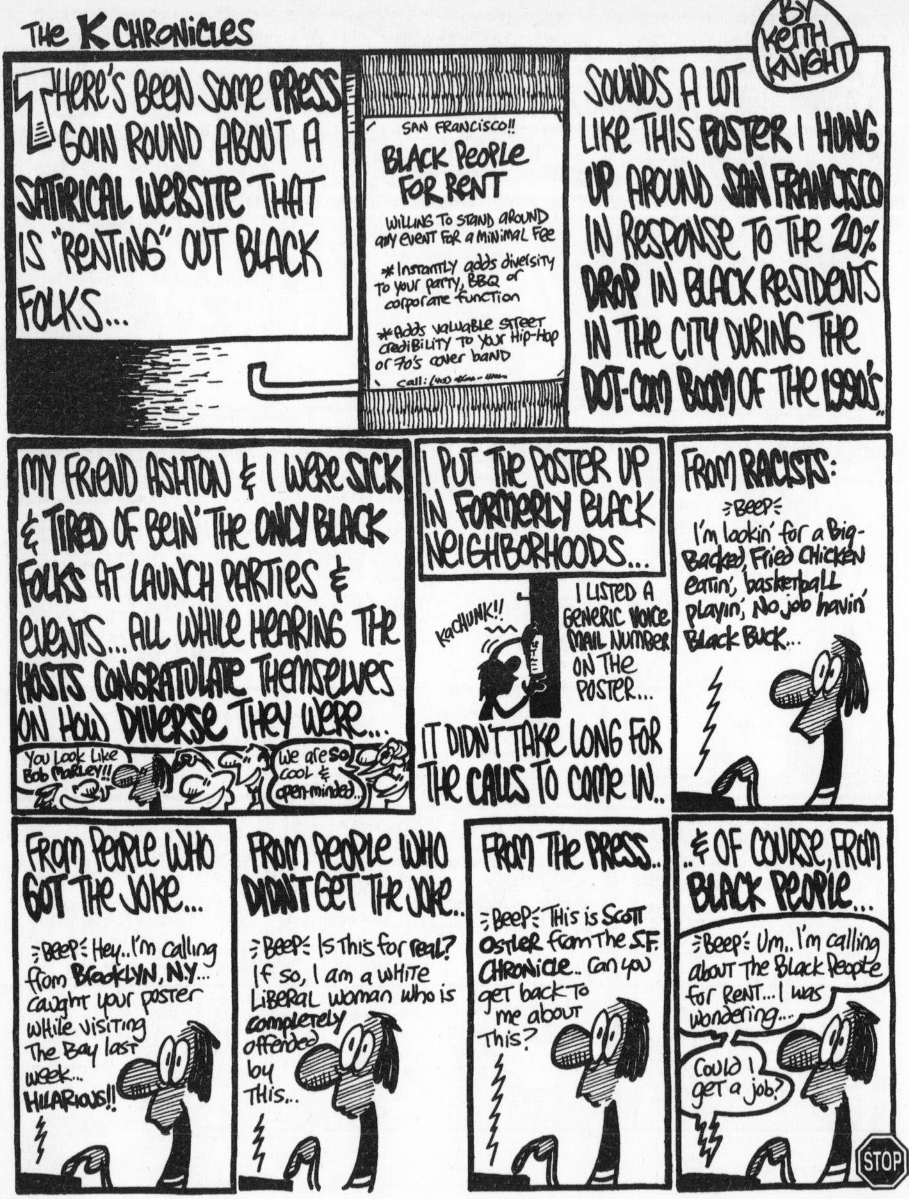
THE K CHRONICLES
BY KEITH KNIGHT
THERE'S BEEN SOME PRESS GOIN ROUND ABOUT A SATIRICAL WEBSITE THAT IS "RENTING" OUT BLACK FOLKS...
SAN FRANCISCO!!
BLACK PEOPLE FOR RENT
WILLING TO STAND AROUND ANY EVENT FOR A MINIMAL FEE
* INSTANTLY ADDS DIVERSITY TO YOUR PARTY, BBQ OR CORPORATE FUNCTION
* ADDS VALUABLE STREET CREDIBILITY TO YOUR HIP-HOP OR 70'S COVER BAND
SOUNDS A LOT LIKE THIS POSTER I HUNG UP AROUND SAN FRANCISCO IN RESPONSE TO THE 20% DROP IN BLACK RESIDENTS IN THE CITY DURING THE DOT-COM BOOM OF THE 1990'S.
MY FRIEND ASHTON & I WERE SICK & TIRED OF BEIN' THE ONLY BLACK FOLKS AT LAUNCH PARTIES & EVENTS... ALL WHILE HEARING THE HOSTS CONGRATULATE THEMSELVES ON HOW DIVERSE THEY WERE...
YOU LOOK LIKE BOB MARLEY!!
WE ARE SO COOL & OPEN-MINDED...
I PUT THE POSTER UP IN FORMERLY BLACK NEIGHBORHOODS...
KACHUNK!!
I LISTED A GENERIC VOICE MAIL NUMBER ON THE POSTER...
IT DIDN'T TAKE LONG FOR THE CALLS TO COME IN..
FROM RACISTS:
BEEP
I'M LOOKIN' FOR A BIG-BACKED, FRIED CHICKEN EATIN', BASKETBALL PLAYIN', NO JOB HAVIN' BLACK BUCK...
FROM PEOPLE WHO GOT THE JOKE...
BEEP HEY.. I'M CALLING FROM BROOKLYN, N.Y... CAUGHT YOUR POSTER WHILE VISITING THE BAY LAST WEEK... HILARIOUS!!
FROM PEOPLE WHO DIDN'T GET THE JOKE..
BEEP IS THIS FOR REAL? IF SO, I AM A WHITE LIBERAL WOMAN WHO IS COMPLETELY OFFENDED BY THIS...
FROM THE PRESS..
BEEP THIS IS SCOTT OSTLER FROM THE S.F. CHRONICLE.. CAN YOU GET BACK TO ME ABOUT THIS?
..& OF COURSE, FROM BLACK PEOPLE...
BEEP UM.. I'M CALLING ABOUT THE BLACK PEOPLE FOR RENT... I WAS WONDERING....
COULD I GET A JOB?
STOP

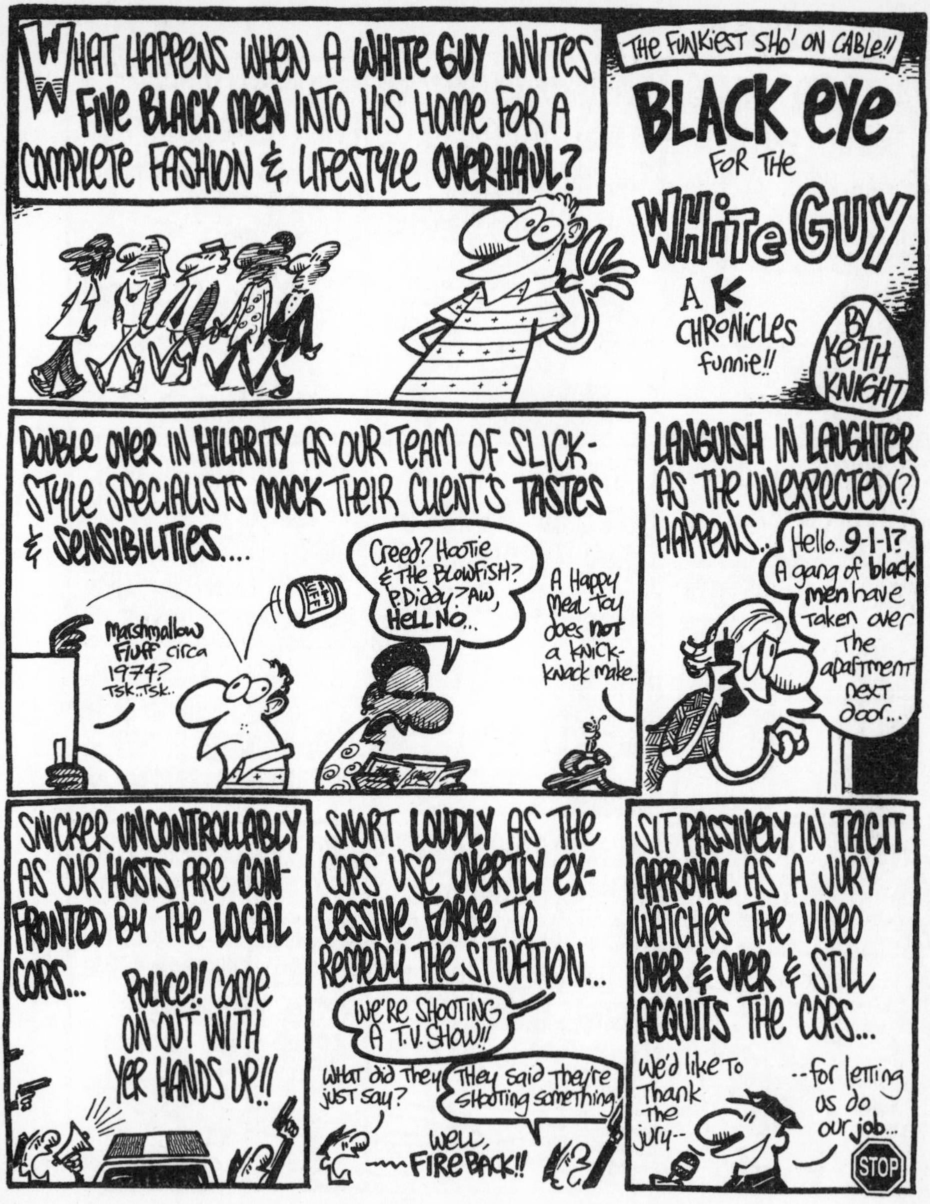
WHAT HAPPENS WHEN A WHITE GUY INVITES FIVE BLACK MEN INTO HIS HOME FOR A COMPLETE FASHION & LIFESTYLE OVERHAUL?
THE FUNKIEST SHO' ON CABLE!!
BLACK eye FOR THE WHITe GUY
A K CHRONICLES funnie!!
BY KEITH KNIGHT
DOUBLE OVER IN HILARITY AS OUR TEAM OF SLICK-STYLE SPECIALISTS MOCK THEIR CLIENT'S TASTES & SENSIBILITIES....
Marshmallow Fluff circa 1974? Tsk..Tsk..
Creed? Hootie & THE BLOWFISH? P.Diddy? AW, HELL NO...
A Happy Meal Toy does not a KNICK-KNACK make..
LANGUISH IN LAUGHTER AS THE UNEXPECTED(?) HAPPENS..
Hello..9-1-1? A gang of black men have taken over the apartment next door...
SNICKER UNCONTROLLABLY AS OUR HOSTS ARE CON-FRONTED BY THE LOCAL COPS...
POLICE!! COME ON OUT WITH YER HANDS UP!!
SNORT LOUDLY AS THE COPS USE OVERTLY EX-CESSIVE FORCE TO REMEDY THE SITUATION...
WE'RE SHOOTING A T.V. SHOW!!
WHAT did THEY JUST SAY?
THEY said they're SHOOTING SOMETHING.
WELL, FIRE BACK!!
SIT PASSIVELY IN TACIT APPROVAL AS A JURY WATCHES THE VIDEO OVER & OVER & STILL ACQUITS THE COPS...
We'd like To Thank The jury--
--for letting us do our job...
STOP

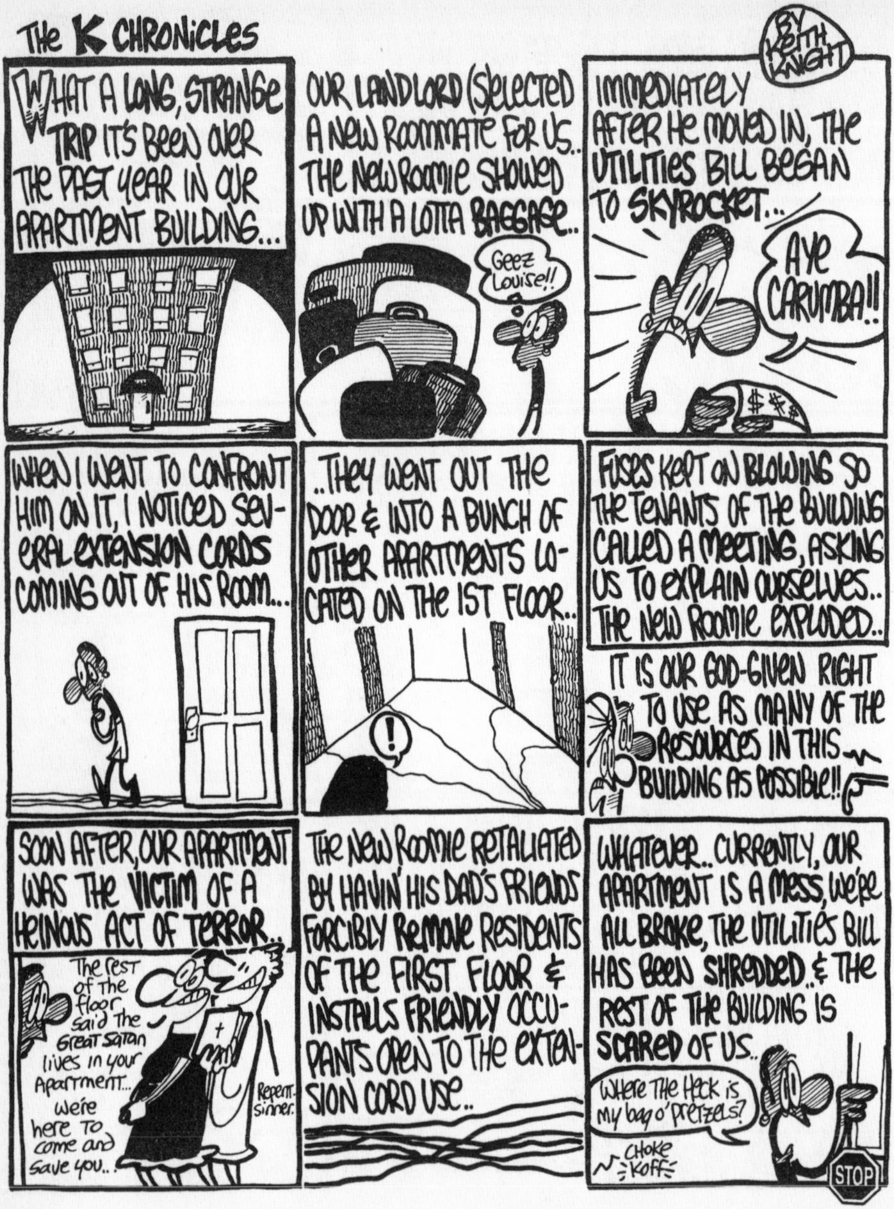
The K Chronicles
By Keith Knight
What a long, strange trip it's been over the past year in our apartment building...
Our landlord (s)elected a new roommate for us.. The new roomie showed up with a lotta baggage..
Geez Louise!!
Immediately after he moved in, the utilities bill began to skyrocket...
Aye Carumba!!
When I went to confront him on it, I noticed several extension cords coming out of his room...
..They went out the door & into a bunch of other apartments located on the 1st floor..
!
Fuses kept on blowing so the tenants of the building called a meeting, asking us to explain ourselves.. The new roomie exploded..
It is our God-given right to use as many of the resources in this building as possible!!
Soon after, our apartment was the victim of a heinous act of terror..
The rest of the floor said the Great Satan lives in your apartment... We're here to come and save you...
Repent sinner.
The new roomie retaliated by havin' his dad's friends forcibly remove residents of the first floor & installs friendly occupants open to the extension cord use..
Whatever.. Currently, our apartment is a mess, we're all broke, the utilities bill has been shredded.. & the rest of the building is scared of us..
Where the heck is my bag o' pretzels?
Choke koff
STOP

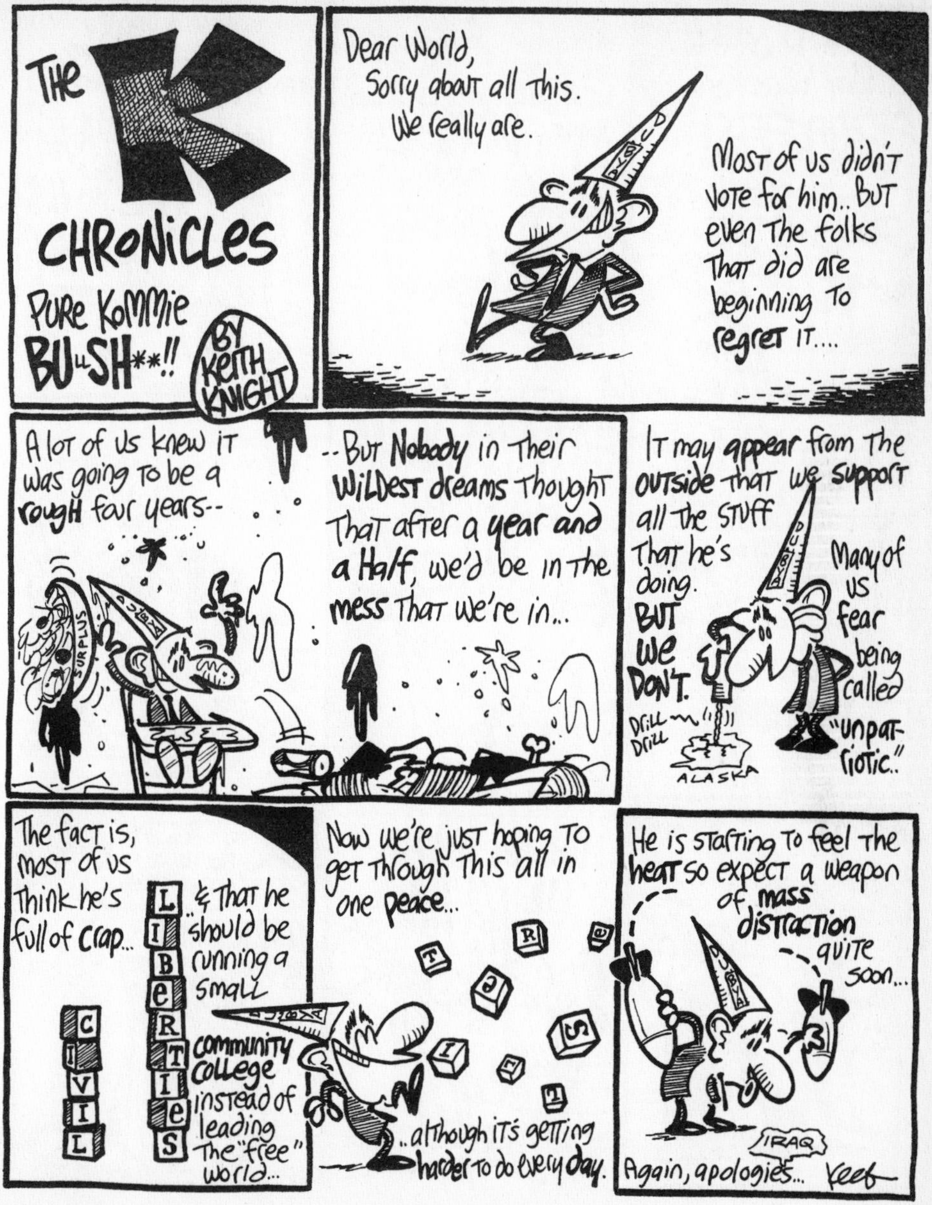

THE K CHRONICLES
Pure Kommie BU"SH**!!
BY KEITH KNIGHT
Dear World, Sorry about all this. We really are.
DUBYA
Most of us didn't vote for him.. But even the folks that did are beginning to regret it....
A lot of us knew it was going to be a rough four years--
SURPLUS
--But Nobody in their WILDEST dreams thought that after a year and a Half, we'd be in the mess that we're in...
It may appear from the OUTSIDE that we support all the STUFF that he's doing.
BUT WE DON'T.
Many of us fear being called "unpatriotic."
DRILL DRILL
ALASKA
The fact is, most of us think he's full of crap...
& that he should be running a small community college instead of leading the "free" world...
CIVIL
LIBERTIES
Now we're just hoping to get through this all in one peace...
..although it's getting harder to do every day.
He is starting to feel the heat so expect a weapon of mass distraction quite soon...
IRAQ
Again, apologies... Keef

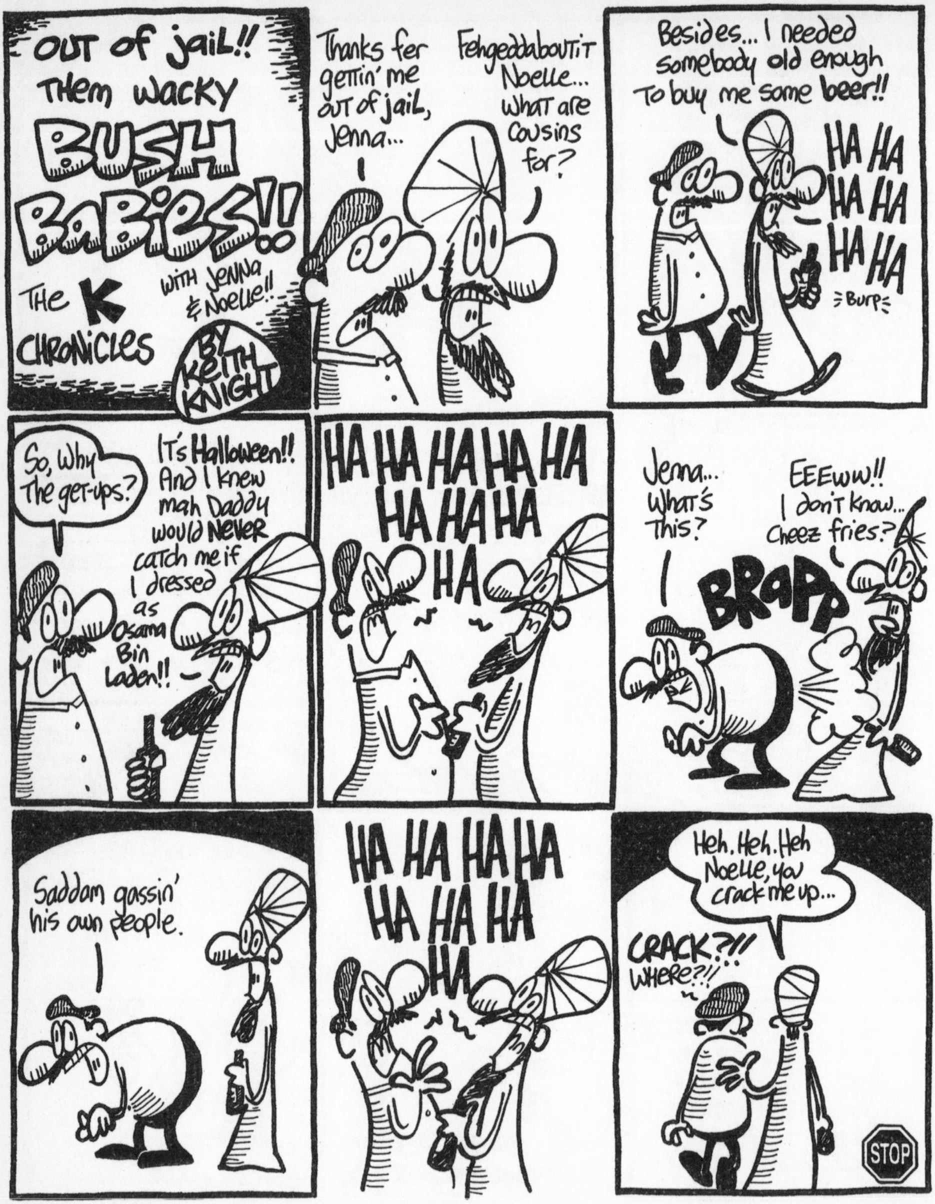
OUT of jaiL!! THEm WACKY BUSH BaBies!!
THE K CHRONICLES
WITH JENNA & NOELLE!!
BY KEITH KNIGHT
Thanks fer gettin' me out of jail, Jenna...
Fehgeddaboutit Noelle... what are cousins for?
Besides... I needed somebody old enough to buy me some beer!!
HA HA HA HA HA HA
BURP
So, why the get-ups?
It's Halloween!! And I knew mah Daddy would NEVER catch me if I dressed as Osama Bin Laden!!
HA HA HA HA HA HA HA HA HA
Jenna... What's this?
BRAPP
EEEWW!! I don't know... Cheez fries?
Saddam gassin' his own people.
HA HA HA HA HA HA HA HA
Heh. Heh. Heh Noelle, you crack me up...
CRACK?!! WHERE?!!
STOP

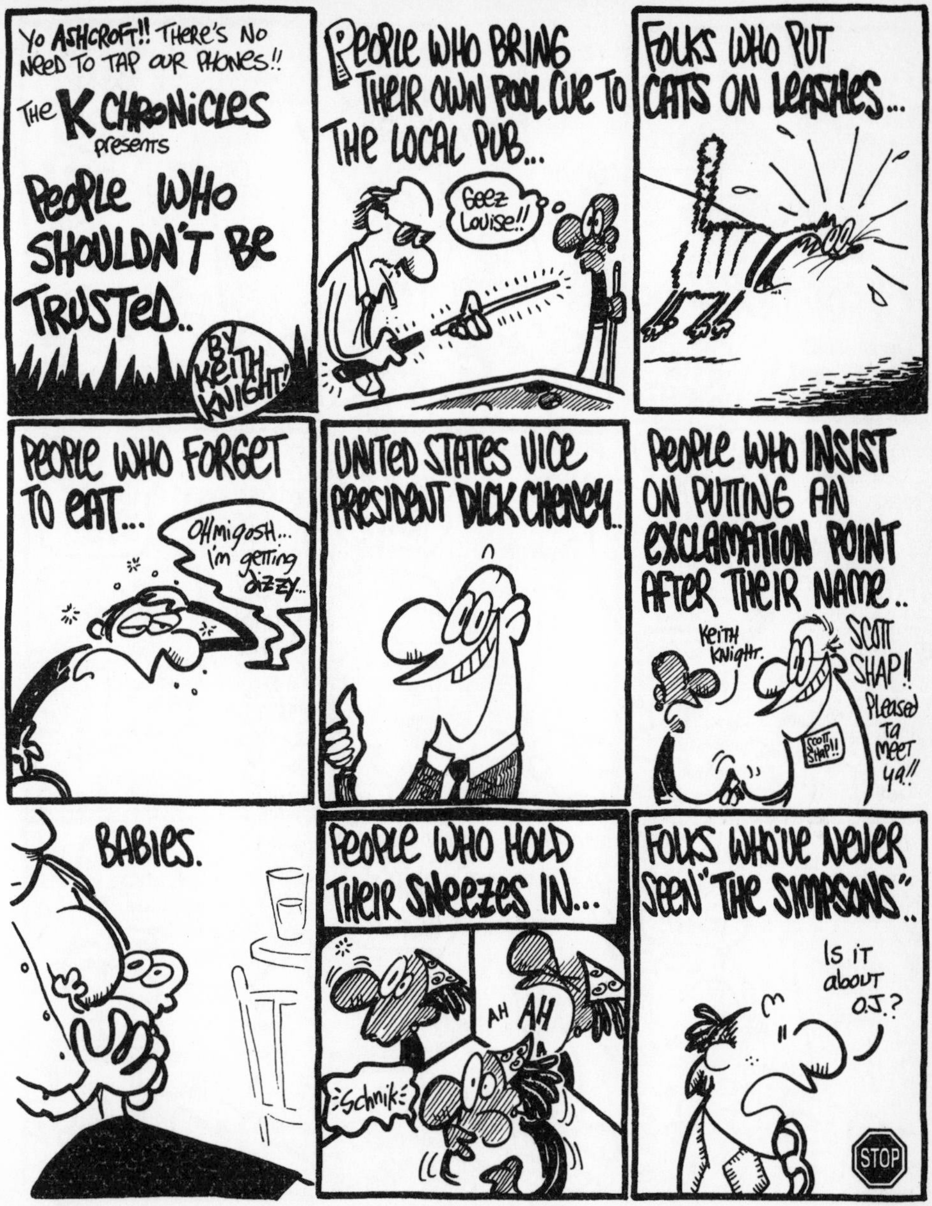
Yo ASHCROFT!! THERE'S NO NEED TO TAP OUR PHONES!!
THE K CHRONICLES presents
PEOPLE WHO SHOULDN'T BE TRUSTED..
BY KEITH KNIGHT!
PEOPLE WHO BRING THEIR OWN POOL CUE TO THE LOCAL PUB...
Geez Louise!!
FOLKS WHO PUT CATS ON LEASHES...
PEOPLE WHO FORGET TO EAT...
OHmigosH... I'm getting dizzy...
UNITED STATES VICE PRESIDENT DICK CHENEY..
PEOPLE WHO INSIST ON PUTTING AN EXCLAMATION POINT AFTER THEIR NAME..
KEITH KNIGHT.
SCOTT SHAP!! Pleased ta meet ya!!
SCOTT SHAP!!
BABIES.
PEOPLE WHO HOLD THEIR SNEEZES IN...
AH AH
Schnik
FOLKS WHO'VE NEVER SEEN "THE SIMPSONS"..
Is it about O.J.?
STOP

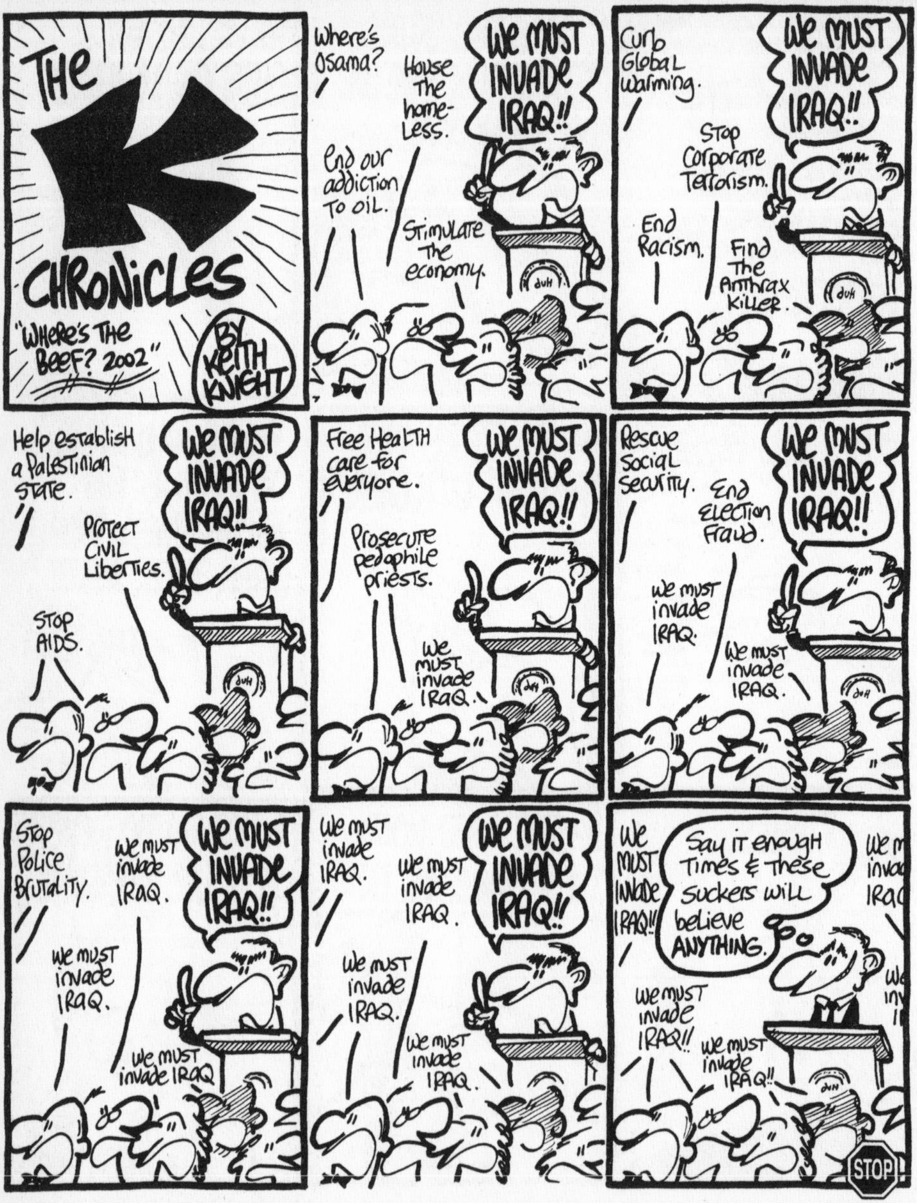
THE K CHRONICLES
"WHERE'S THE BEEF? 2002"
BY KEITH KNIGHT
Where's Osama?
House the homeless.
End our addiction to oil.
Stimulate the economy.
WE MUST INVADE IRAQ!!
duH
Curb Global warming.
Stop Corporate Terrorism.
End Racism.
Find the Anthrax Killer.
WE MUST INVADE IRAQ!!
duH
Help establish a Palestinian state.
Protect Civil Liberties.
STOP AIDS.
WE MUST INVADE IRAQ!!
duH
Free Health care for everyone.
Prosecute pedophile priests.
We must invade IRAQ.
WE MUST INVADE IRAQ!!
duH
Rescue social security.
End Election Fraud.
We must invade IRAQ.
We must invade IRAQ.
WE MUST INVADE IRAQ!!
duH
Stop Police Brutality.
We must invade IRAQ.
We must invade IRAQ.
We must invade IRAQ
WE MUST INVADE IRAQ!!
We must invade IRAQ.
We must invade IRAQ.
We must invade IRAQ.
We must invade IRAQ.
WE MUST INVADE IRAQ!!
We MUST INVADE IRAQ!!
Say it enough times & these suckers will believe ANYTHING.
We must invade IRAQ!!
We must invade IRAQ!!
duH
STOP!

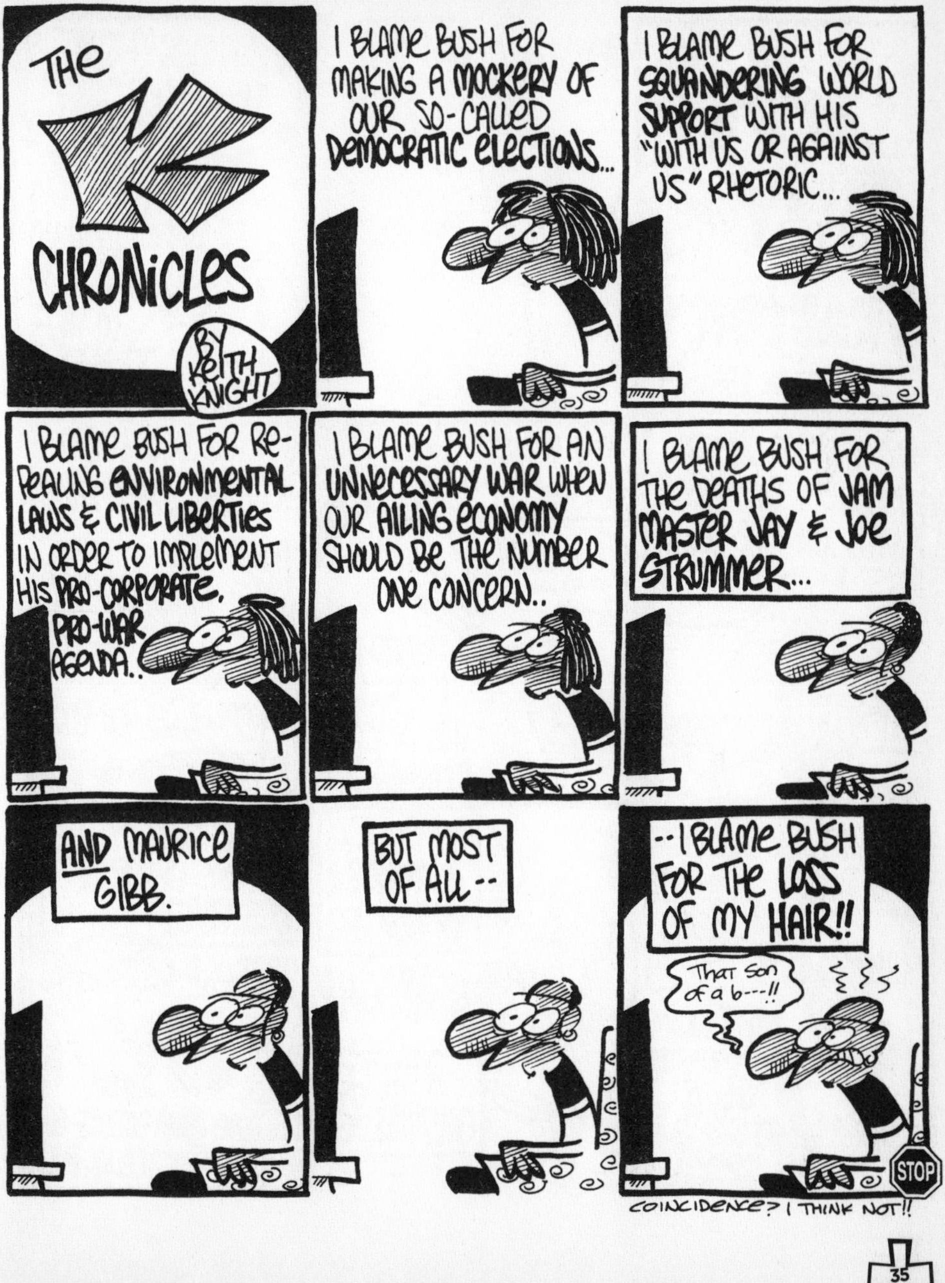
THE K CHRONICLES
BY KEITH KNIGHT
I BLAME BUSH FOR MAKING A MOCKERY OF OUR SO-CALLED DEMOCRATIC ELECTIONS...
I BLAME BUSH FOR SQUANDERING WORLD SUPPORT WITH HIS "WITH US OR AGAINST US" RHETORIC...
I BLAME BUSH FOR REPEALING ENVIRONMENTAL LAWS & CIVIL LIBERTIES IN ORDER TO IMPLEMENT HIS PRO-CORPORATE, PRO-WAR AGENDA..
I BLAME BUSH FOR AN UNNECESSARY WAR WHEN OUR AILING ECONOMY SHOULD BE THE NUMBER ONE CONCERN..
I BLAME BUSH FOR THE DEATHS OF JAM MASTER JAY & JOE STRUMMER...
AND MAURICE GIBB.
BUT MOST OF ALL--
--I BLAME BUSH FOR THE LOSS OF MY HAIR!!
That son of a b---!!
STOP
COINCIDENCE? I THINK NOT!!

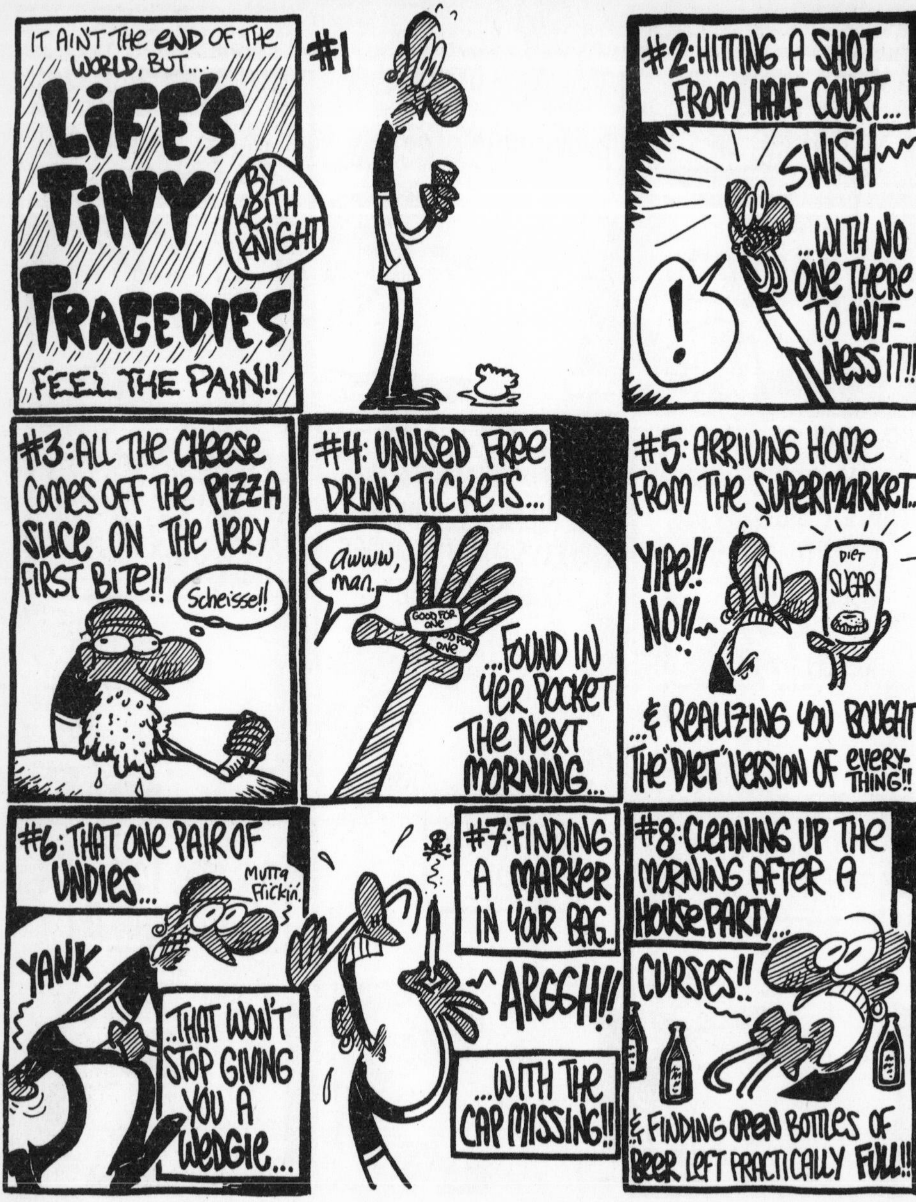
IT AIN'T THE END OF THE WORLD, BUT....
LIFE'S TINY TRAGEDIES
BY KEITH KNIGHT
FEEL THE PAIN!!
#1
#2: HITTING A SHOT FROM HALF COURT...
SWISH
!
...WITH NO ONE THERE TO WITNESS IT!!
#3: ALL THE CHEESE COMES OFF THE PIZZA SLICE ON THE VERY FIRST BITE!!
Scheisse!!
#4: UNUSED FREE DRINK TICKETS...
awww, man.
GOOD FOR ONE
GOOD FOR ONE
...FOUND IN YER POCKET THE NEXT MORNING...
#5: ARRIVING HOME FROM THE SUPERMARKET..
YIPE!! NO!!
DIET SUGAR
...& REALIZING YOU BOUGHT THE "DIET" VERSION OF EVERYTHING!!
#6: THAT ONE PAIR OF UNDIES...
Mutta Frickin'
YANK
..THAT WON'T STOP GIVING YOU A WEDGIE...
#7: FINDING A MARKER IN YOUR BAG..
ARGGH!!
...WITH THE CAP MISSING!!
#8: CLEANING UP THE MORNING AFTER A HOUSE PARTY...
CURSES!!
& FINDING OPEN BOTTLES OF BEER LEFT PRACTICALLY FULL!!

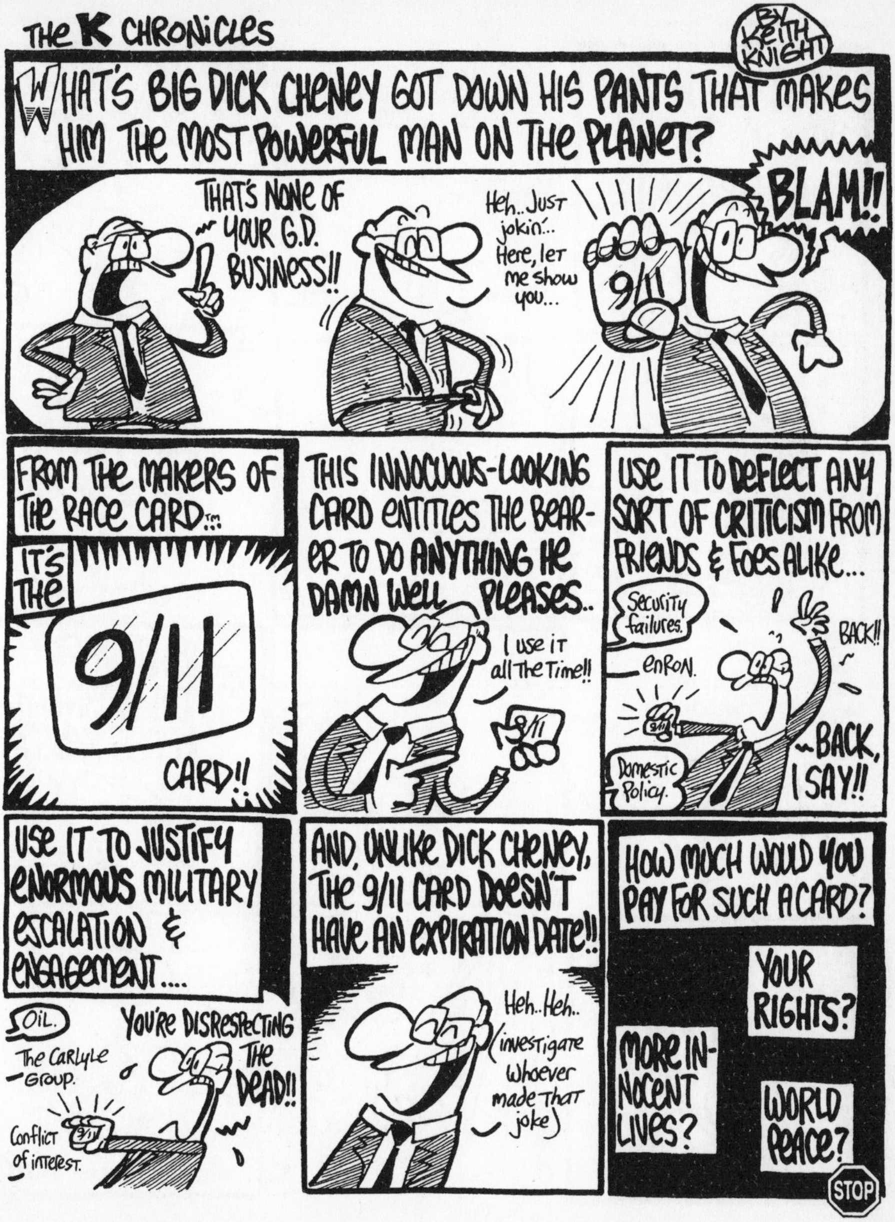
THE K CHRONICLES
BY KEITH KNIGHT
WHAT'S BIG DICK CHENEY GOT DOWN HIS PANTS THAT MAKES HIM THE MOST POWERFUL MAN ON THE PLANET?
THAT'S NONE OF YOUR G.D. BUSINESS!!
Heh.. JUST jokin'... Here, let me show you...
9/11
BLAM!!
FROM THE MAKERS OF THE RACE CARD...™
IT'S THE 9/11 CARD!!
THIS INNOCUOUS-LOOKING CARD ENTITLES THE BEARER TO DO ANYTHING HE DAMN WELL PLEASES..
I use it all the time!!
9/11
USE IT TO DEFLECT ANY SORT OF CRITICISM FROM FRIENDS & FOES ALIKE...
Security failures.
Enron.
Domestic Policy.
BACK!!
BACK, I SAY!!
USE IT TO JUSTIFY ENORMOUS MILITARY ESCALATION & ENGAGEMENT....
Oil.
The Carlyle Group.
Conflict of interest.
YOU'RE DISRESPECTING THE DEAD!!
AND, UNLIKE DICK CHENEY, THE 9/11 CARD DOESN'T HAVE AN EXPIRATION DATE!!
Heh.. Heh..
(investigate whoever made that joke)
HOW MUCH WOULD YOU PAY FOR SUCH A CARD?
YOUR RIGHTS?
MORE INNOCENT LIVES?
WORLD PEACE?
STOP

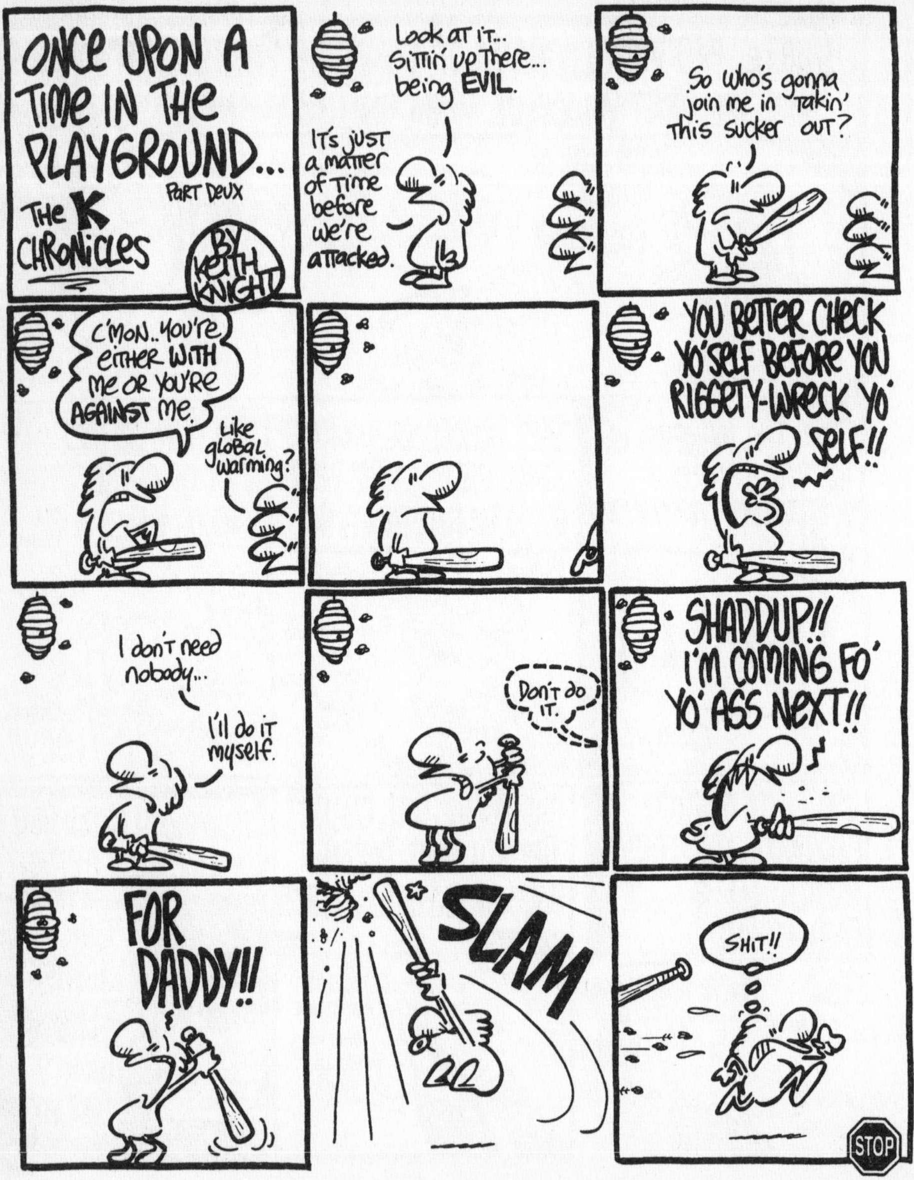
ONCE UPON A TIME IN THE PLAYGROUND...
PART DEUX
THE K CHRONICLES
BY KEITH KNIGHT
Look at it... Sittin' up there... being EVIL.
It's just a matter of time before we're attacked.
So who's gonna join me in takin' this sucker out?
C'MON.. YOU'RE EITHER WITH ME OR YOU'RE AGAINST ME.
Like global warming?
YOU BETTER CHECK YO'SELF BEFORE YOU RIGGETY-WRECK YO' SELF!!
I don't need nobody...
I'll do it myself.
Don't do it.
SHADDUP!! I'M COMING FO' YO' ASS NEXT!!
FOR DADDY!!
SLAM
SHIT!!
STOP

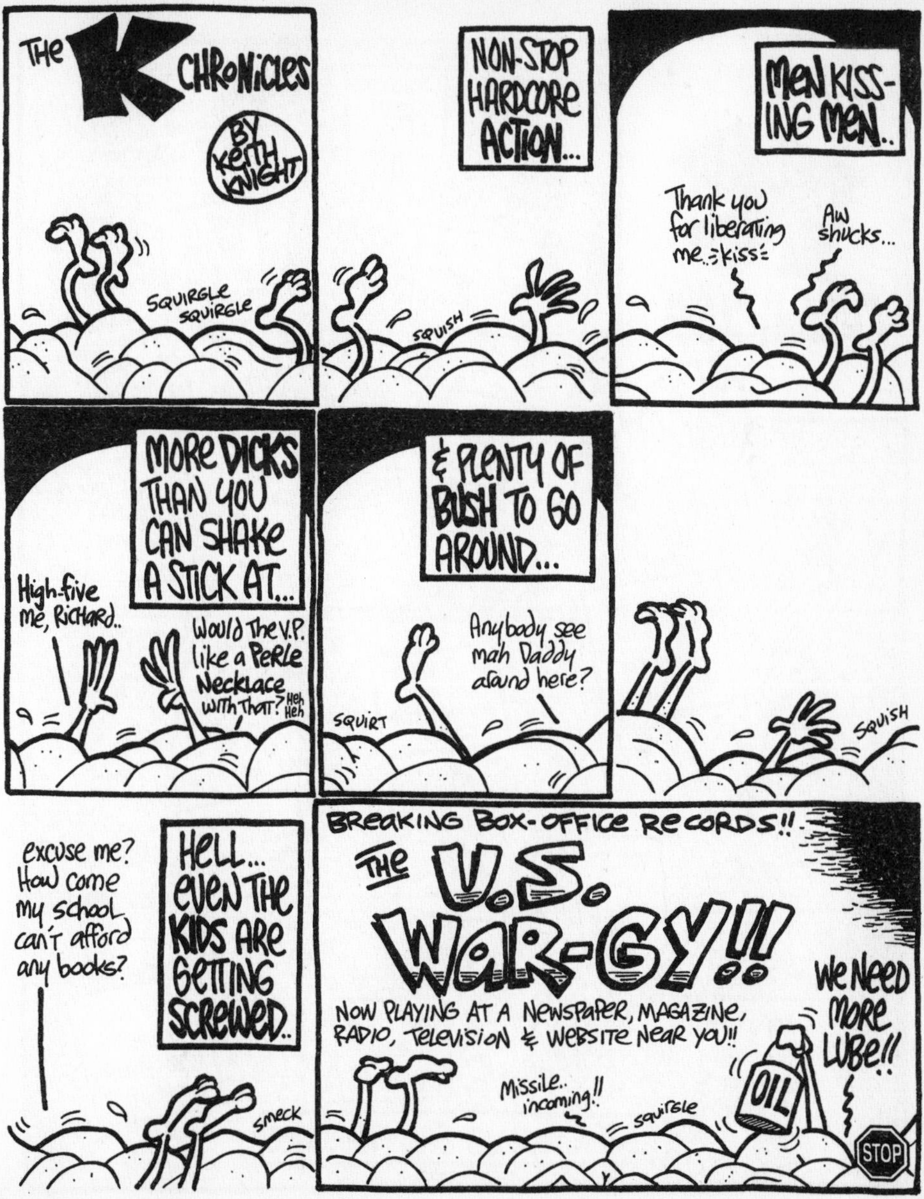
THE K CHRONICLES
BY KEITH KNIGHT
SQUIRGLE SQUIRGLE
NON-STOP HARDCORE ACTION...
SQUISH
MEN KISSING MEN..
Thank you for liberating me.. kiss
Aw shucks...
MORE DICKS THAN YOU CAN SHAKE A STICK AT...
High-five me, Richard..
Would the V.P. like a Perle Necklace with that?
Heh Heh
& PLENTY OF BUSH TO GO AROUND...
Anybody see mah Daddy around here?
SQUIRT
SQUISH
excuse me? How come my school can't afford any books?
HELL... EVEN THE KIDS ARE GETTING SCREWED..
SMECK
BREAKING BOX-OFFICE RECORDS!!
THE U.S. WAR-GY!!
NOW PLAYING AT A NEWSPAPER, MAGAZINE, RADIO, TELEVISION & WEBSITE NEAR YOU!!
We NEED MORE LUBE!!
OIL
Missile.. incoming!!
squirgle
STOP

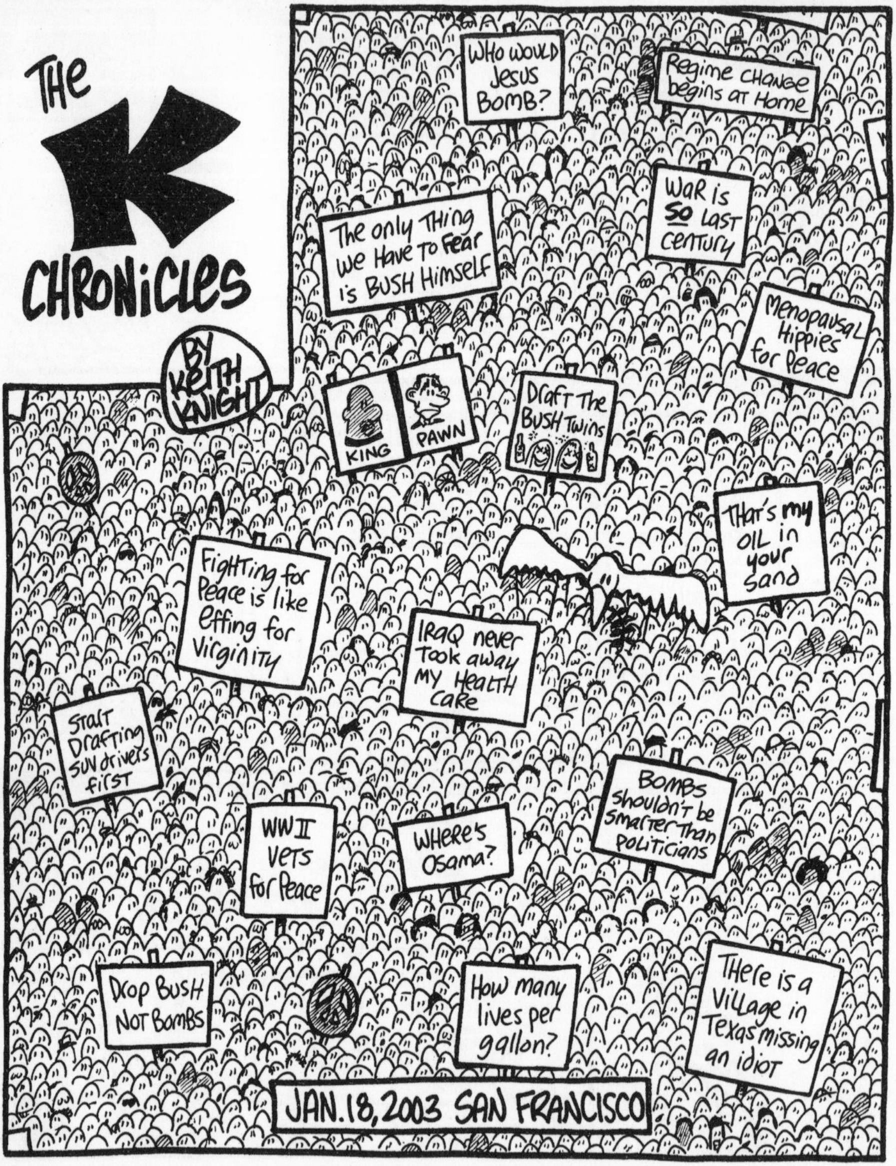
THE K CHRONICLES
BY KEITH KNIGHT
WHO WOULD JESUS BOMB?
Regime change begins at Home
The only THING we Have to Fear is BUSH Himself
WaR is SO LasT century
Menopausal Hippies for Peace
KING
PAWN
Draft The BUSH Twins
THaT's my OIL in your Sand
FighTing for Peace is like effing for Virginity
IRaQ never Took away MY HeaLTH care
Start DrafTing SUV drivers first
WW II VeTS for Peace
WHeRe's Osama?
BOMBS shouldn't be smarTer Than POLITICIANS
Drop BUSH NOT BOMBS
How many lives per gallon?
THere is a Village in Texas missing an idioT
JAN. 18, 2003 SAN FRANCISCO

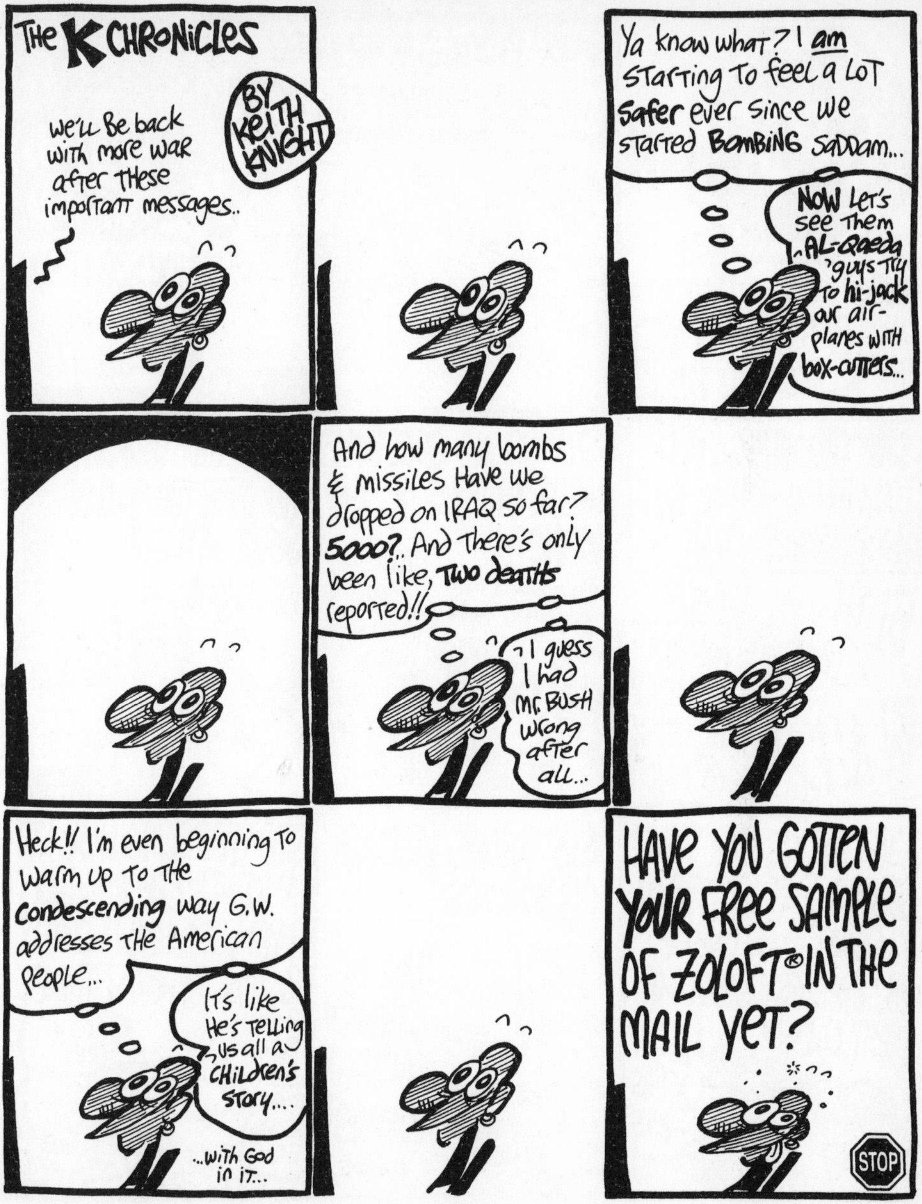
THE K CHRONICLES
BY KEITH KNIGHT
we'll Be back with more war after these important messages..
Ya know what? I am starting to feel a LOT Safer ever since we started BOMBING SADDAM...
NOW Let's see them AL-Qaeda guys try to hi-jack our air-planes with box-cutters...
And how many bombs & missiles Have we dropped on IRAQ so far? 5000?.. And there's only been like, TWO deaths reported!!
I guess I had Mr. BUSH wrong after all...
Heck!! I'm even beginning to warm up to the condescending way G.W. addresses the American people...
It's like He's telling us all a CHILdren's story....
...with God in it...
HAVE YOU GOTTEN YOUR FREE SAMPLE OF ZOLOFT® IN THE MAIL YET?
STOP

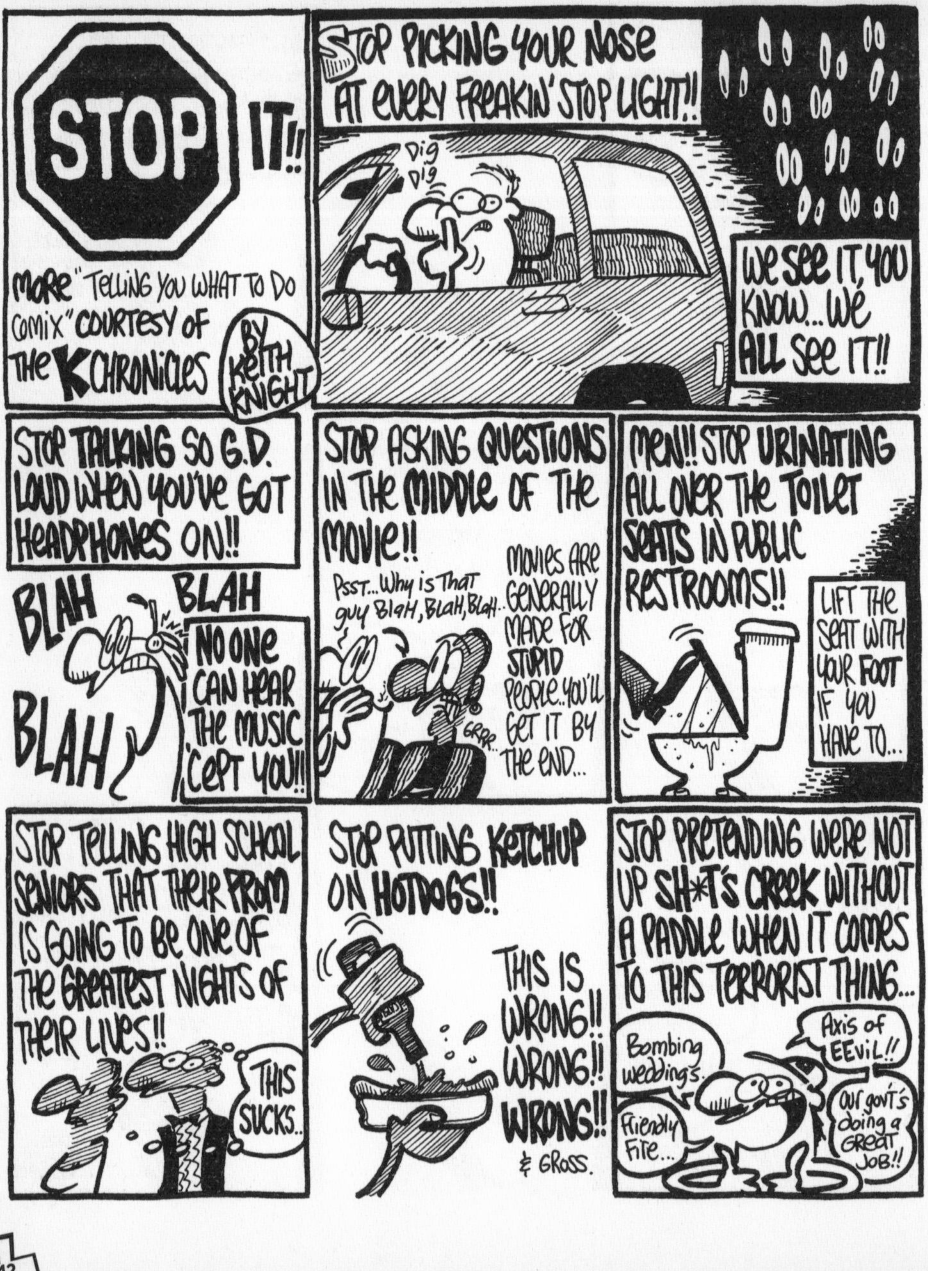
STOP IT!!
MORE "TELLING YOU WHAT TO DO COMIX" COURTESY OF THE K CHRONICLES
BY KEITH KNIGHT
STOP PICKING YOUR NOSE AT EVERY FREAKIN' STOP LIGHT!!
DIG DIG
WE SEE IT, YOU KNOW... WE ALL SEE IT!!
STOP TALKING SO G.D. LOUD WHEN YOU'VE GOT HEADPHONES ON!!
BLAH BLAH BLAH BLAH
NO ONE CAN HEAR THE MUSIC 'CEPT YOU!!
STOP ASKING QUESTIONS IN THE MIDDLE OF THE MOVIE!!
PSST... WHY IS THAT GUY BLAH, BLAH, BLAH...
GRRR...
MOVIES ARE GENERALLY MADE FOR STUPID PEOPLE... YOU'LL GET IT BY THE END...
MEN!! STOP URINATING ALL OVER THE TOILET SEATS IN PUBLIC RESTROOMS!!
LIFT THE SEAT WITH YOUR FOOT IF YOU HAVE TO...
STOP TELLING HIGH SCHOOL SENIORS THAT THEIR PROM IS GOING TO BE ONE OF THE GREATEST NIGHTS OF THEIR LIVES!!
THIS SUCKS...
STOP PUTTING KETCHUP ON HOTDOGS!!
THIS IS WRONG!! WRONG!! WRONG!!
& GROSS.
STOP PRETENDING WE'RE NOT UP SH*T'S CREEK WITHOUT A PADDLE WHEN IT COMES TO THIS TERRORIST THING...
Bombing weddings.
Axis of EEviL!!
Friendly Fire...
Our govt's doing a GREAT JOB!!

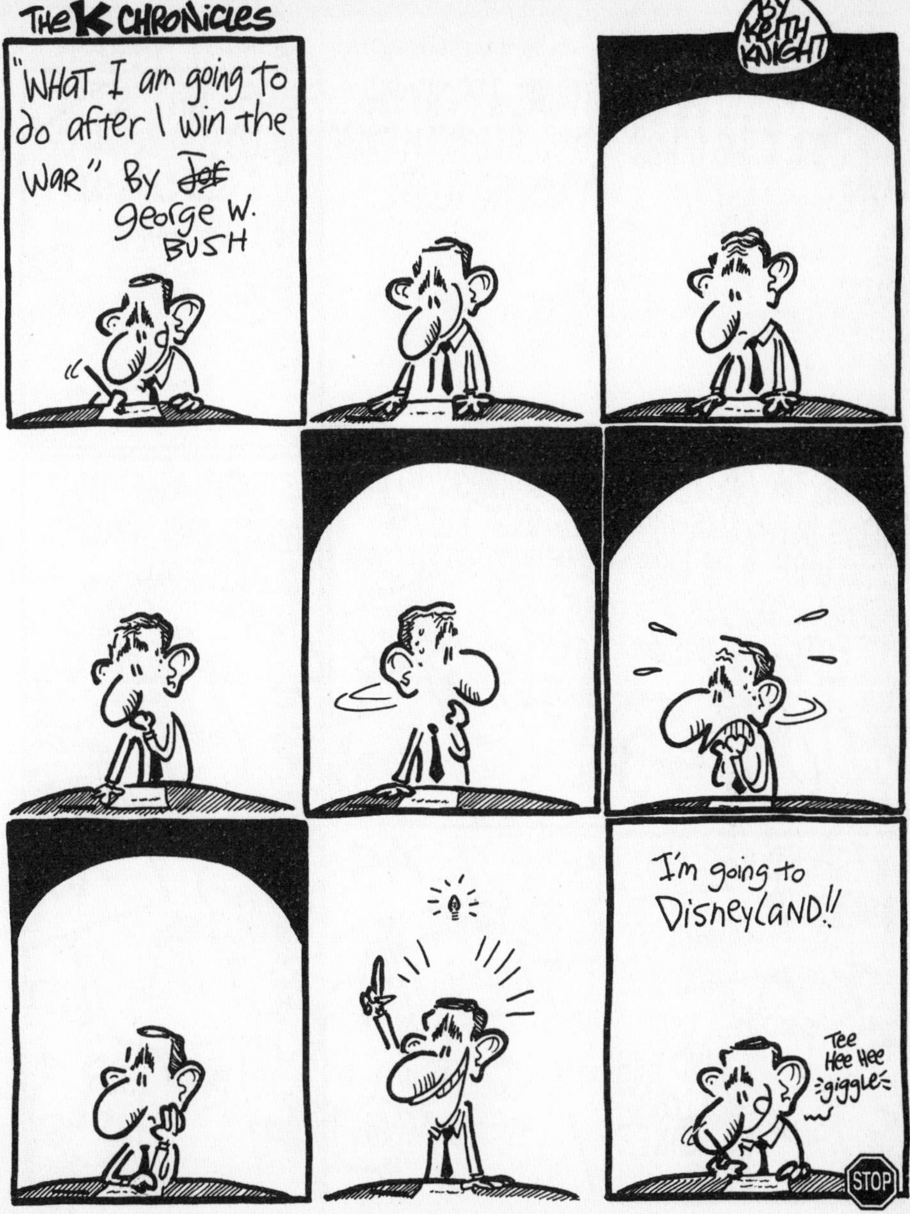
THE K CHRONICLES
BY KEITH KNIGHT
"WHAT I am going to do after I win the war" By Joe George W. BUSH
I'm going to DISNEYLAND!!
Tee Hee Hee
giggle
STOP

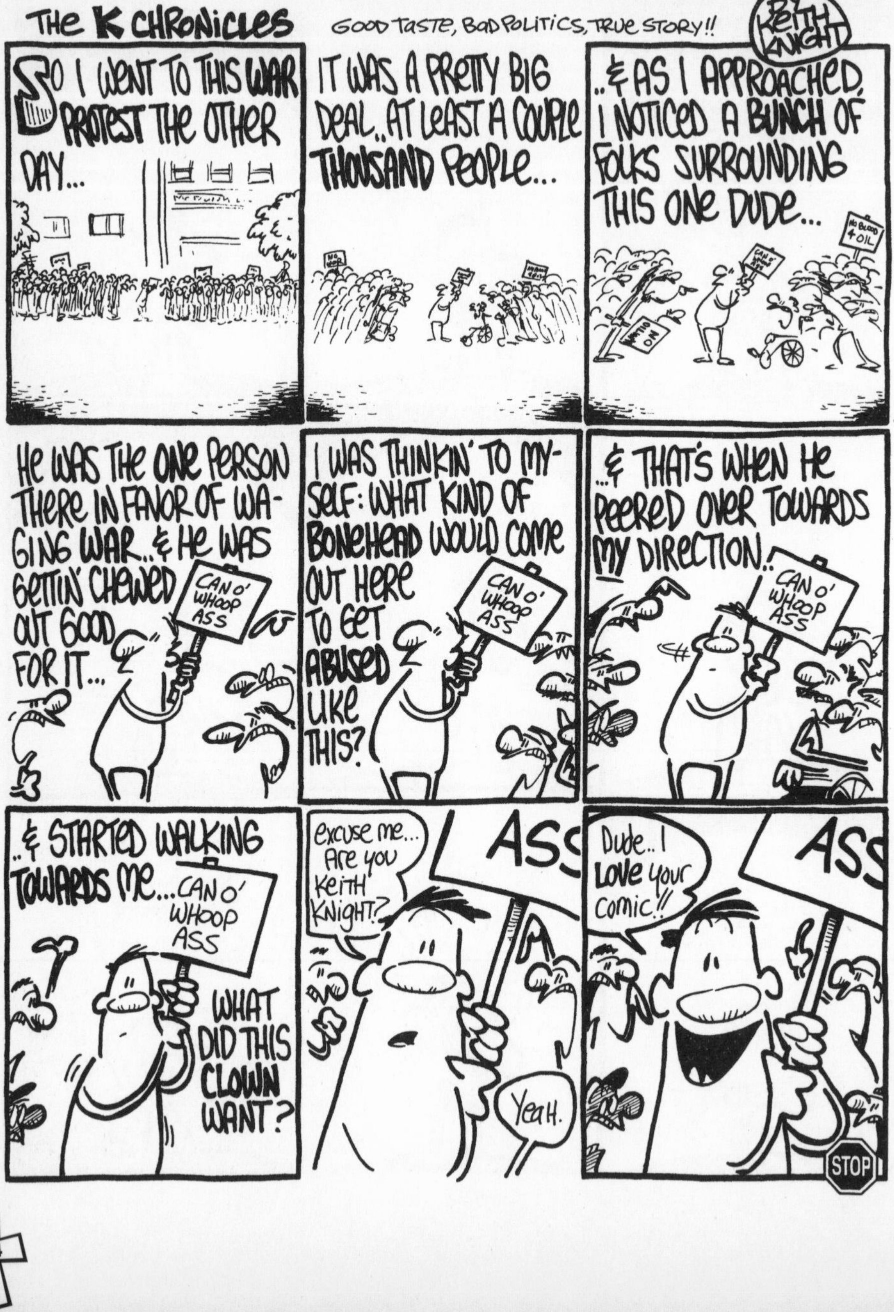
THE K CHRONICLES
GOOD TASTE, BAD POLITICS, TRUE STORY!!
BY KEITH KNIGHT
SO I WENT TO THIS WAR PROTEST THE OTHER DAY...
IT WAS A PRETTY BIG DEAL.. AT LEAST A COUPLE THOUSAND PEOPLE...
..& AS I APPROACHED, I NOTICED A BUNCH OF FOLKS SURROUNDING THIS ONE DUDE...
NO BLOOD 4 OIL
HE WAS THE ONE PERSON THERE IN FAVOR OF WAGING WAR..& HE WAS GETTIN' CHEWED OUT GOOD FOR IT...
CAN O' WHOOP ASS
I WAS THINKIN' TO MYSELF: WHAT KIND OF BONEHEAD WOULD COME OUT HERE TO GET ABUSED LIKE THIS?
CAN O' WHOOP ASS
...& THAT'S WHEN HE PEERED OVER TOWARDS MY DIRECTION..
CAN O' WHOOP ASS
..& STARTED WALKING TOWARDS ME...
CAN O' WHOOP ASS
WHAT DID THIS CLOWN WANT?
excuse me... Are you Keith Knight?
ASS
YeaH.
Dude.. I Love your comic!!
ASS
STOP

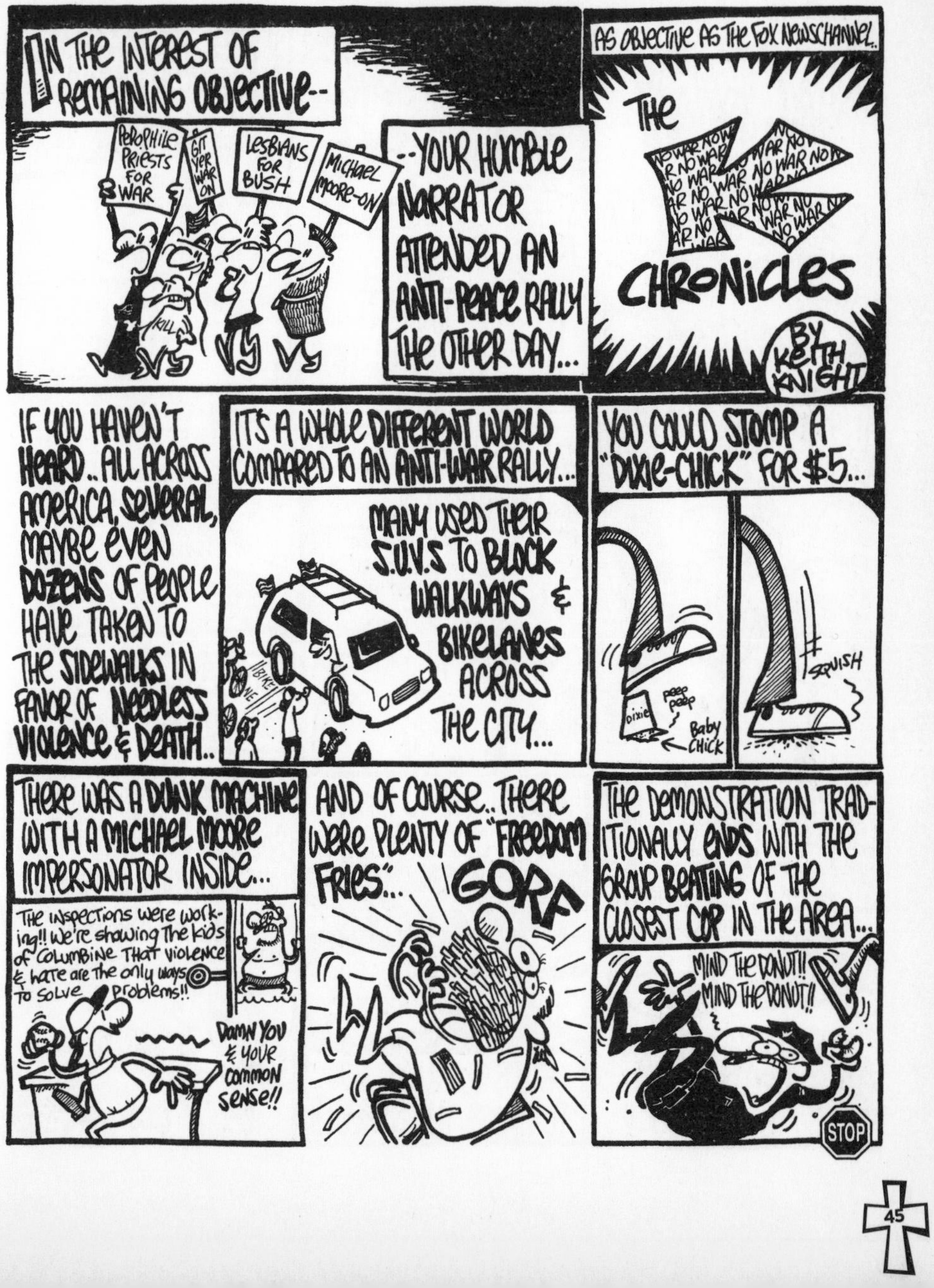

IN THE INTEREST OF REMAINING OBJECTIVE--
PEDOPHILE PRIESTS FOR WAR
GIT YER WAR ON
LESBIANS FOR BUSH
MICHAEL MOORE-ON
KILL
--YOUR HUMBLE NARRATOR ATTENDED AN ANTI-PEACE RALLY THE OTHER DAY...
AS OBJECTIVE AS THE FOX NEWSCHANNEL..
THE
NO WAR NO WAR NO WAR
CHRONICLES
BY KEITH KNIGHT
IF YOU HAVEN'T HEARD.. ALL ACROSS AMERICA, SEVERAL, MAYBE EVEN DOZENS OF PEOPLE HAVE TAKEN TO THE SIDEWALKS IN FAVOR OF NEEDLESS VIOLENCE & DEATH..
IT'S A WHOLE DIFFERENT WORLD COMPARED TO AN ANTI-WAR RALLY...
MANY USED THEIR S.U.V.S TO BLOCK WALKWAYS & BIKELANES ACROSS THE CITY...
BIKE
YOU COULD STOMP A "DIXIE-CHICK" FOR $5...
peep peep
dixie
Baby Chick
SQUISH
THERE WAS A DUNK MACHINE WITH A MICHAEL MOORE IMPERSONATOR INSIDE...
The inspections were working!! We're showing the kids of Columbine that violence & hate are the only ways to solve problems!!
DAMN YOU & YOUR COMMON SENSE!!
AND OF COURSE.. THERE WERE PLENTY OF "FREEDOM FRIES"..
GORF
THE DEMONSTRATION TRADITIONALLY ENDS WITH THE GROUP BEATING OF THE CLOSEST COP IN THE AREA...
MIND THE DONUT!! MIND THE DONUT!!
STOP

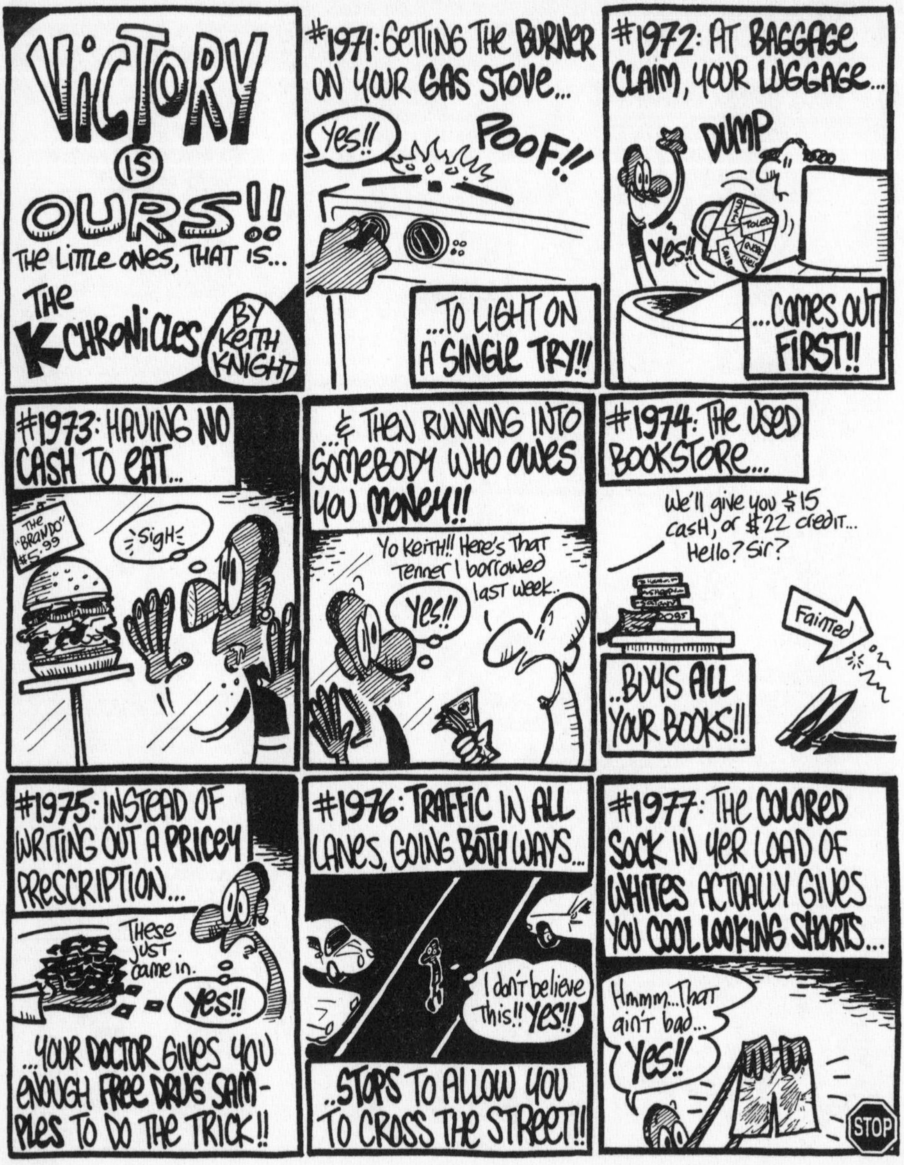
VICTORY IS OURS!!
THE LITTLE ONES, THAT IS...
THE K CHRONICLES
BY KEITH KNIGHT
#1971: GETTING THE BURNER ON YOUR GAS STOVE...
Yes!!
POOF!!
...TO LIGHT ON A SINGLE TRY!!
#1972: AT BAGGAGE CLAIM, YOUR LUGGAGE...
DUMP
Yes!!
TOLEDO
...COMES OUT FIRST!!
#1973: HAVING NO CASH TO EAT...
THE "BRANDO" $5.99
SIGH
...& THEN RUNNING INTO SOMEBODY WHO OWES YOU MONEY!!
Yo KEITH!! Here's That Tenner I borrowed last week..
Yes!!
#1974: THE USED BOOKSTORE...
We'll give you $15 cash, or $22 credit... Hello? Sir?
Fainted
...BUYS ALL YOUR BOOKS!!
#1975: INSTEAD OF WRITING OUT A PRICEY PRESCRIPTION...
These just came in.
Yes!!
...YOUR DOCTOR GIVES YOU ENOUGH FREE DRUG SAMPLES TO DO THE TRICK!!
#1976: TRAFFIC IN ALL LANES, GOING BOTH WAYS...
I don't believe this!! YES!!
...STOPS TO ALLOW YOU TO CROSS THE STREET!!
#1977: THE COLORED SOCK IN YER LOAD OF WHITES ACTUALLY GIVES YOU COOL LOOKING SHORTS...
Hmmm...That ain't bad... Yes!!
STOP

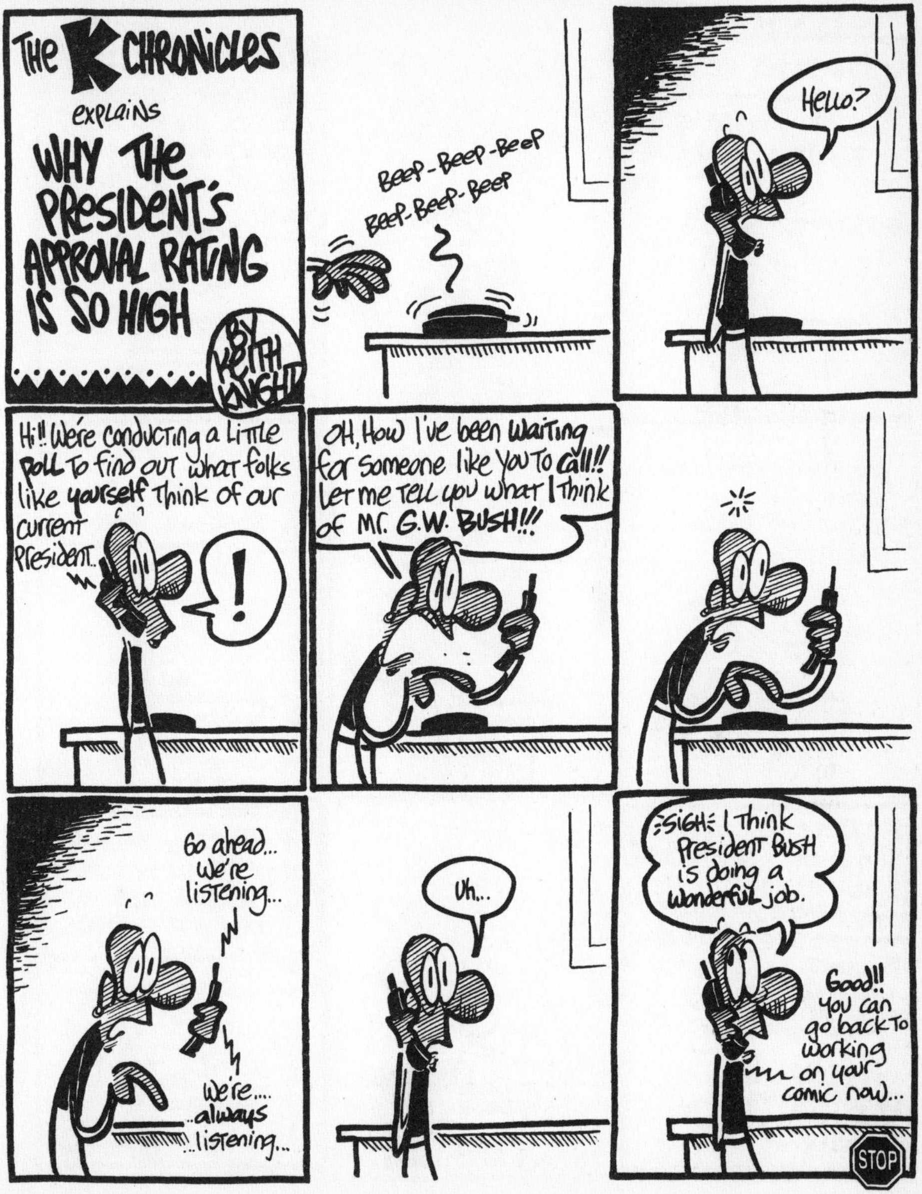
THE K CHRONICLES
explains
WHY THE PRESIDENT'S APPROVAL RATING IS SO HIGH
BY KEITH KNIGHT!!
Beep-Beep-Beep
Beep-Beep-Beep
Hello?
Hi!! We're conducting a little poll to find out what folks like yourself think of our current President..
!
OH, How I've been waiting for someone like you to call!! Let me tell you what I think of Mr. G.W. BUSH!!!
Go ahead... We're listening...
We're.... ...always ...listening...
Uh...
:SIGH: I think President BUSH is doing a Wonderful job.
Good!! You can go back to working on your comic now...
STOP

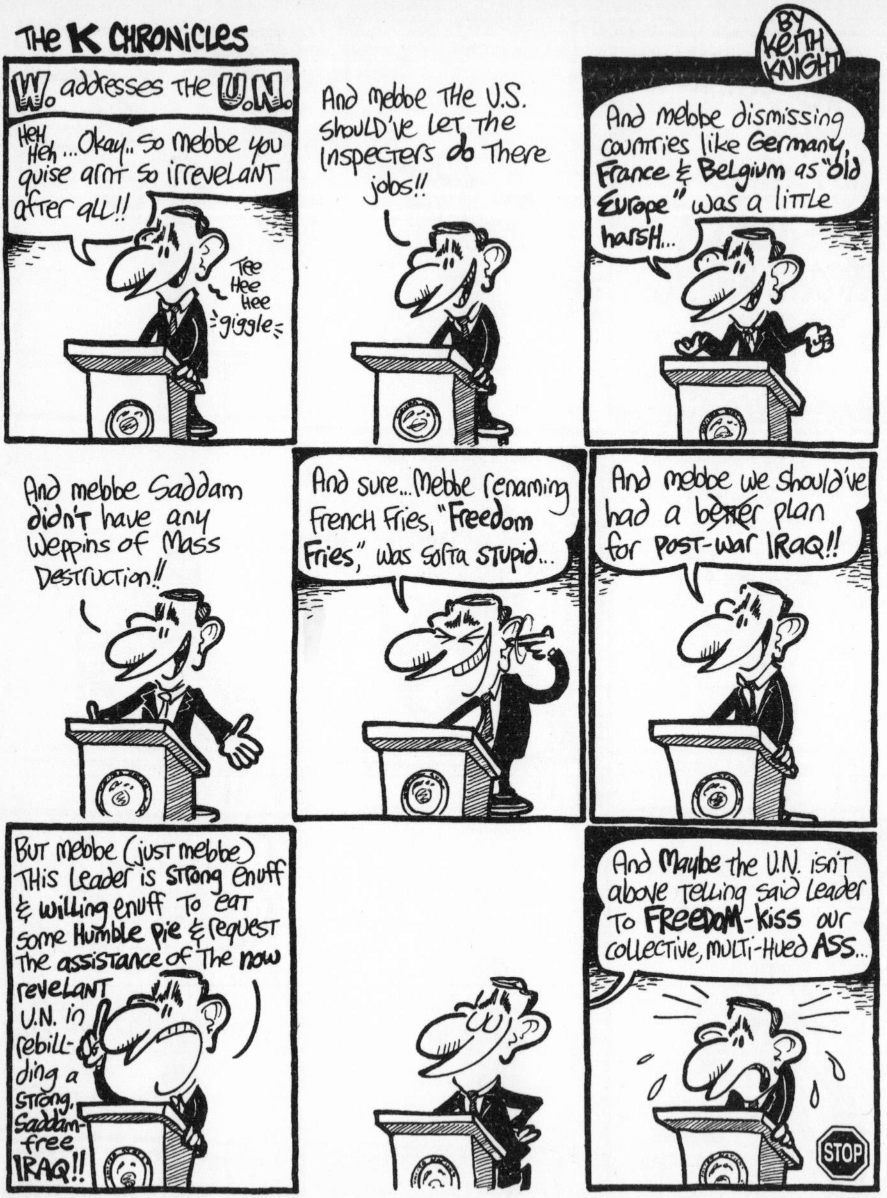
THE K CHRONICLES
BY KEITH KNIGHT
W. addresses THE U.N.
HeH Heh ...Okay.. So mebbe you guise arnt so irrevelant after all!!
Tee Hee Hee
giggle
And mebbe THE U.S. should've let the inspecters do there jobs!!
And mebbe dismissing countries like Germany, France & Belgium as "old Europe" was a little harsH...
And mebbe Saddam didn't have any Weppins of Mass Destruction!!
And sure... Mebbe renaming French Fries, "Freedom Fries," was sorta STUPID...
And mebbe we should've had a better plan for POST-war IRAQ!!
BUT mebbe (just mebbe) THis Leader is STRONG enuff & willing enuff To eat some Humble pie & request The assistance of The now revelant U.N. in rebill-ding a strong, Saddam-free IRAQ!!
And Maybe the U.N. isn't above Telling said Leader To FREEDOM-kiss our collective, MULTI-Hued ASS...
STOP

Whenever I come across somebody in a military uniform, I make it a point to acknowledge the sacrifice they're making for this country...
Let me profusely apologize on behalf of the American people for your Commander-in-Chief...
Yeah... He's sure keepin' us busy..
THE K CHRONICLES
This one's for the U.S. men & women serving overseas!!!
By Keith Knight
He's already cut veteran's benefits..He wanted to cut military pay..& He's motivating opposing factions by telling them to--
Bring it on!! Tee Hee Hee giggle
Statements like that remind me of loudmouth pro athletes..at least once a year, the press asks a player of a heavily favored team about an upcoming opponent...
So..what dya think their chances are against you next week?
(A real arrogant & smug answer that the opposing coach can use to motivate his players)
Whatever happened to good old-fashioned humility? Whatever happened to--
Speak softly & carry a big stick!!
Here's an idea: if Mr. AWOL decides to don another military uniform & play fly-boy for another photo-op, I suggest that the pilot take him to Iraq, drop him off, & bring one of our soldiers home to their family..
Hey!! Whoa!! Where are we going, soldier?
Just a little detour, Mr. President...
STOP

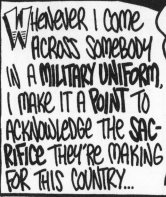

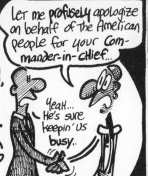

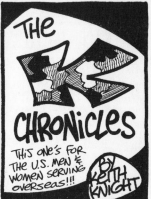

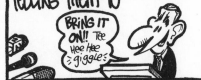

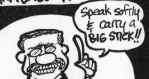

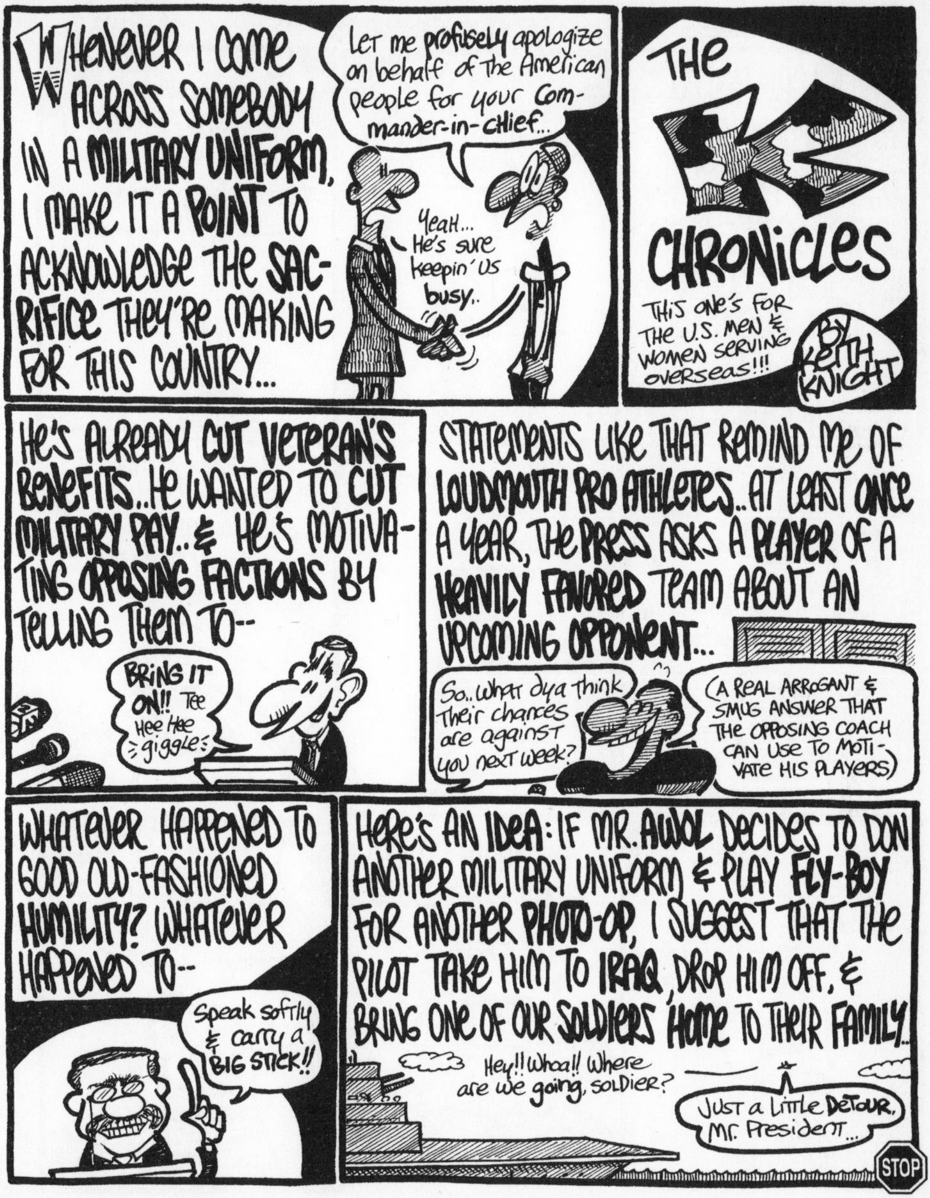

THE K CHRONICLES "A TALE OF TWO GEORGES"

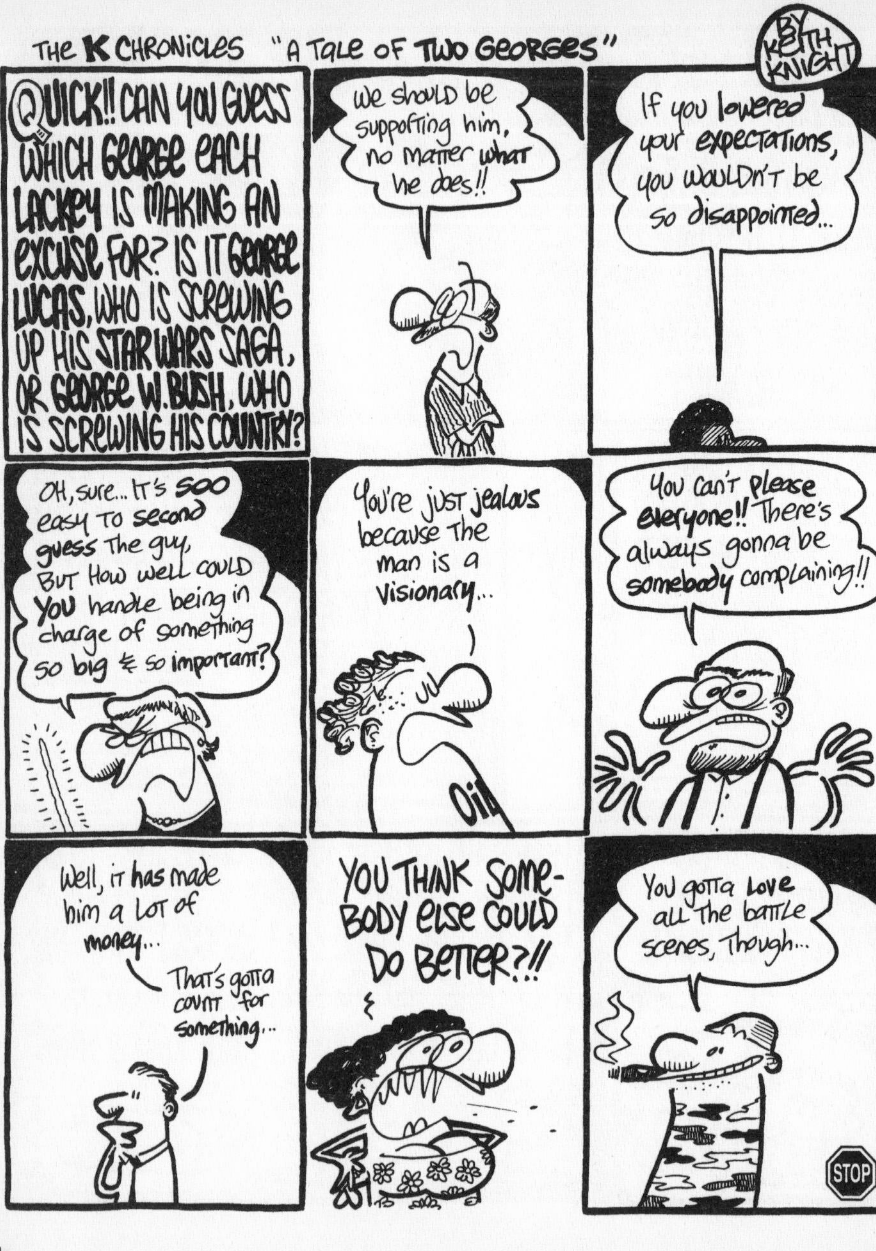
BY KEITH KNIGHT
QUICK!! CAN YOU GUESS WHICH GEORGE EACH LACKEY IS MAKING AN EXCUSE FOR? IS IT GEORGE LUCAS, WHO IS SCREWING UP HIS STAR WARS SAGA, OR GEORGE W. BUSH, WHO IS SCREWING HIS COUNTRY?
We should be supporting him, no matter what he does!!
If you lowered your expectations, you wouldn't be so disappointed...
Oh, sure... It's soo easy to second guess the guy, but how well could you handle being in charge of something so big & so important?
You're just jealous because the man is a visionary...
Oil
You can't please everyone!! There's always gonna be somebody complaining!!
Well, it has made him a lot of money...
That's gotta count for something...
YOU THINK SOMEBODY ELSE COULD DO BETTER?!!
You gotta love all the battle scenes, though...
STOP

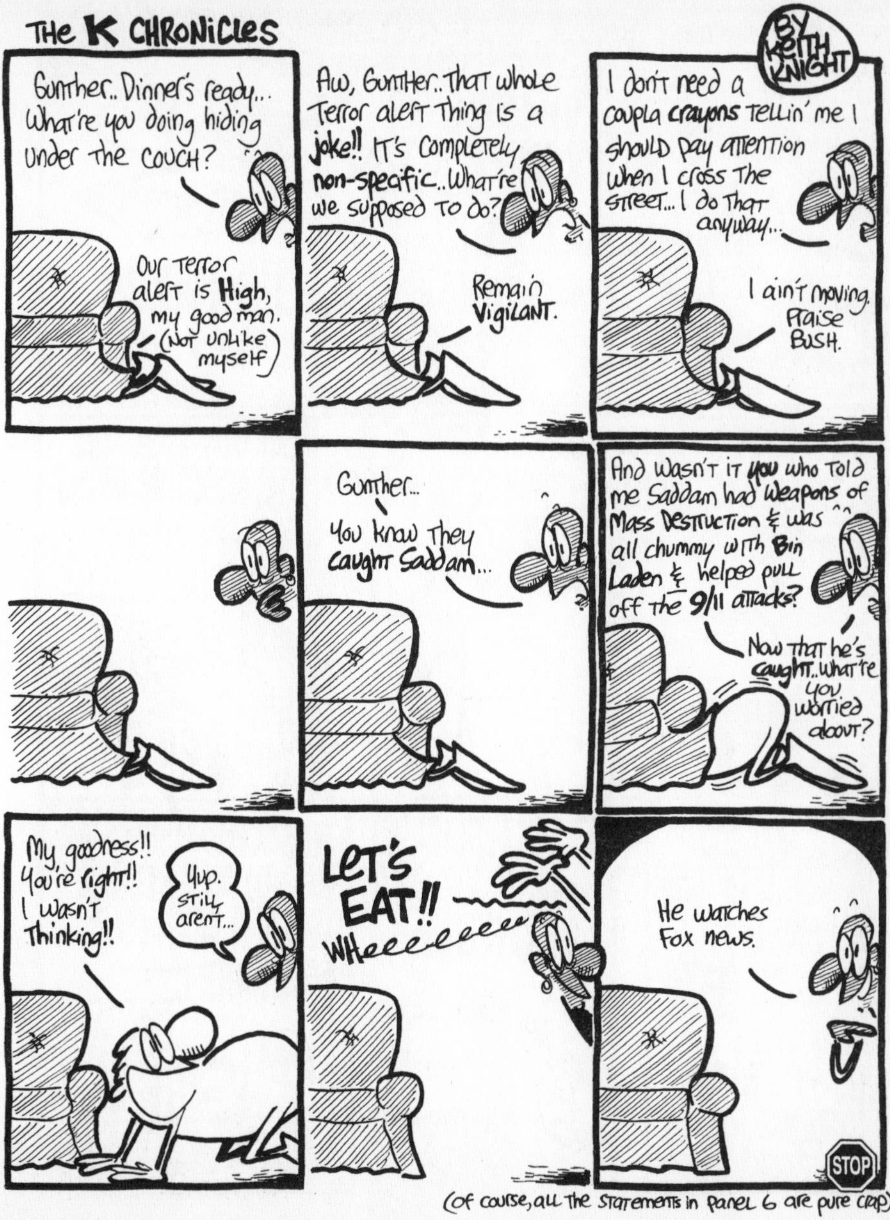
THE K CHRONICLES
BY KEITH KNIGHT
Gunther.. Dinner's ready... What're you doing hiding under the couch?
Our terror alert is High, my good man. (Not unlike myself)
Aw, Gunther.. That whole terror alert thing is a joke!! It's completely non-specific.. What're we supposed to do?
Remain Vigilant.
I don't need a coupla crayons tellin' me I should pay attention when I cross the street... I do that anyway...
I ain't moving. Praise Bush.
Gunther...
You know they caught Saddam...
And wasn't it you who told me Saddam had Weapons of Mass Destruction & was all chummy with Bin Laden & helped pull off the 9/11 attacks?
Now that he's caught.. what're you worried about?
My goodness!! You're right!! I wasn't thinking!!
Yup. Still aren't...
LET'S EAT!!
WHeeeeeeee
He watches Fox news.
STOP

(Of course, all the statements in panel 6 are pure crap)

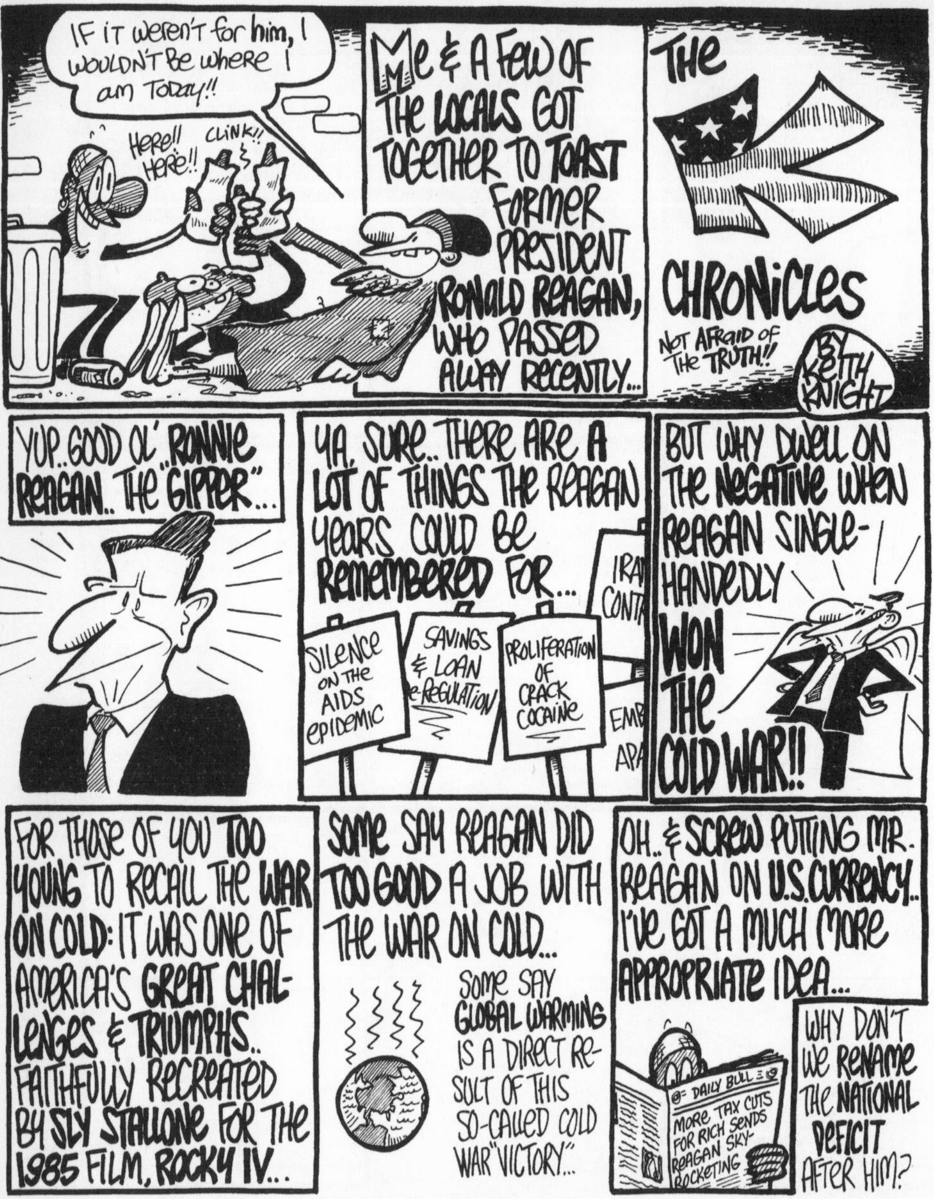

IF IT weren't for him, I WOULDN'T Be where I am TODAY!!
Here!! Here!!
CLINK!!
Me & A Few OF THE LOCALS GOT TOGETHER TO TOAST FORMER PRESIDENT RONALD REAGAN, WHO PASSED AWAY RECENTLY...
THE
CHRONICLES
NOT AFRAID OF THE TRUTH!!
BY KEITH KNIGHT
YUP..GOOD OL' RONNIE REAGAN.. THE "GIPPER"...
YA, SURE.. THERE ARE A LOT OF THINGS THE REAGAN YEARS COULD BE REMEMBERED FOR...
SILENCE ON THE AIDS EPIDEMIC
SAVINGS & LOAN DE-REGULATION
PROLIFERATION OF CRACK COCAINE
BUT WHY DWELL ON THE NEGATIVE WHEN REAGAN SINGLE-HANDEDLY WON THE COLD WAR!!
FOR THOSE OF YOU TOO YOUNG TO RECALL THE WAR ON COLD: IT WAS ONE OF AMERICA'S GREAT CHALLENGES & TRIUMPHS.. FAITHFULLY RECREATED BY SLY STALLONE FOR THE 1985 FILM, ROCKY IV...
SOME SAY REAGAN DID TOO GOOD A JOB WITH THE WAR ON COLD...
SOME SAY GLOBAL WARMING IS A DIRECT RESULT OF THIS SO-CALLED COLD WAR "VICTORY"...
OH..& SCREW PUTTING MR. REAGAN ON U.S. CURRENCY.. I'VE GOT A MUCH MORE APPROPRIATE IDEA...
DAILY BULL
MORE TAX CUTS FOR RICH SENDS REAGAN SKY-ROCKETING
WHY DON'T WE RENAME THE NATIONAL DEFICIT AFTER HIM?

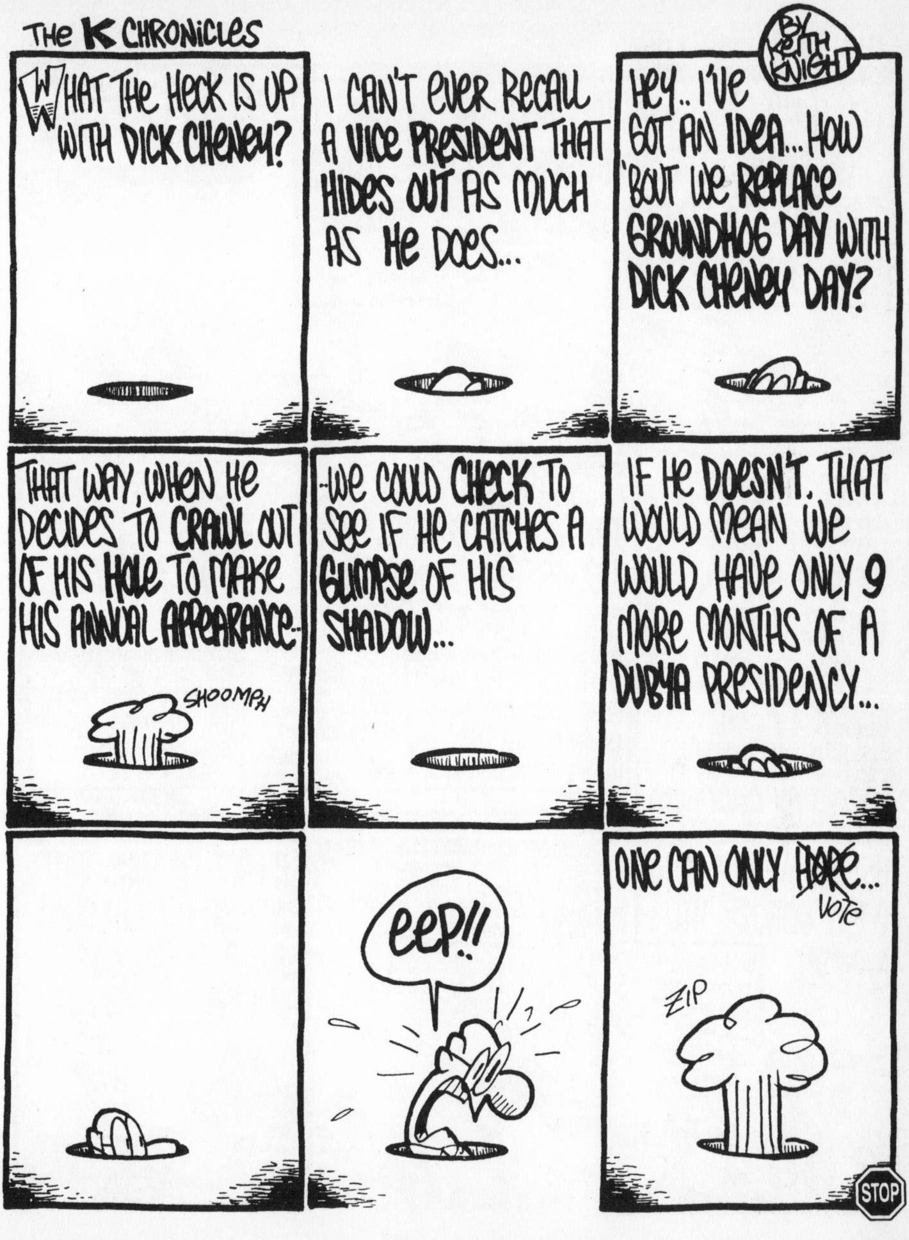
THE K CHRONICLES
BY KEITH KNIGHT
WHAT THE HECK IS UP WITH DICK CHENEY?
I CAN'T EVER RECALL A VICE PRESIDENT THAT HIDES OUT AS MUCH AS HE DOES...
HEY.. I'VE GOT AN IDEA... HOW 'BOUT WE REPLACE GROUNDHOG DAY WITH DICK CHENEY DAY?
THAT WAY, WHEN HE DECIDES TO CRAWL OUT OF HIS HOLE TO MAKE HIS ANNUAL APPEARANCE..
SHOOMPH
..WE COULD CHECK TO SEE IF HE CATCHES A GLIMPSE OF HIS SHADOW...
IF HE DOESN'T, THAT WOULD MEAN WE WOULD HAVE ONLY 9 MORE MONTHS OF A DUBYA PRESIDENCY...
EEP!!
ONE CAN ONLY HOPE...
VOTE
ZIP
STOP

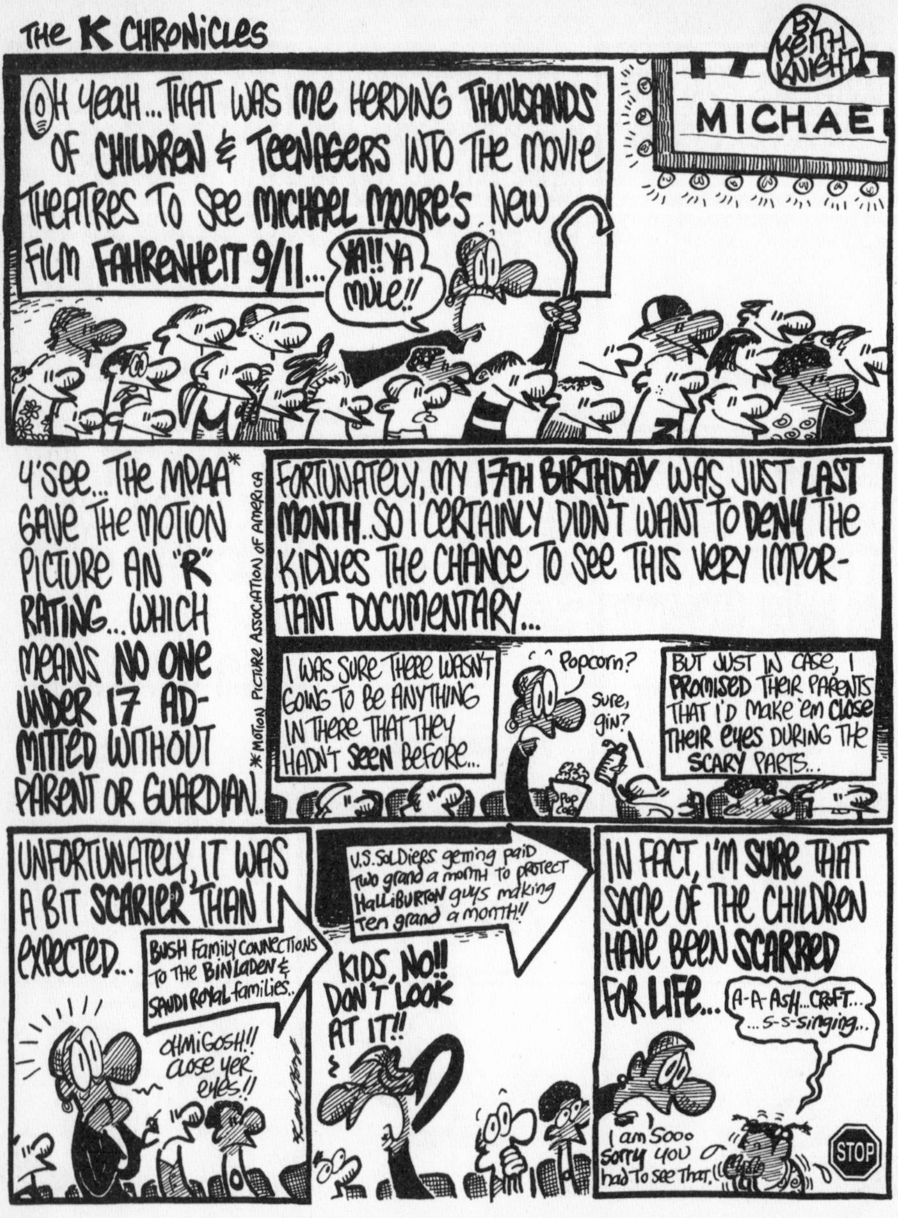
THE K CHRONICLES
BY KEITH KNIGHT
MICHAE
OH YEAH... THAT WAS ME HERDING THOUSANDS OF CHILDREN & TEENAGERS INTO THE MOVIE THEATRES TO SEE MICHAEL MOORE'S NEW FILM FAHRENHEIT 9/11...
YA!! YA MULE!!
Y'SEE... THE MPAA* GAVE THE MOTION PICTURE AN "R" RATING... WHICH MEANS NO ONE UNDER 17 ADMITTED WITHOUT PARENT OR GUARDIAN..
*MOTION PICTURE ASSOCIATION OF AMERICA
FORTUNATELY, MY 17TH BIRTHDAY WAS JUST LAST MONTH.. SO I CERTAINLY DIDN'T WANT TO DENY THE KIDDIES THE CHANCE TO SEE THIS VERY IMPORTANT DOCUMENTARY...
I WAS SURE THERE WASN'T GOING TO BE ANYTHING IN THERE THAT THEY HADN'T SEEN BEFORE...
Popcorn?
Sure, gin?
POP CORN
BUT JUST IN CASE, I PROMISED THEIR PARENTS THAT I'D MAKE 'EM CLOSE THEIR EYES DURING THE SCARY PARTS...
UNFORTUNATELY, IT WAS A BIT SCARIER THAN I EXPECTED...
BUSH FAMILY CONNECTIONS TO THE BIN LADEN & SAUDI ROYAL FAMILIES..
OHMIGOSH!! CLOSE YER EYES!!
U.S. SOLDIERS GETTING PAID TWO GRAND A MONTH TO PROTECT HALLIBURTON GUYS MAKING TEN GRAND A MONTH!!
KIDS, NO!! DON'T LOOK AT IT!!
IN FACT, I'M SURE THAT SOME OF THE CHILDREN HAVE BEEN SCARRED FOR LIFE...
A-A-ASH... CROFT... ...S-S-SINGING...
I am Sooo sorry you had to see that.
STOP

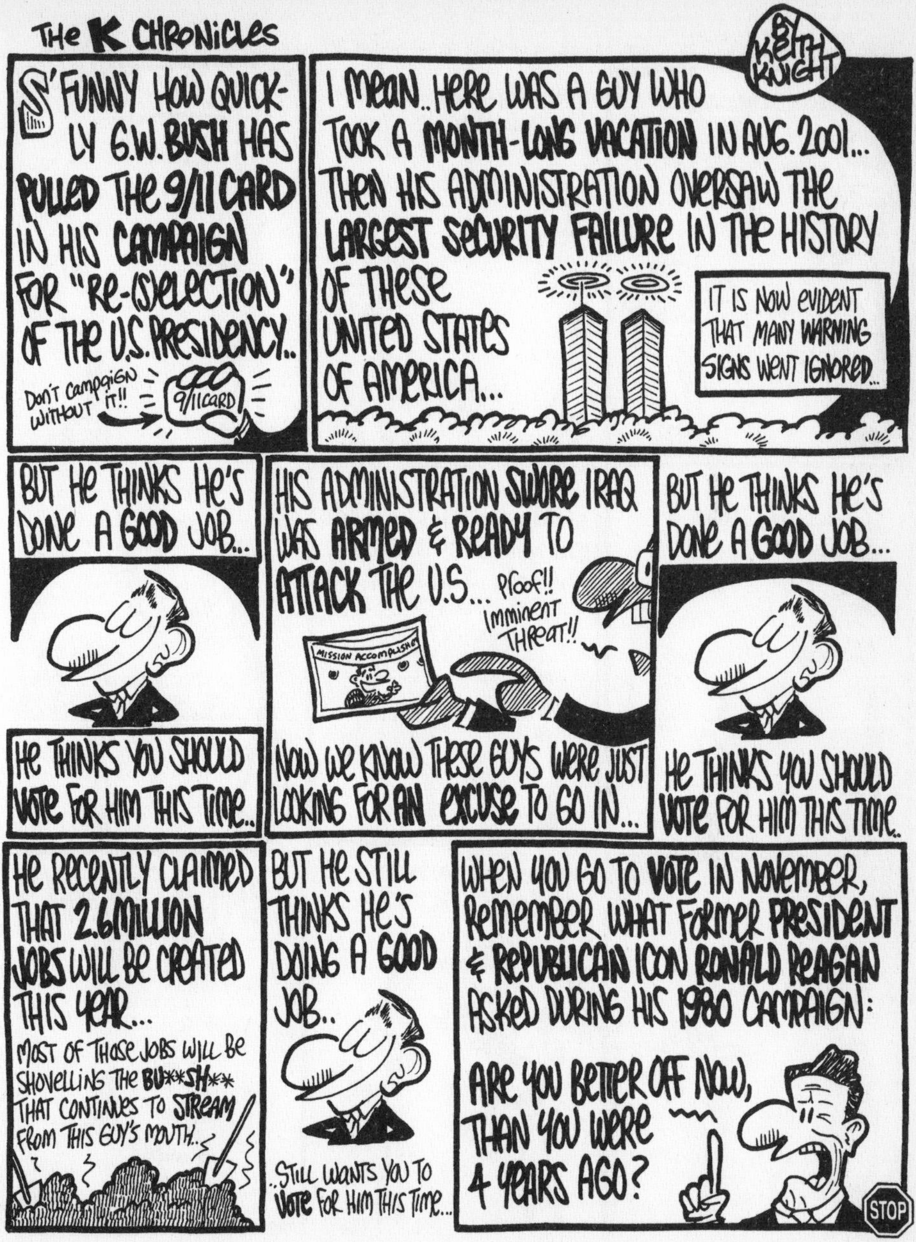
The K Chronicles
By Keith Knight
S'FUNNY HOW QUICKLY G.W. BUSH HAS PULLED THE 9/11 CARD IN HIS CAMPAIGN FOR "RE-(S)ELECTION" OF THE U.S. PRESIDENCY..
DON'T CAMPAIGN WITHOUT IT!!
9/11 CARD
I MEAN.. HERE WAS A GUY WHO TOOK A MONTH-LONG VACATION IN AUG. 2001... THEN HIS ADMINISTRATION OVERSAW THE LARGEST SECURITY FAILURE IN THE HISTORY OF THESE UNITED STATES OF AMERICA...
IT IS NOW EVIDENT THAT MANY WARNING SIGNS WENT IGNORED...
BUT HE THINKS HE'S DONE A GOOD JOB...
HE THINKS YOU SHOULD VOTE FOR HIM THIS TIME..
HIS ADMINISTRATION SWORE IRAQ WAS ARMED & READY TO ATTACK THE U.S...
PROOF!! IMMINENT THREAT!!
MISSION ACCOMPLISHED
NOW WE KNOW THESE GUYS WERE JUST LOOKING FOR AN EXCUSE TO GO IN...
BUT HE THINKS HE'S DONE A GOOD JOB...
HE THINKS YOU SHOULD VOTE FOR HIM THIS TIME..
HE RECENTLY CLAIMED THAT 2.6 MILLION JOBS WILL BE CREATED THIS YEAR...
MOST OF THOSE JOBS WILL BE SHOVELLING THE BU**SH** THAT CONTINUES TO STREAM FROM THIS GUY'S MOUTH..
BUT HE STILL THINKS HE'S DOING A GOOD JOB..
..STILL WANTS YOU TO VOTE FOR HIM THIS TIME...
WHEN YOU GO TO VOTE IN NOVEMBER, REMEMBER WHAT FORMER PRESIDENT & REPUBLICAN ICON RONALD REAGAN ASKED DURING HIS 1980 CAMPAIGN:
ARE YOU BETTER OFF NOW, THAN YOU WERE 4 YEARS AGO?
STOP

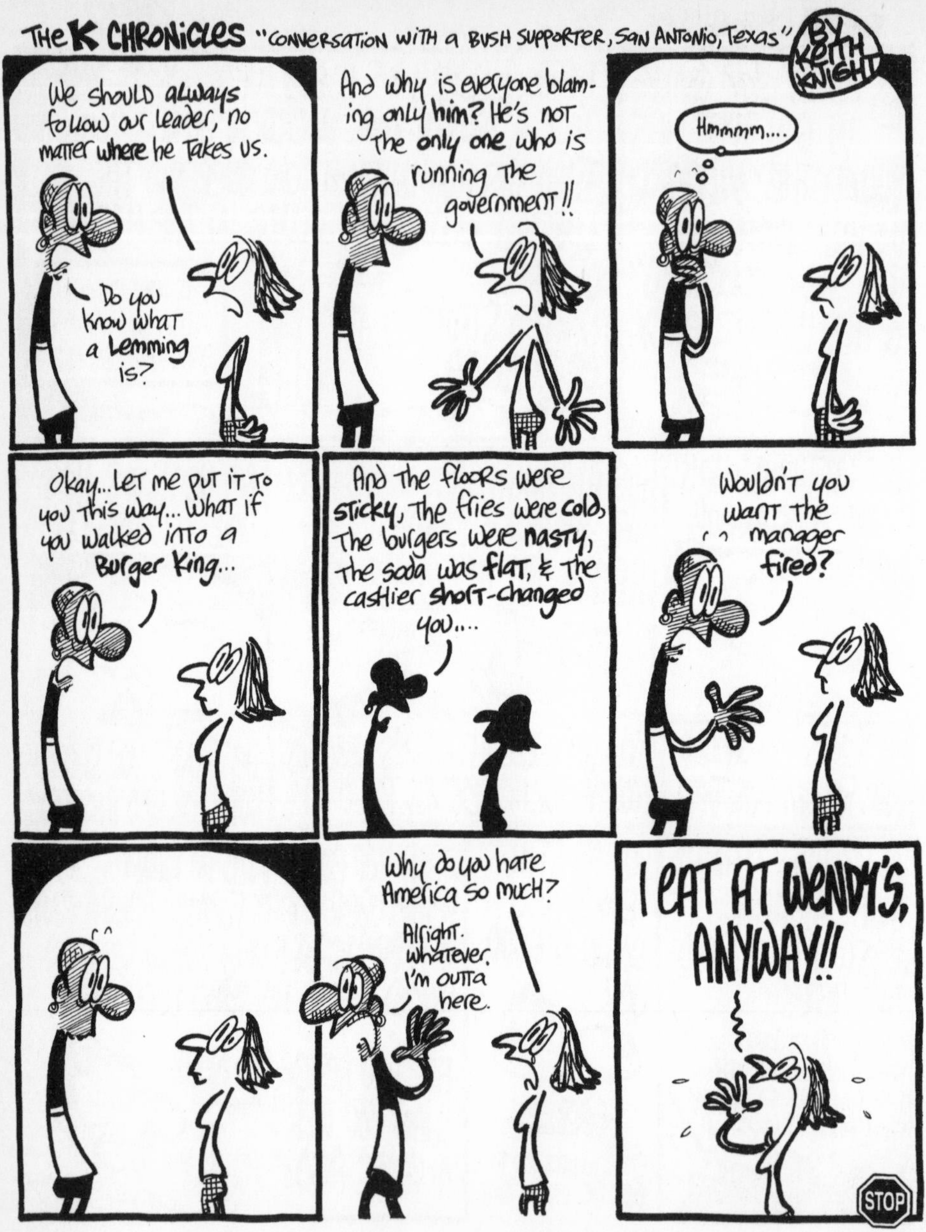
THE K CHRONICLES "CONVERSATION WITH A BUSH SUPPORTER, SAN ANTONIO, TEXAS"
BY KEITH KNIGHT
We should always follow our leader, no matter where he takes us.
Do you know what a Lemming is?
And why is everyone blaming only him? He's not the only one who is running the government!!
Hmmmm....
Okay... let me put it to you this way... what if you walked into a Burger King...
And the floors were sticky, the fries were cold, the burgers were nasty, the soda was flat, & the cashier short-changed you....
Wouldn't you want the manager fired?
Why do you hate America so much?
Alright. whatever. I'm outta here.
I EAT AT WENDY'S, ANYWAY!!
STOP

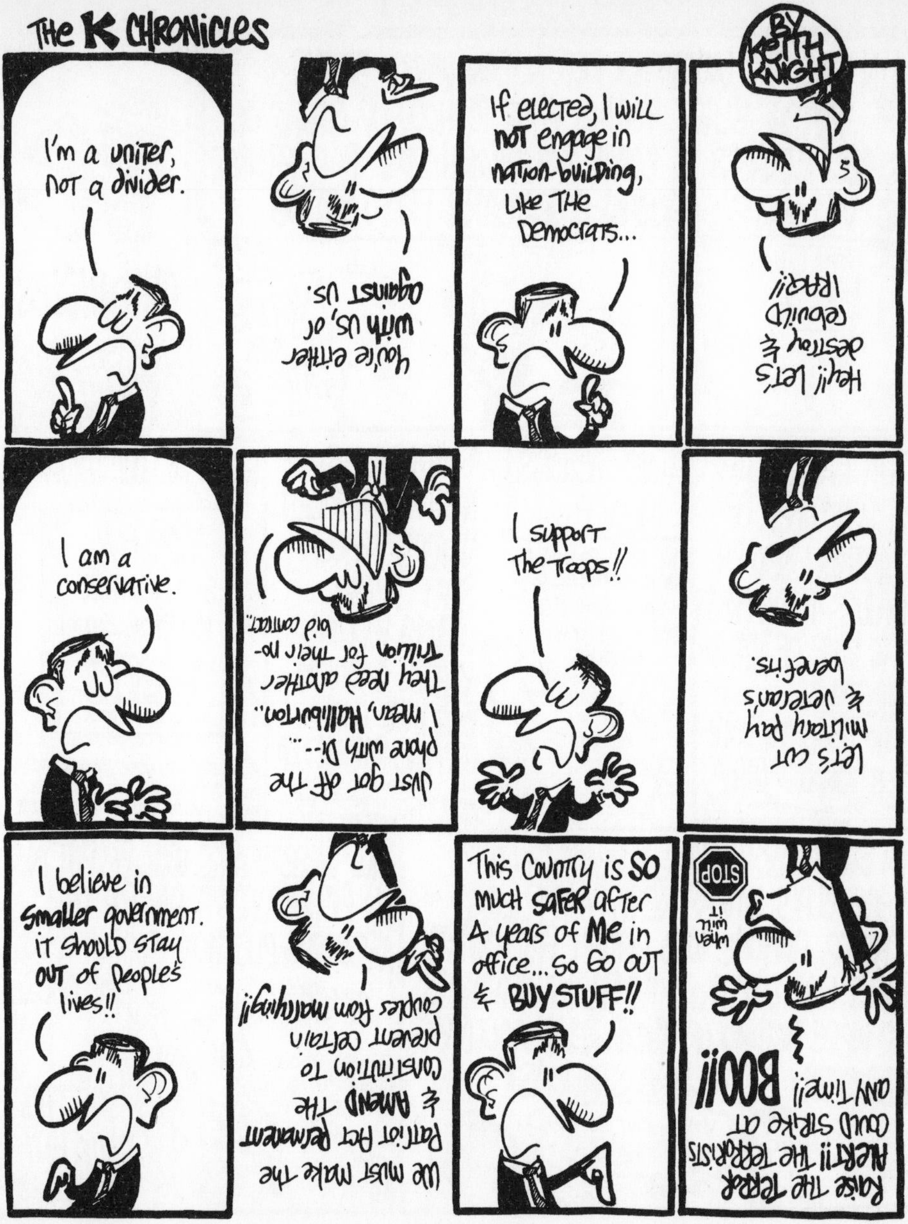
The K Chronicles
By Keith Knight
I'm a uniter, not a divider.
You're either with us, or against us.
If elected, I will not engage in nation-building, like the Democrats...
Hey!! Let's destroy & rebuild IRAQ!!
I am a conservative.
Just got off the phone with Di--... I mean, Halliburton... They need another Trillion for their no-bid contract.
I support the Troops!!
Let's cut military pay & veteran's benefits.
I believe in smaller government. It should stay out of people's lives!!
We must make the Patriot Act permanent & AMEND the Constitution to prevent certain couples from marrying!!
This Country is SO much SAFER after 4 years of ME in office... So GO OUT & BUY STUFF!!
STOP
when will it
Raise the TERROR ALERT!! The terrorists could strike at any time!! BOO!!

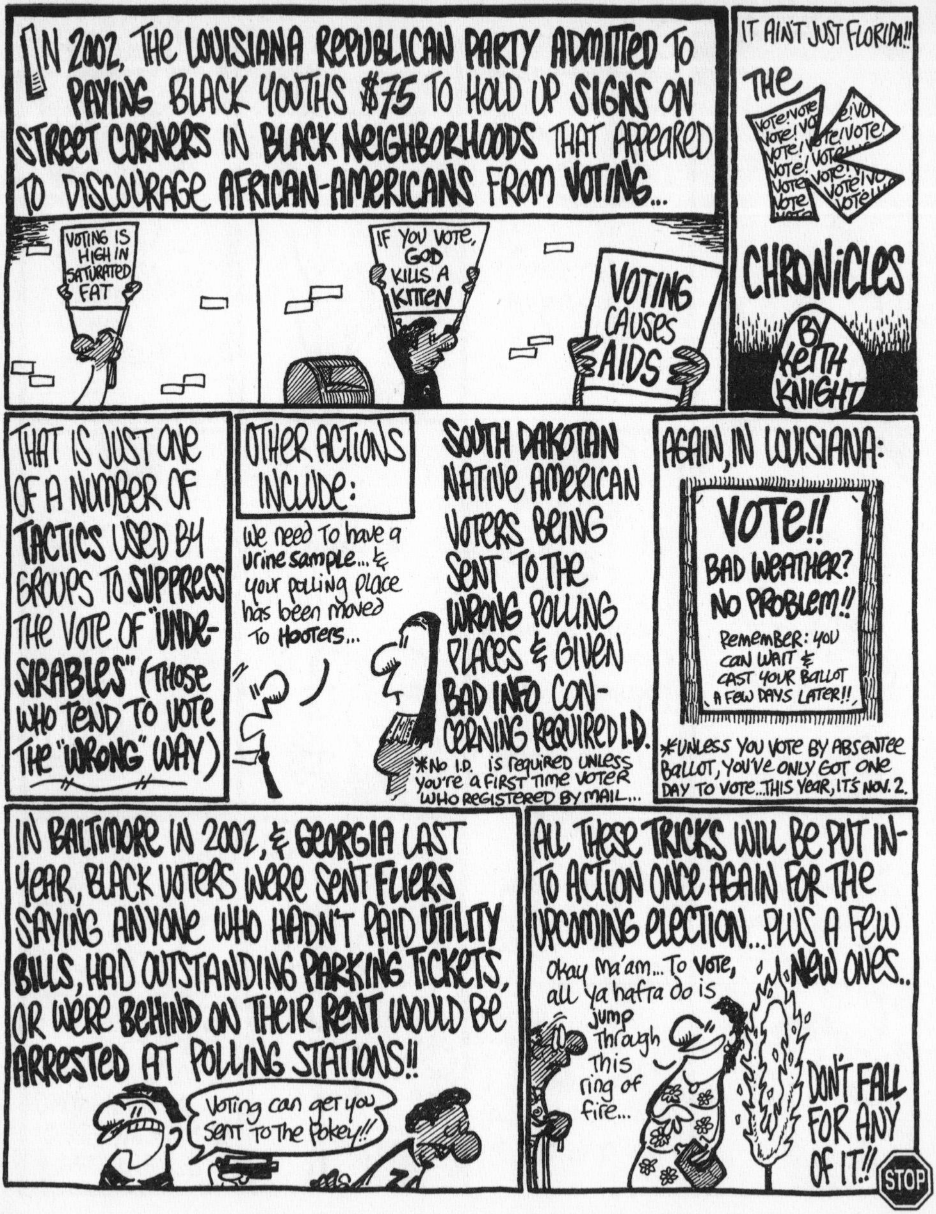
IN 2002, THE LOUISIANA REPUBLICAN PARTY ADMITTED TO PAYING BLACK YOUTHS $75 TO HOLD UP SIGNS ON STREET CORNERS IN BLACK NEIGHBORHOODS THAT APPEARED TO DISCOURAGE AFRICAN-AMERICANS FROM VOTING...
VOTING IS HIGH IN SATURATED FAT
IF YOU VOTE, GOD KILLS A KITTEN
VOTING CAUSES AIDS
IT AIN'T JUST FLORIDA!!
THE K CHRONICLES
BY KEITH KNIGHT
THAT IS JUST ONE OF A NUMBER OF TACTICS USED BY GROUPS TO SUPPRESS THE VOTE OF "UNDE-SIRABLES" (THOSE WHO TEND TO VOTE THE "WRONG" WAY)
OTHER ACTIONS INCLUDE:
We need to have a urine sample... & your polling place has been moved to Hooters...
SOUTH DAKOTAN NATIVE AMERICAN VOTERS BEING SENT TO THE WRONG POLLING PLACES & GIVEN BAD INFO CON-CERNING REQUIRED I.D.
*No I.D. is required unless you're a first time voter who registered by mail...
AGAIN, IN LOUISIANA:
VOTE!! BAD WEATHER? NO PROBLEM!!
Remember: you can wait & cast your ballot a few days later!!
*Unless you vote by absentee ballot, you've only got one day to vote...This year, it's Nov. 2.
IN BALTIMORE IN 2002, & GEORGIA LAST YEAR, BLACK VOTERS WERE SENT FLIERS SAYING ANYONE WHO HADN'T PAID UTILITY BILLS, HAD OUTSTANDING PARKING TICKETS, OR WERE BEHIND ON THEIR RENT WOULD BE ARRESTED AT POLLING STATIONS!!
Voting can get you sent to the Pokey!!
ALL THESE TRICKS WILL BE PUT INTO ACTION ONCE AGAIN FOR THE UPCOMING ELECTION...PLUS A FEW NEW ONES..
Okay Ma'am... To vote, all ya hafta do is jump through this ring of fire...
DON'T FALL FOR ANY OF IT!!
STOP

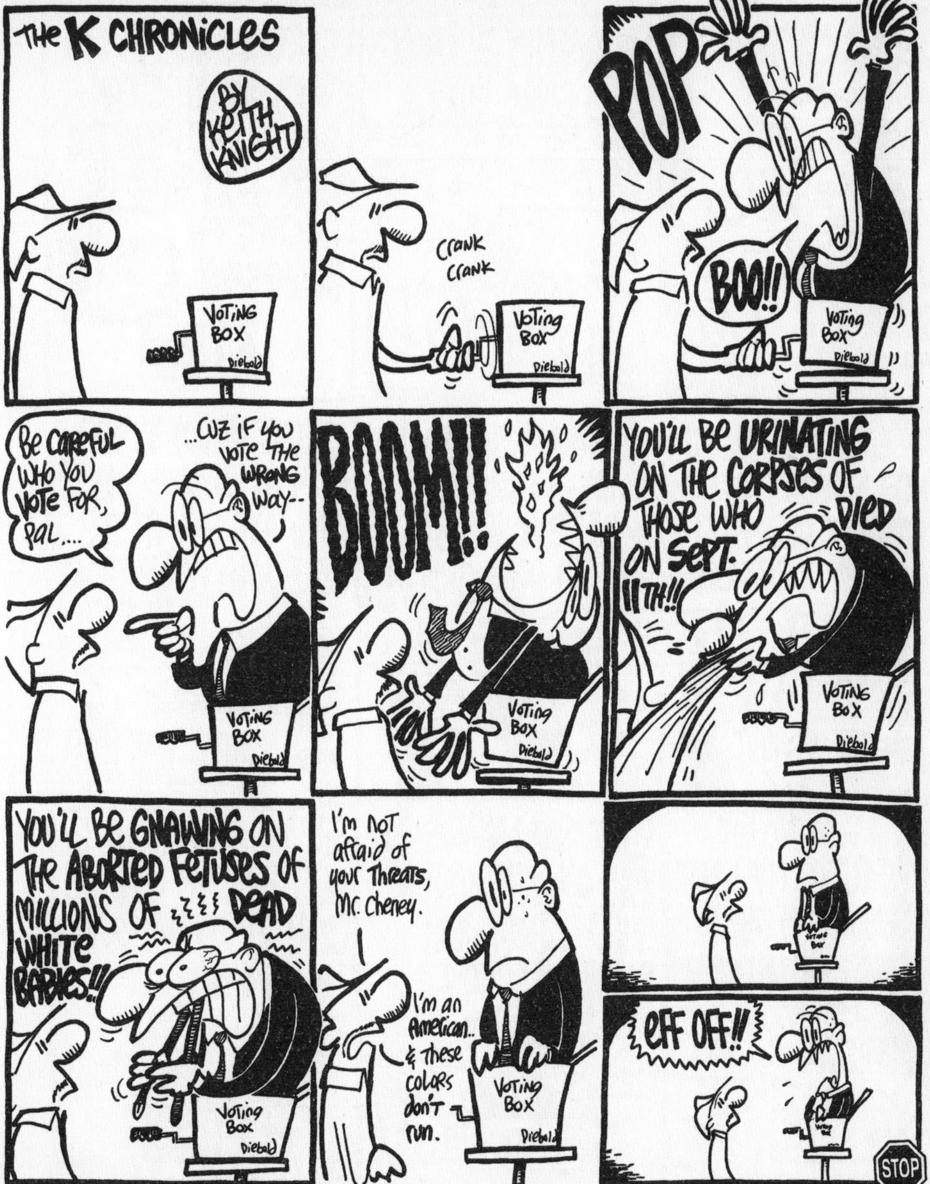
The K Chronicles
By Keith Knight
Voting Box
Diebold
Crank
Crank
POP
BOO!!
Be careful who you vote for, pal....
...cuz if you vote the wrong way--
BOOM!!
You'll be urinating on the corpses of those who died on Sept. 11th!!
You'll be gnawing on the aborted fetuses of millions of dead white babies!!
I'm not afraid of your threats, Mr. Cheney.
I'm an American.. & these colors don't run.
eff off!!
STOP

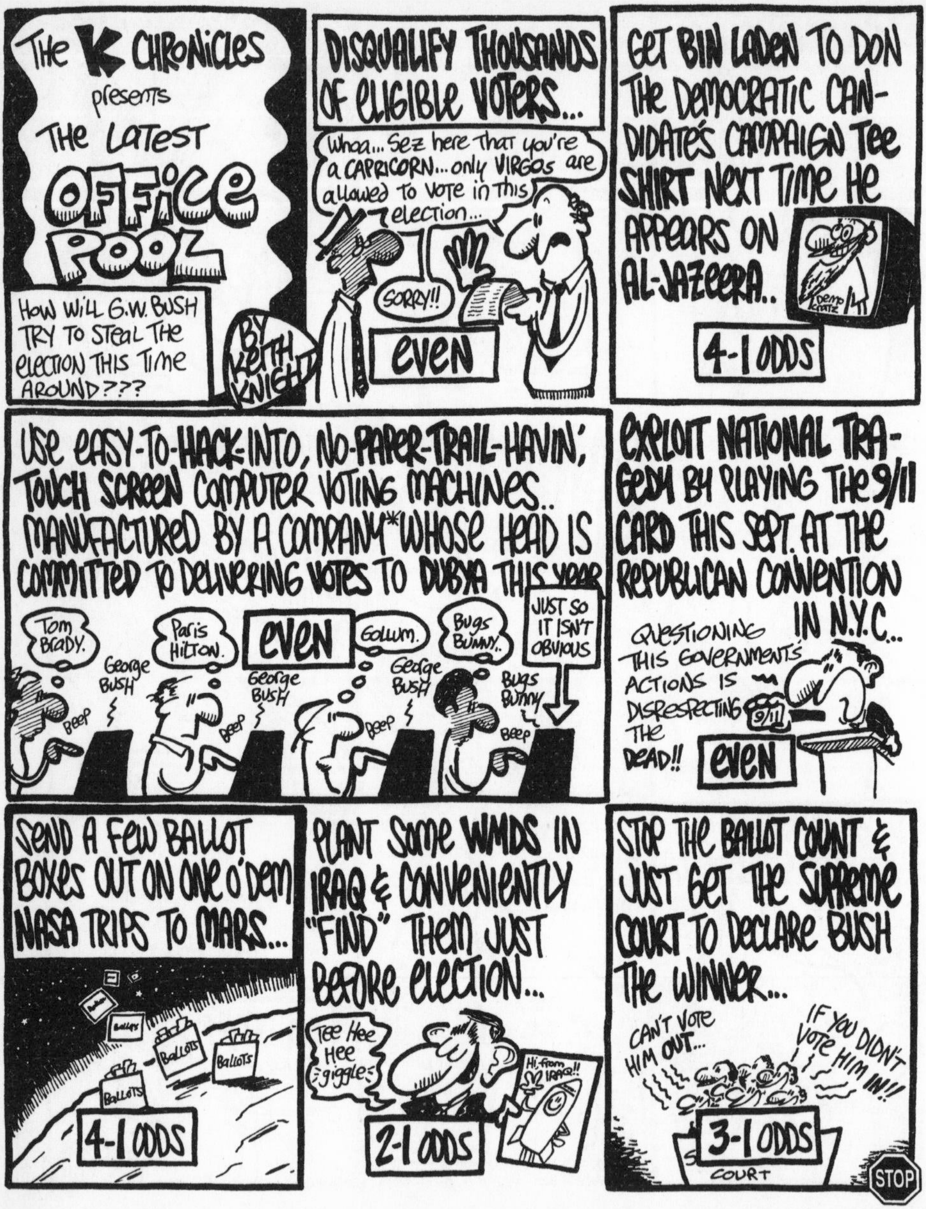
THE K CHRONICLES
presents
THE LATEST
OFFICE POOL
HOW WILL G.W. BUSH TRY TO STEAL THE ELECTION THIS TIME AROUND???
BY KEITH KNIGHT
DISQUALIFY THOUSANDS OF ELIGIBLE VOTERS...
Whoa... Sez here that you're a CAPRICORN... only VIRGOS are allowed to vote in this election...
SORRY!!
EVEN
GET BIN LADEN TO DON THE DEMOCRATIC CANDIDATE'S CAMPAIGN TEE SHIRT NEXT TIME HE APPEARS ON AL-JAZEERA...
DEMO CRATZ
4-1 ODDS
USE EASY-TO-HACK-INTO, NO-PAPER-TRAIL-HAVIN', TOUCH SCREEN COMPUTER VOTING MACHINES.. MANUFACTURED BY A COMPANY* WHOSE HEAD IS COMMITTED TO DELIVERING VOTES TO DUBYA THIS YEAR
Tom Brady.
George Bush
BEEP
Paris Hilton.
George Bush
BEEP
EVEN
Golum.
George Bush
BEEP
Bugs Bunny..
Bugs Bunny
BEEP
JUST SO IT ISN'T OBVIOUS
EXPLOIT NATIONAL TRAGEDY BY PLAYING THE 9/11 CARD THIS SEPT. AT THE REPUBLICAN CONVENTION IN N.Y.C...
QUESTIONING THIS GOVERNMENT'S ACTIONS IS DISRESPECTING THE DEAD!!
9/11
EVEN
SEND A FEW BALLOT BOXES OUT ON ONE O'DEM NASA TRIPS TO MARS...
BALLOTS
BALLOTS
BALLOTS
BALLOTS
4-1 ODDS
PLANT SOME WMDS IN IRAQ & CONVENIENTLY "FIND" THEM JUST BEFORE ELECTION...
Tee Hee Hee giggle
Hi-from IRAQ!!
2-1 ODDS
STOP THE BALLOT COUNT & JUST GET THE SUPREME COURT TO DECLARE BUSH THE WINNER...
CAN'T VOTE HIM OUT...
IF YOU DIDN'T VOTE HIM IN!!
3-1 ODDS
COURT
STOP

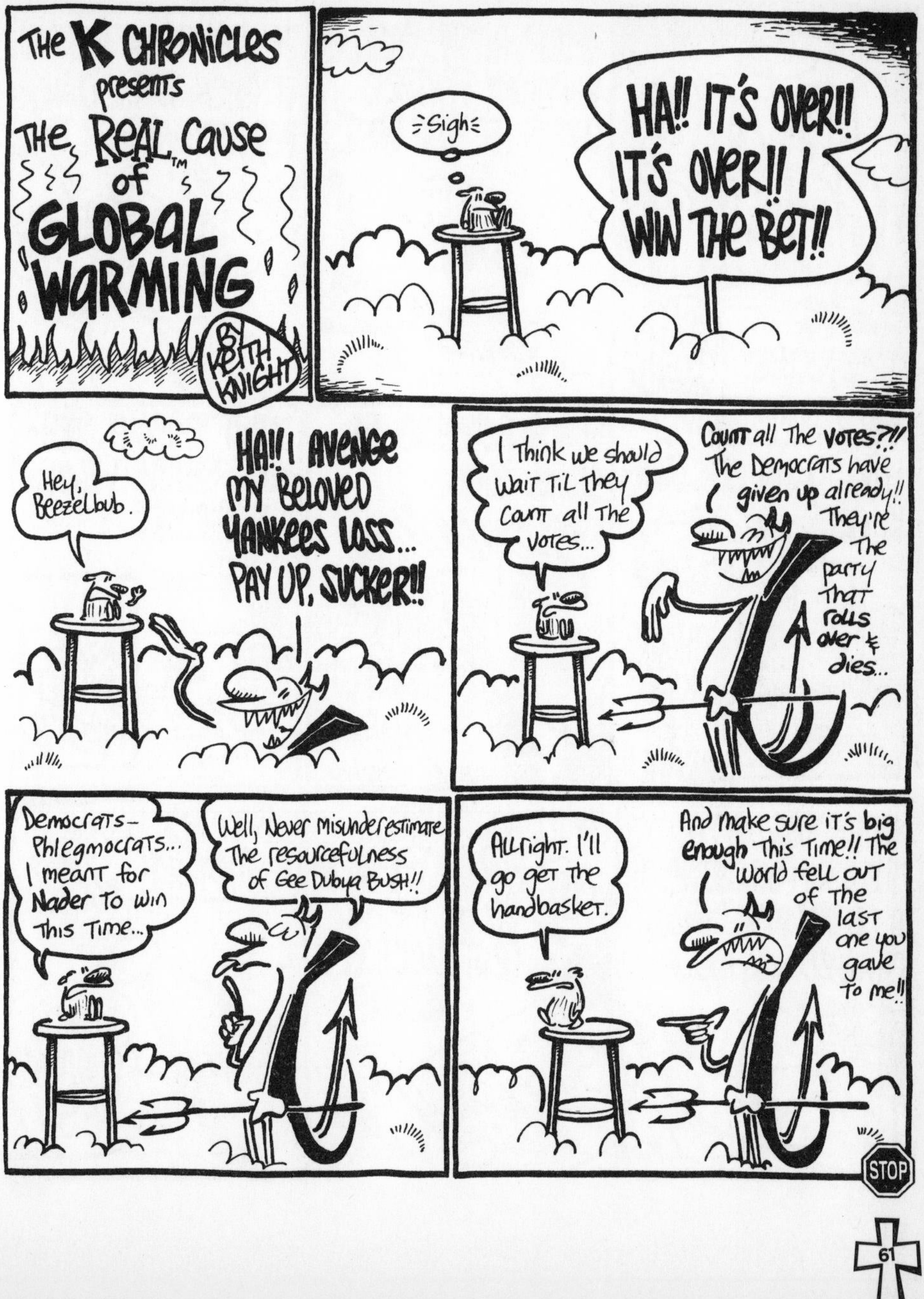
THE K CHRONICLES presents
THE REAL™ Cause of GLOBAL WARMING
BY KEITH KNIGHT
Sigh
HA!! IT'S OVER!! IT'S OVER!! I WIN THE BET!!
Hey, Beezelbub.
HA!! I AVENGE MY BELOVED YANKEES LOSS... PAY UP, SUCKER!!
I Think we should wait til they count all the votes...
Count all The VOTES?!! The Democrats have given up already!! They're The party That rolls over & dies...
Democrats— Phlegmocrats... I meant for Nader to win This Time...
Well, Never misunderestimate The resourcefulness of Gee Dubya BUSH!!
Allright. I'll go get the handbasket.
And make sure it's big enough This Time!! The world fell out of The last one you gave to me!!
STOP

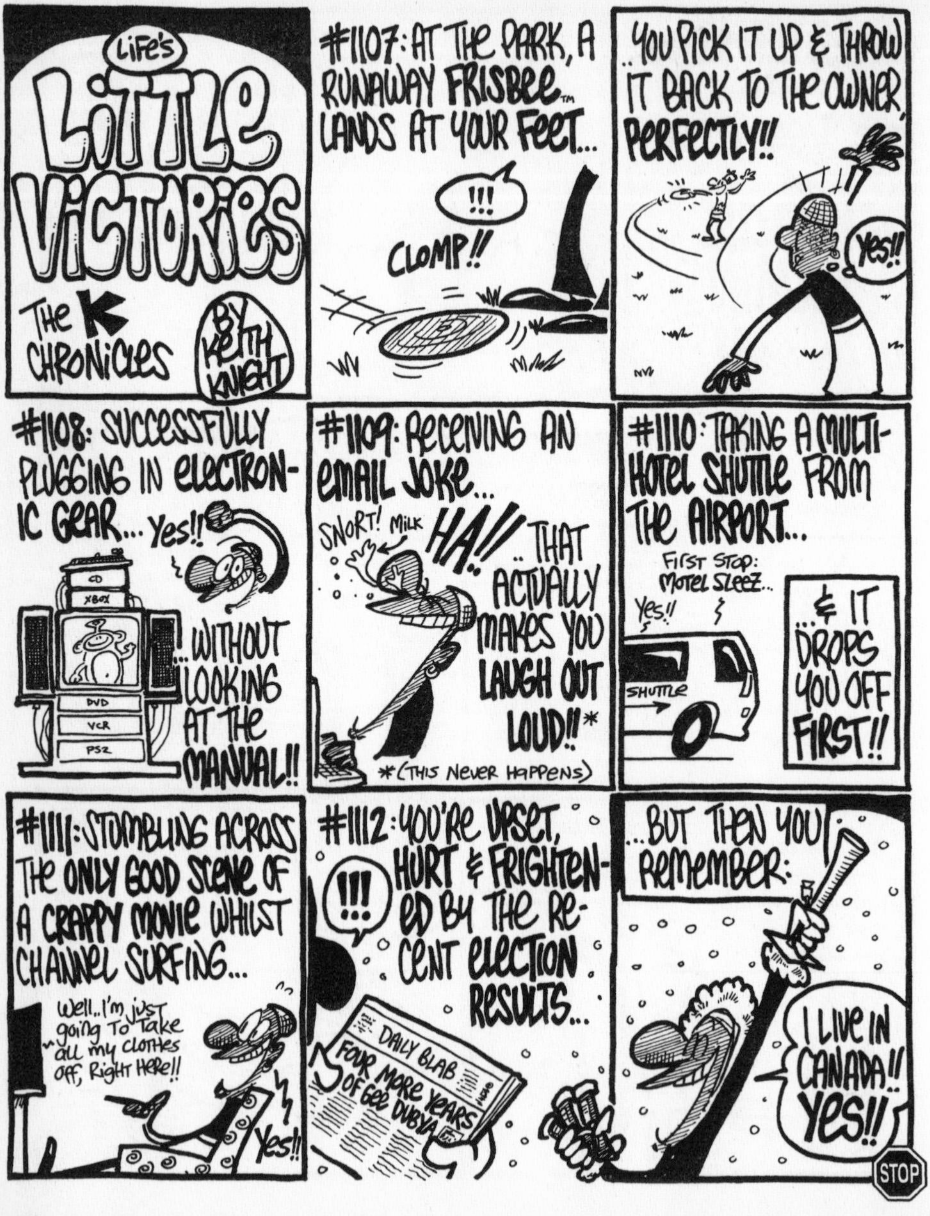
LIFE'S LITTLE VICTORIES
THE K CHRONICLES
BY KEITH KNIGHT
#1107: AT THE PARK, A RUNAWAY FRISBEE™ LANDS AT YOUR FEET...
!!!
CLOMP!!
...YOU PICK IT UP & THROW IT BACK TO THE OWNER, PERFECTLY!!
YES!!
#1108: SUCCESSFULLY PLUGGING IN ELECTRONIC GEAR... YES!!
CD
XBOX
DVD
VCR
PS2
...WITHOUT LOOKING AT THE MANUAL!!
#1109: RECEIVING AN EMAIL JOKE...
SNORT! MILK
HA!!
...THAT ACTUALLY MAKES YOU LAUGH OUT LOUD!!*
*(THIS NEVER HAPPENS)
#1110: TAKING A MULTI-HOTEL SHUTTLE FROM THE AIRPORT...
FIRST STOP: MOTEL SLEEZ...
YES!!
SHUTTLE
...& IT DROPS YOU OFF FIRST!!
#1111: STUMBLING ACROSS THE ONLY GOOD SCENE OF A CRAPPY MOVIE WHILST CHANNEL SURFING...
Well.. I'm just going to take all my clothes off, right here!!
YES!!
#1112: YOU'RE UPSET, HURT & FRIGHTENED BY THE RECENT ELECTION RESULTS...
!!!
DAILY BLAB
FOUR MORE YEARS OF GEE DUBYA
...BUT THEN YOU REMEMBER:
I LIVE IN CANADA!!.. YES!!
STOP

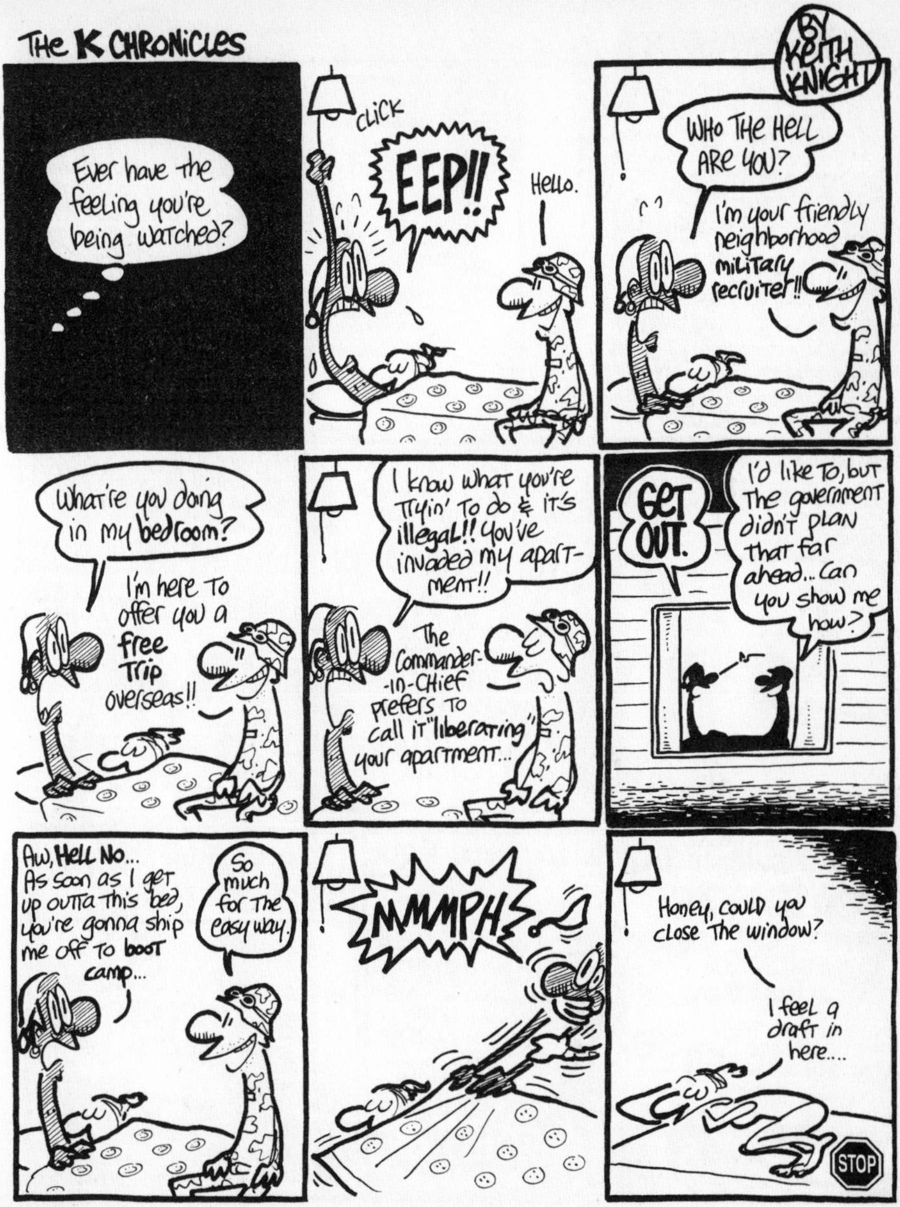

The K CHRONICLES
BY KEITH KNIGHT
Ever have the feeling you're being watched?
CLICK
EEP!!
Hello.
WHO THE HELL ARE YOU?
I'm your friendly neighborhood military recruiter!!
What're you doing in my bedroom?
I'm here to offer you a free Trip overseas!!
I know what you're Tryin' To do & it's illegal!! You've invaded my apartment!!
The Commander-in-Chief prefers to call it "liberating" your apartment...
GET OUT.
I'd like to, but the government didn't plan that far ahead... Can you show me how?
Aw, Hell No... As soon as I get up outta this bed, you're gonna ship me off to boot camp...
So much for the easy way.
MMMPH
Honey, could you close the window?
I feel a draft in here....
STOP

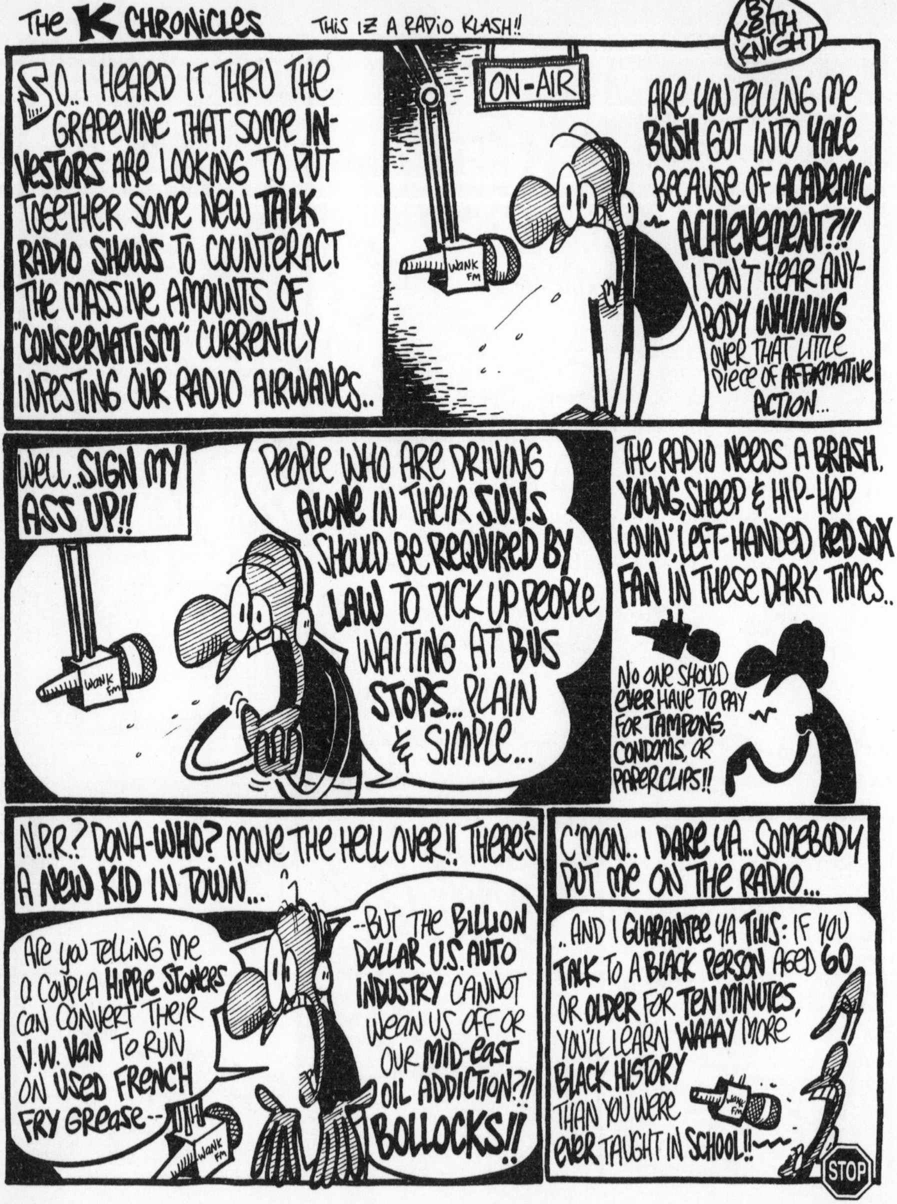
THE K CHRONICLES
THIS IZ A RADIO KLASH!!
BY KEITH KNIGHT
SO.. I HEARD IT THRU THE GRAPEVINE THAT SOME INVESTORS ARE LOOKING TO PUT TOGETHER SOME NEW TALK RADIO SHOWS TO COUNTERACT THE MASSIVE AMOUNTS OF "CONSERVATISM" CURRENTLY INFESTING OUR RADIO AIRWAVES..
ON-AIR
WANK FM
ARE YOU TELLING ME BUSH GOT INTO YALE BECAUSE OF ACADEMIC ACHIEVEMENT?!! I DON'T HEAR ANYBODY WHINING OVER THAT LITTLE PIECE OF AFFIRMATIVE ACTION...
WELL.. SIGN MY ASS UP!!
PEOPLE WHO ARE DRIVING ALONE IN THEIR S.U.V.S SHOULD BE REQUIRED BY LAW TO PICK UP PEOPLE WAITING AT BUS STOPS... PLAIN & SIMPLE...
THE RADIO NEEDS A BRASH, YOUNG, SHEEP & HIP-HOP LOVIN', LEFT-HANDED RED SOX FAN IN THESE DARK TIMES..
NO ONE SHOULD EVER HAVE TO PAY FOR TAMPONS, CONDOMS, OR PAPERCLIPS!!
N.P.R.? DONA-WHO? MOVE THE HELL OVER!! THERE'S A NEW KID IN TOWN...
ARE YOU TELLING ME A COUPLA HIPPIE STONERS CAN CONVERT THEIR V.W. VAN TO RUN ON USED FRENCH FRY GREASE--
--BUT THE BILLION DOLLAR U.S. AUTO INDUSTRY CANNOT WEAN US OFF OF OUR MID-EAST OIL ADDICTION?!! BOLLOCKS!!
C'MON.. I DARE YA.. SOMEBODY PUT ME ON THE RADIO...
..AND I GUARANTEE YA THIS: IF YOU TALK TO A BLACK PERSON AGED 60 OR OLDER FOR TEN MINUTES, YOU'LL LEARN WAAAY MORE BLACK HISTORY THAN YOU WERE EVER TAUGHT IN SCHOOL!!
STOP

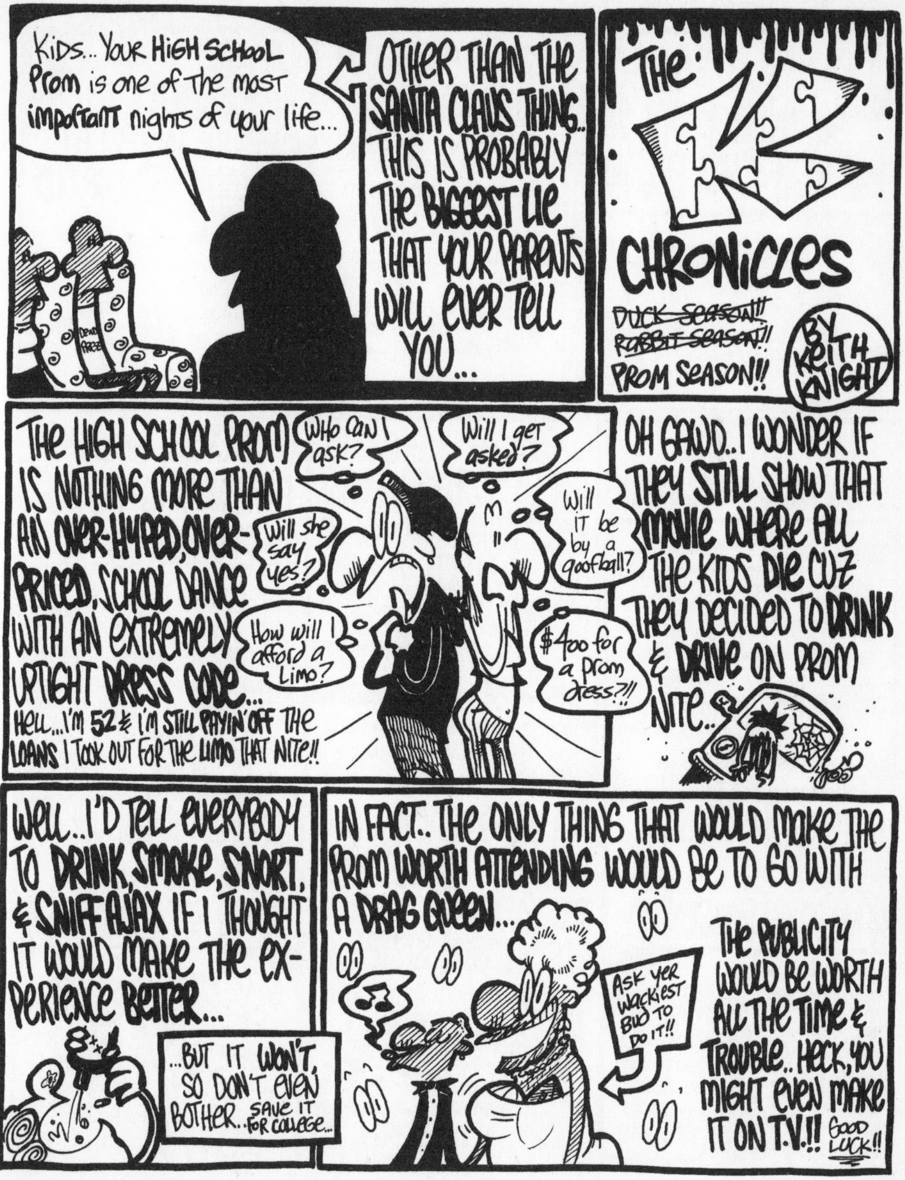

KIDS... YOUR HIGH SCHOOL Prom is one of THE MOST important nights of your life...
OTHER THAN THE SANTA CLAUS THING.. THIS IS PROBABLY THE BIGGEST LIE THAT YOUR PARENTS WILL EVER TELL YOU...
THE K CHRONICLES
DUCK SEASON!!
RABBIT SEASON!!
PROM SEASON!!
BY KEITH KNIGHT
THE HIGH SCHOOL PROM IS NOTHING MORE THAN AN OVER-HYPED, OVER-PRICED, SCHOOL DANCE WITH AN EXTREMELY UPTIGHT DRESS CODE...
HELL...I'M 52 & I'M STILL PAYIN' OFF THE LOANS I TOOK OUT FOR THE LIMO THAT NITE!!
Who can I ask?
Will I get asked?
Will she say yes?
Will it be by a goofball!?
How will I afford a limo?
$400 for a prom dress?!!
OH GAWD..I WONDER IF THEY STILL SHOW THAT MOVIE WHERE ALL THE KIDS DIE CUZ THEY DECIDED TO DRINK & DRIVE ON PROM NITE...
WELL...I'D TELL EVERYBODY TO DRINK, SMOKE, SNORT, & SNIFF AJAX IF I THOUGHT IT WOULD MAKE THE EX-PERIENCE BETTER...
...BUT IT WON'T, SO DON'T EVEN BOTHER... SAVE IT FOR COLLEGE...
IN FACT.. THE ONLY THING THAT WOULD MAKE THE PROM WORTH ATTENDING WOULD BE TO GO WITH A DRAG QUEEN...
ASK YER WACKIEST BUD TO DO IT!!
THE PUBLICITY WOULD BE WORTH ALL THE TIME & TROUBLE.. HECK, YOU MIGHT EVEN MAKE IT ON T.V.!!
GOOD LUCK!!

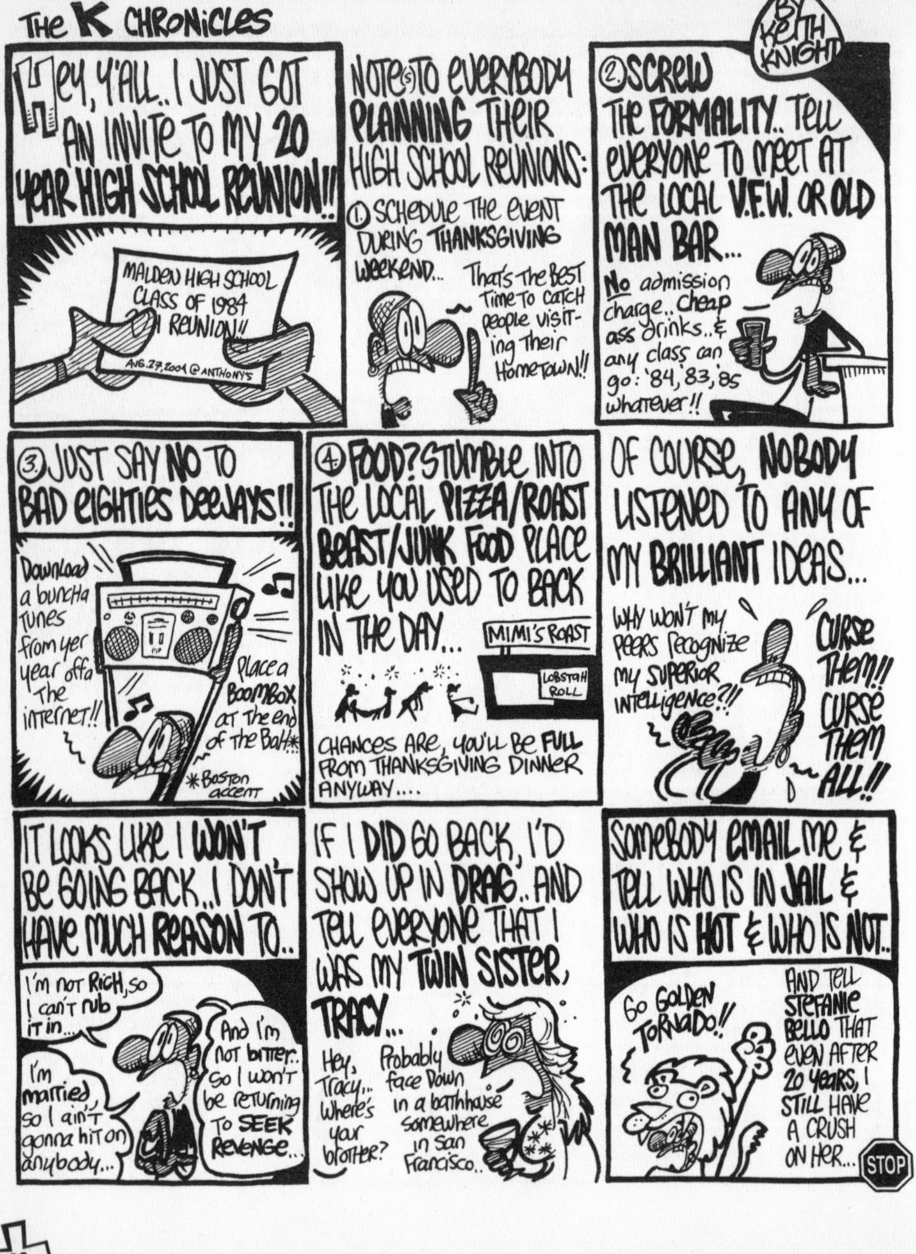
The K Chronicles
By Keith Knight
Hey, y'all.. I just got an invite to my 20 year high school reunion!!..
MALDEN HIGH SCHOOL
CLASS OF 1984
REUNION!!
AUG. 27, 2004 @ ANTHONY'S
Note(s) to everybody planning their high school reunions:
1. Schedule the event during Thanksgiving weekend..
That's the best time to catch people visiting their hometown!!
2. Screw the formality.. tell everyone to meet at the local V.F.W. or old man bar...
No admission charge.. cheap ass drinks.. & any class can go: '84, '83, '85 whatever!!
3. Just say no to bad eighties deejays!!
Download a buncha tunes from yer year offa the internet!!
Place a boombox at the end of the bah!*
*Boston accent
4. Food? Stumble into the local pizza/roast beast/junk food place like you used to back in the day...
MIMI'S ROAST
LOBSTAH ROLL
Chances are, you'll be full from Thanksgiving dinner anyway....
Of course, nobody listened to any of my brilliant ideas...
Why won't my peers recognize my superior intelligence?!!
Curse them!! Curse them! Curse them all!!
It looks like I won't be going back.. I don't have much reason to..
I'm not rich, so I can't rub it in...
I'm married, so I ain't gonna hit on anybody...
And I'm not bitter.. so I won't be returning to seek revenge...
If I did go back, I'd show up in drag.. and tell everyone that I was my twin sister, Tracy...
Hey, Tracy.. where's your brother?
Probably face down in a bathhouse somewhere in San Francisco..
Somebody email me & tell who is in jail & who is hot & who is not..
Go Golden Tornado!!
And tell Stefanie Bello that even after 20 years, I still have a crush on her...
STOP

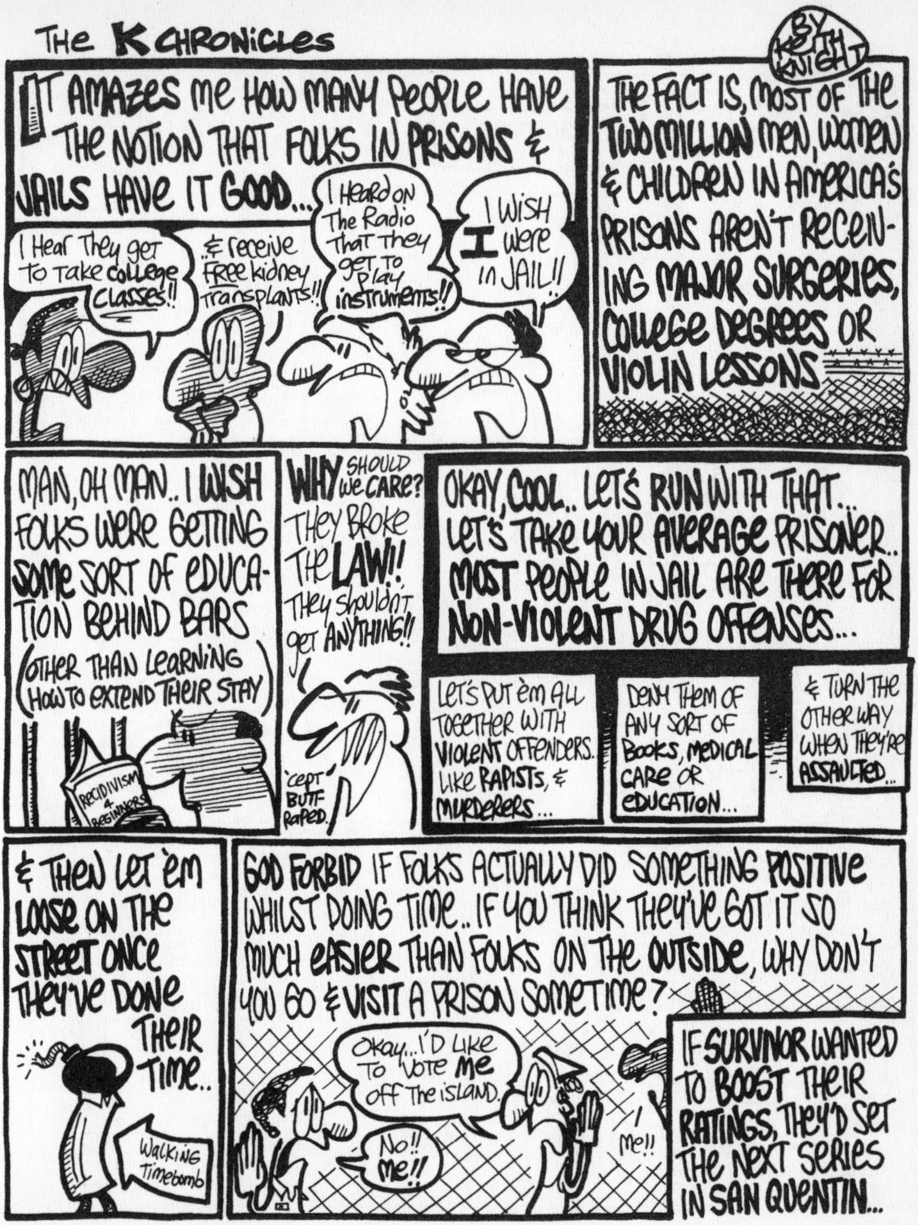
THE K CHRONICLES
BY KEITH KNIGHT
IT AMAZES ME HOW MANY PEOPLE HAVE THE NOTION THAT FOLKS IN PRISONS & JAILS HAVE IT GOOD...
I Hear They get to Take college classes!!
...& receive Free kidney transplants!!
I Heard on The Radio that They get to play instruments!!
I WISH I were in JAIL!!
THE FACT IS, MOST OF THE TWO MILLION MEN, WOMEN & CHILDREN IN AMERICA'S PRISONS AREN'T RECEIVING MAJOR SURGERIES, COLLEGE DEGREES OR VIOLIN LESSONS
MAN, OH MAN.. I WISH FOLKS WERE GETTING SOME SORT OF EDUCATION BEHIND BARS (OTHER THAN LEARNING HOW TO EXTEND THEIR STAY)
RECIDIVISM 4 BEGINNERS
WHY SHOULD WE CARE? THEY BROKE THE LAW!! THEY SHOULDN'T GET ANYTHING!!
'CEPT BUTT RAPED.
OKAY, COOL.. LET'S RUN WITH THAT... LET'S TAKE YOUR AVERAGE PRISONER.. MOST PEOPLE IN JAIL ARE THERE FOR NON-VIOLENT DRUG OFFENSES...
LET'S PUT 'EM ALL TOGETHER WITH VIOLENT OFFENDERS. LIKE RAPISTS, & MURDERERS...
DENY THEM OF ANY SORT OF BOOKS, MEDICAL CARE OR EDUCATION...
& TURN THE OTHER WAY WHEN THEY'RE ASSAULTED...
& THEN LET 'EM LOOSE ON THE STREET ONCE THEY'VE DONE THEIR TIME...
WALKING Timebomb
GOD FORBID IF FOLKS ACTUALLY DID SOMETHING POSITIVE WHILST DOING TIME.. IF YOU THINK THEY'VE GOT IT SO MUCH EASIER THAN FOLKS ON THE OUTSIDE, WHY DON'T YOU GO & VISIT A PRISON SOMETIME?
Okay...I'D LIKE TO VOTE ME OFF The island.
No!! me!!
I me!!
IF SURVIVOR WANTED TO BOOST THEIR RATINGS, THEY'D SET THE NEXT SERIES IN SAN QUENTIN...

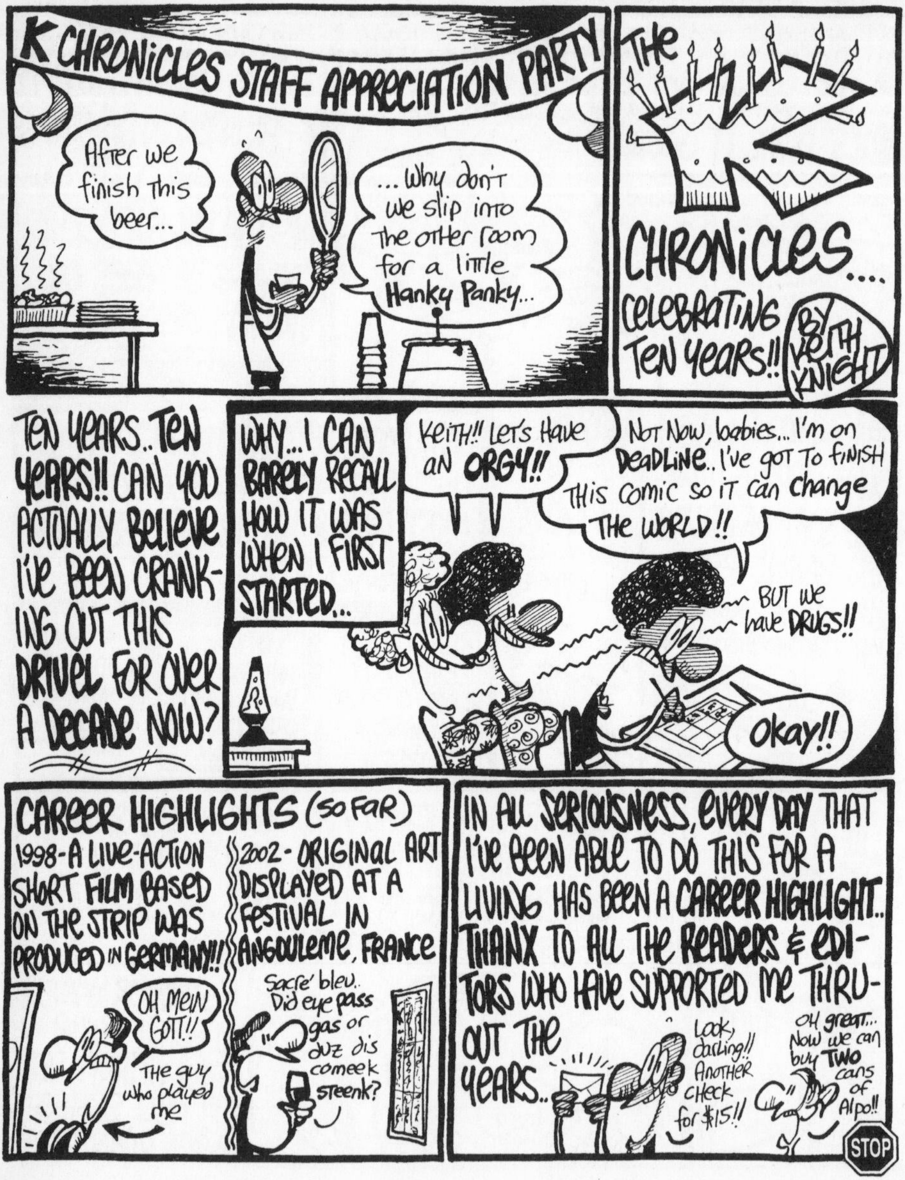
K CHRONICLES STAFF APPRECIATION PARTY
After we finish this beer...
...Why don't we slip into the other room for a little Hanky Panky...
THE K CHRONICLES.... CELEBRATING TEN YEARS!!
BY KEITH KNIGHT
TEN YEARS.. TEN YEARS!! CAN YOU ACTUALLY BELIEVE I'VE BEEN CRANK-ING OUT THIS DRIVEL FOR OVER A DECADE NOW?
WHY...I CAN BARELY RECALL HOW IT WAS WHEN I FIRST STARTED...
KEITH!! LET'S HAVE AN ORGY!!
NOT NOW, babies... I'M ON DEADLINE.. I'VE GOT TO FINISH THIS COMIC SO IT CAN CHANGE THE WORLD!!
BUT WE have DRUGS!!
Okay!!
CAREER HIGHLIGHTS (SO FAR)
1998-A LIVE-ACTION SHORT FILM BASED ON THE STRIP WAS PRODUCED IN GERMANY!!
OH MEIN GOTT!!
THE guy who played me
2002-ORIGINAL ART DISPLAYED AT A FESTIVAL IN ANGOULEME, FRANCE
Sacre' bleu.. Did eye pass gas or duz dis comeek steenk?
IN ALL SERIOUSNESS, EVERY DAY THAT I'VE BEEN ABLE TO DO THIS FOR A LIVING HAS BEEN A CAREER HIGHLIGHT.. THANX TO ALL THE READERS & EDI-TORS WHO HAVE SUPPORTED ME THRU-OUT THE YEARS..
Look, darling!! Another check for $15!!
OH great... Now we can buy TWO cans of Alpo!!
STOP

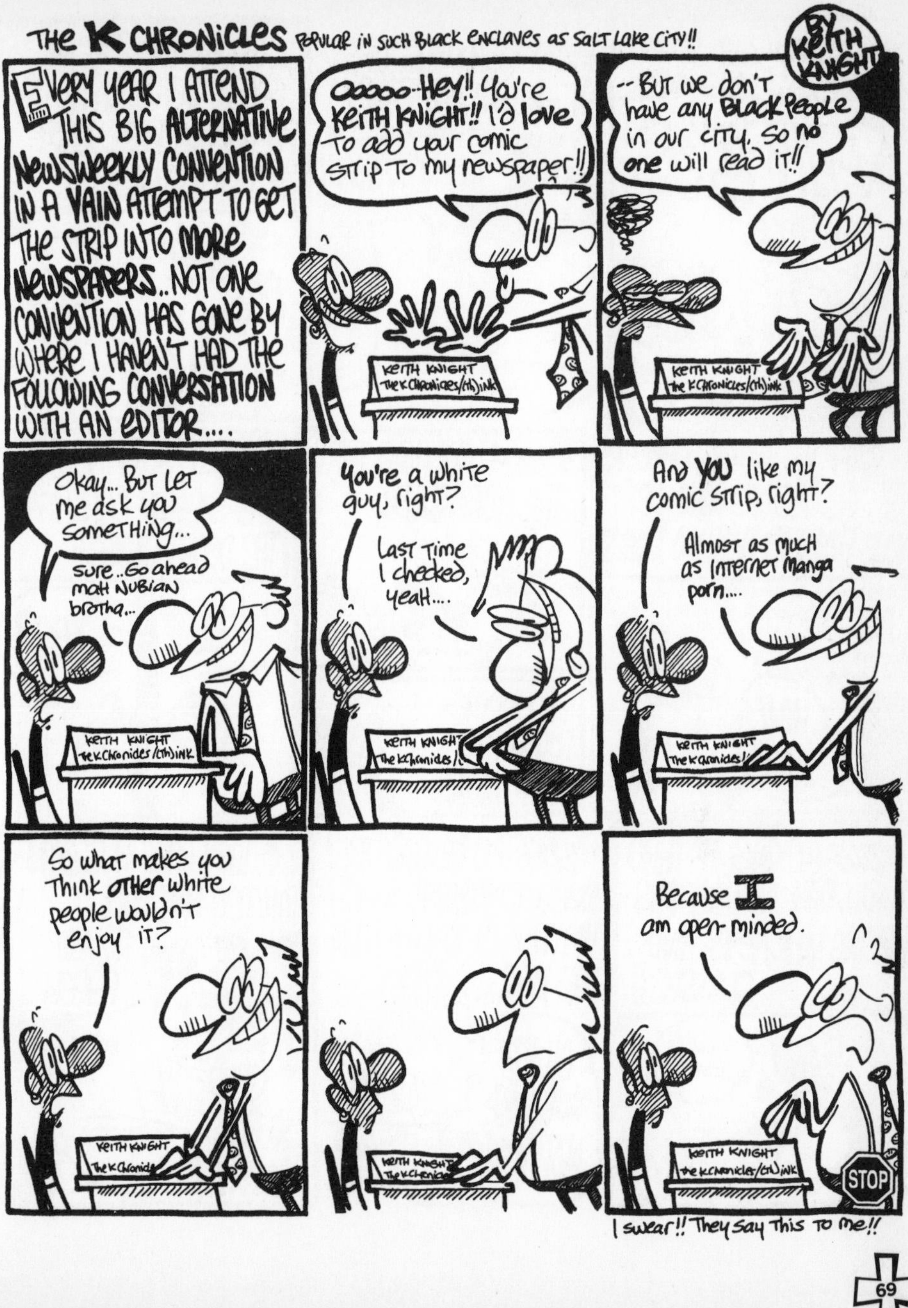
THE K CHRONICLES POPULAR IN SUCH BLACK ENCLAVES AS SALT LAKE CITY!!
BY KEITH KNIGHT
EVERY YEAR I ATTEND THIS BIG ALTERNATIVE NEWSWEEKLY CONVENTION IN A VAIN ATTEMPT TO GET THE STRIP INTO MORE NEWSPAPERS... NOT ONE CONVENTION HAS GONE BY WHERE I HAVEN'T HAD THE FOLLOWING CONVERSATION WITH AN EDITOR....
Ooooo-Hey!! You're Keith Knight!! I'd love to add your comic strip to my newspaper!!
KEITH KNIGHT The K Chronicles/(th)ink
-- But we don't have any Black People in our city, so no one will read it!!
KEITH KNIGHT The K Chronicles/(th)ink
Okay... But let me ask you something...
Sure.. Go ahead mah Nubian brotha...
KEITH KNIGHT The K Chronicles/(th)ink
You're a white guy, right?
Last time I checked, yeah....
KEITH KNIGHT The K Chronicles
And YOU like my comic strip, right?
Almost as much as Internet Manga porn....
KEITH KNIGHT The K Chronicles
So what makes you think OTHER white people wouldn't enjoy it?
KEITH KNIGHT The K Chronicles
KEITH KNIGHT The K Chronicles
Because I am open-minded.
KEITH KNIGHT The K Chronicles/(th)ink
STOP
I swear!! They say this to me!!

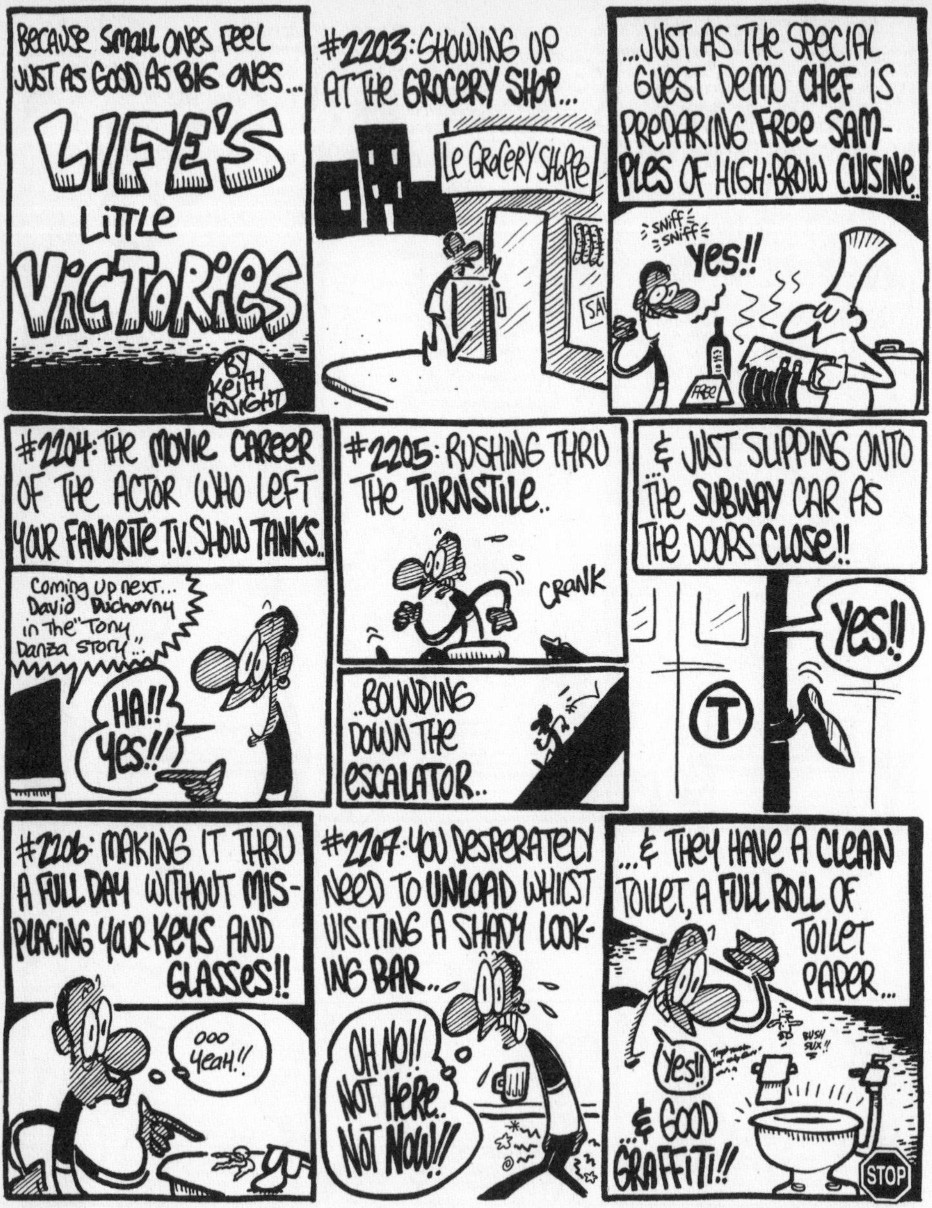

BECAUSE SMALL ONES FEEL JUST AS GOOD AS BIG ONES...
LIFE'S LITTLE VICTORIES
BY KEITH KNIGHT
#2203: SHOWING UP AT THE GROCERY SHOP...
LE GROCERY SHOPPE
...JUST AS THE SPECIAL GUEST DEMO CHEF IS PREPARING FREE SAMPLES OF HIGH-BROW CUISINE..
SNIFF SNIFF
YES!!
FREE
#2204: THE MOVIE CAREER OF THE ACTOR WHO LEFT YOUR FAVORITE T.V. SHOW TANKS..
Coming up next... David Duchovny in the "Tony Danza Story"!...
HA!! YES!!
#2205: RUSHING THRU THE TURNSTILE..
CRANK
..BOUNDING DOWN THE ESCALATOR..
...& JUST SLIPPING ONTO THE SUBWAY CAR AS THE DOORS CLOSE!!
T
YES!!
#2206: MAKING IT THRU A FULL DAY WITHOUT MISPLACING YOUR KEYS AND GLASSES!!
OOO YEAH!!
#2207: YOU DESPERATELY NEED TO UNLOAD WHILST VISITING A SHADY LOOKING BAR...
OH NO!! NOT HERE.. NOT NOW!!
...& THEY HAVE A CLEAN TOILET, A FULL ROLL OF TOILET PAPER...
YES!!
BUSH SUX!!
...& GOOD GRAFFITI!!
STOP

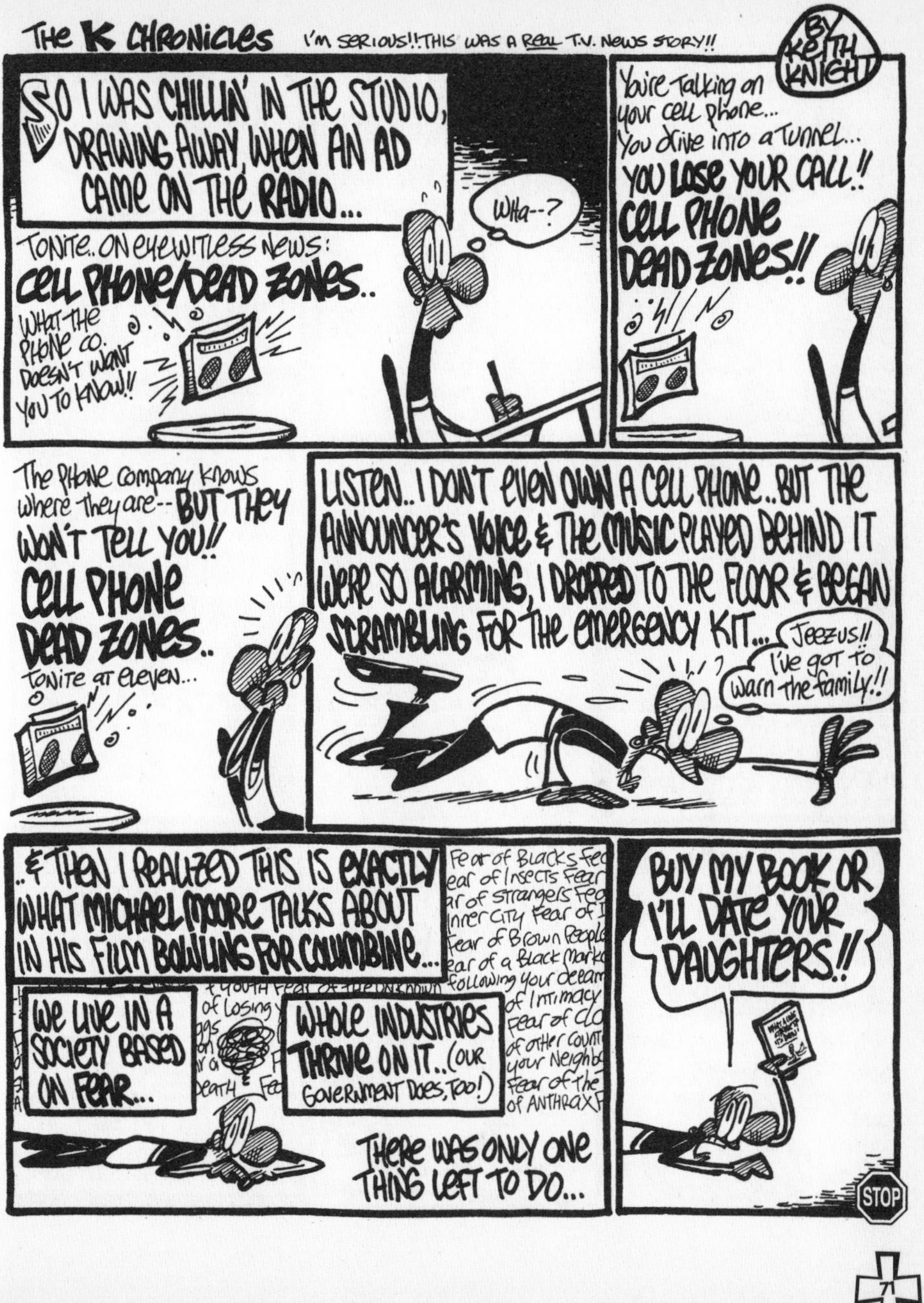
THE K CHRONICLES
I'M SERIOUS!! THIS WAS A REAL T.V. NEWS STORY!!
BY KEITH KNIGHT
SO I WAS CHILLIN' IN THE STUDIO, DRAWING AWAY, WHEN AN AD CAME ON THE RADIO...
TONITE.. ON EYEWITLESS NEWS:
CELL PHONE/DEAD ZONES..
WHAT THE PHONE CO. DOESN'T WANT YOU TO KNOW!!
Wha--?
You're talking on your cell phone... You drive into a tunnel...
YOU LOSE YOUR CALL!..
CELL PHONE DEAD ZONES!!
The phone company knows where they are-- BUT THEY WON'T TELL YOU!!
CELL PHONE DEAD ZONES..
TONITE AT ELEVEN...
LISTEN.. I DON'T EVEN OWN A CELL PHONE.. BUT THE ANNOUNCER'S VOICE & THE MUSIC PLAYED BEHIND IT WERE SO ALARMING, I DROPPED TO THE FLOOR & BEGAN SCRAMBLING FOR THE EMERGENCY KIT...
Jeezus!! I've got to warn the family!!
..& THEN I REALIZED THIS IS EXACTLY WHAT MICHAEL MOORE TALKS ABOUT IN HIS FILM BOWLING FOR COLUMBINE...
Fear of Blacks
Fear of Insects
Fear of Strangers
Inner City
Fear of Brown People
Fear of a Black Market
following your dream
of Intimacy
of other countries
your Neighbor
of ANTHRAX
WE LIVE IN A SOCIETY BASED ON FEAR...
WHOLE INDUSTRIES THRIVE ON IT.. (OUR GOVERNMENT DOES, TOO!)
THERE WAS ONLY ONE THING LEFT TO DO...
BUY MY BOOK OR I'LL DATE YOUR DAUGHTERS!!
STOP

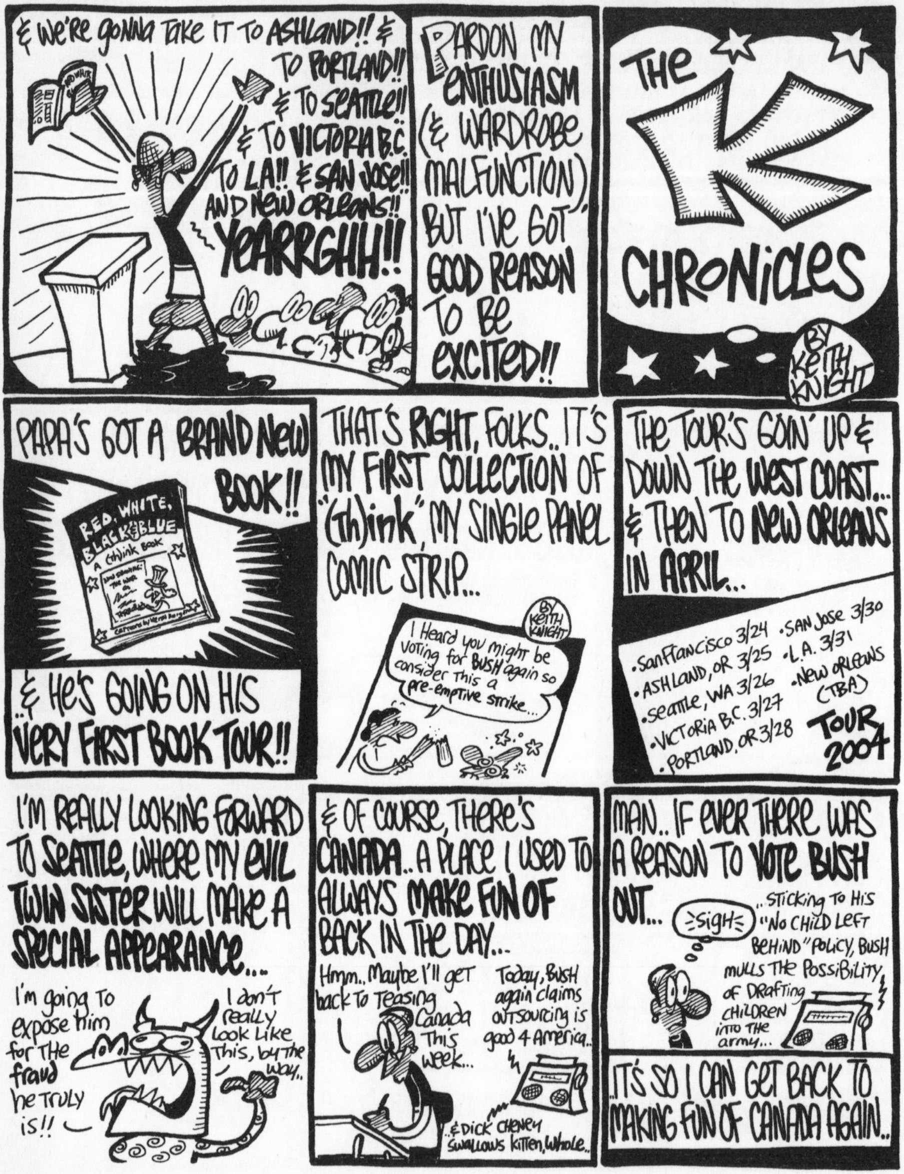
& WE'RE GONNA TAKE IT TO ASHLAND!! & TO PORTLAND!! & TO SEATTLE!! & TO VICTORIA B.C. TO L.A.!! & SAN JOSE!! AND NEW ORLEANS!!
YEARRGHH!!
PARDON MY ENTHUSIASM (& WARDROBE MALFUNCTION), BUT I'VE GOT GOOD REASON TO BE EXCITED!!
THE K CHRONICLES
BY KEITH KNIGHT
PAPA'S GOT A BRAND NEW BOOK!!
RED, WHITE, BLACK & BLUE
A (th)ink BOOK
..& HE'S GOING ON HIS VERY FIRST BOOK TOUR!!
THAT'S RIGHT, FOLKS.. IT'S MY FIRST COLLECTION OF "(th)ink", MY SINGLE PANEL COMIC STRIP...
BY KEITH KNIGHT
I Heard you might be voting for BUSH again so consider this a pre-emptive strike...
THE TOUR'S GOIN' UP & DOWN THE WEST COAST... & THEN TO NEW ORLEANS IN APRIL...
• San Francisco 3/24
• ASHLAND, OR 3/25
• Seattle, WA 3/26
• VICTORIA B.C. 3/27
• PORTLAND, OR 3/28
• SAN Jose 3/30
• L.A. 3/31
• New Orleans (TBA)
TOUR 2004
I'M REALLY LOOKING FORWARD TO SEATTLE, WHERE MY EVIL TWIN SISTER WILL MAKE A SPECIAL APPEARANCE....
I'm going to expose him for the fraud he truly is!!
I don't really look like this, by the way..
& OF COURSE, THERE'S CANADA.. A PLACE I USED TO ALWAYS MAKE FUN OF BACK IN THE DAY...
Hmm.. Maybe I'll get back to teasing Canada this week...
Today, BUSH again claims outsourcing is good 4 America..
..& DICK CHENEY SWALLOWS KITTEN, WHOLE..
MAN.. IF EVER THERE WAS A REASON TO VOTE BUSH OUT...
SIGH
..STICKING TO HIS "NO CHILD LEFT BEHIND" POLICY, BUSH MULLS THE POSSIBILITY OF DRAFTING CHILDREN INTO THE ARMY...
..IT'S SO I CAN GET BACK TO MAKING FUN OF CANADA AGAIN..

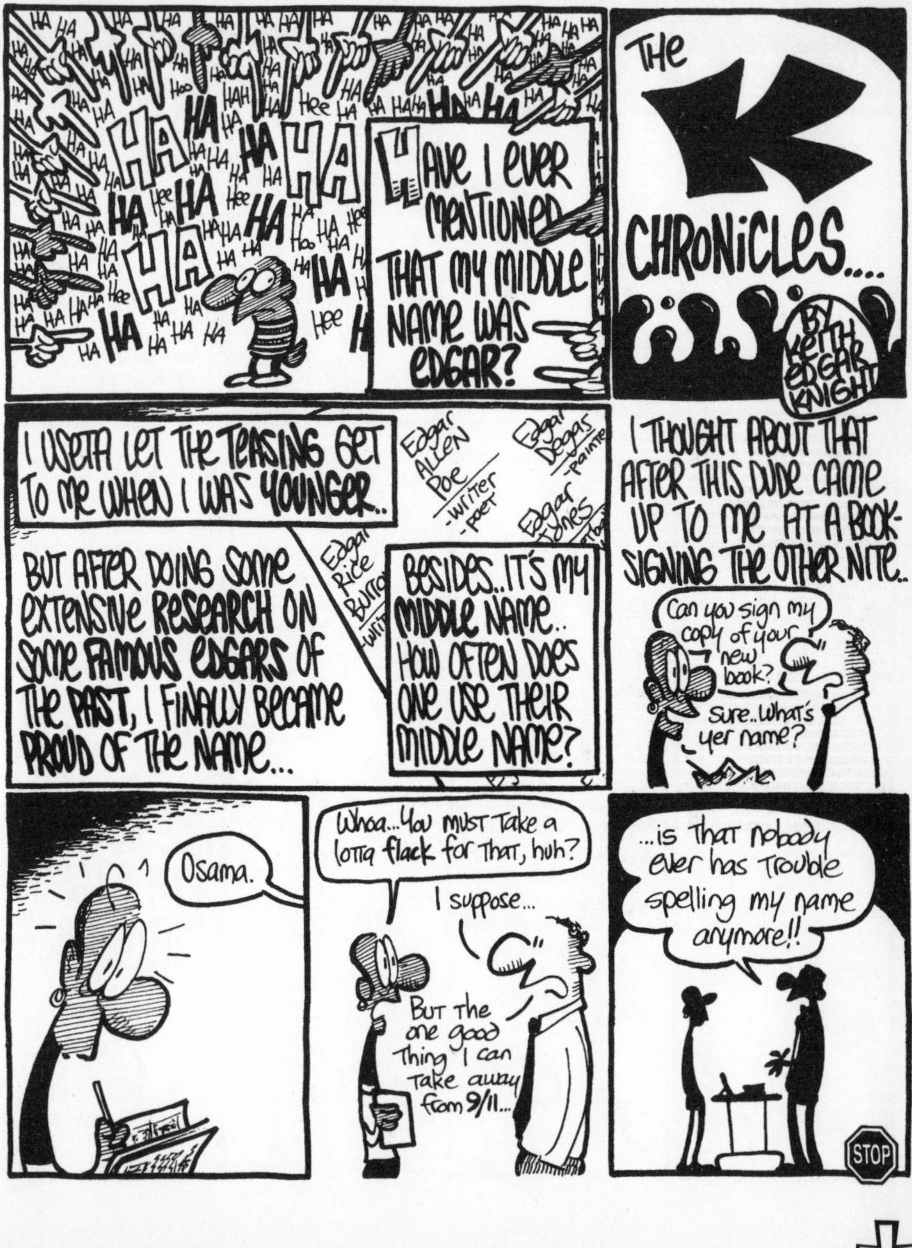
HA HA HA HEE HOO HAH HA
HAVE I EVER MENTIONED THAT MY MIDDLE NAME WAS EDGAR?
THE K CHRONICLES....
BY KEITH EDGAR KNIGHT
I USETA LET THE TEASING GET TO ME WHEN I WAS YOUNGER..
BUT AFTER DOING SOME EXTENSIVE RESEARCH ON SOME FAMOUS EDGARS OF THE PAST, I FINALLY BECAME PROUD OF THE NAME...
Edgar Allen Poe -writer -poet
Edgar Degas
Edgar Rice
BESIDES.. IT'S MY MIDDLE NAME.. HOW OFTEN DOES ONE USE THEIR MIDDLE NAME?
I THOUGHT ABOUT THAT AFTER THIS DUDE CAME UP TO ME AT A BOOK-SIGNING THE OTHER NITE..
Can you sign my copy of your new book?
Sure.. What's yer name?
Osama.
Whoa... You MUST Take a lotta flack for That, huh?
I suppose...
But The one good Thing I can Take away from 9/11...
...is That nobody ever has Trouble spelling my name anymore!!
STOP

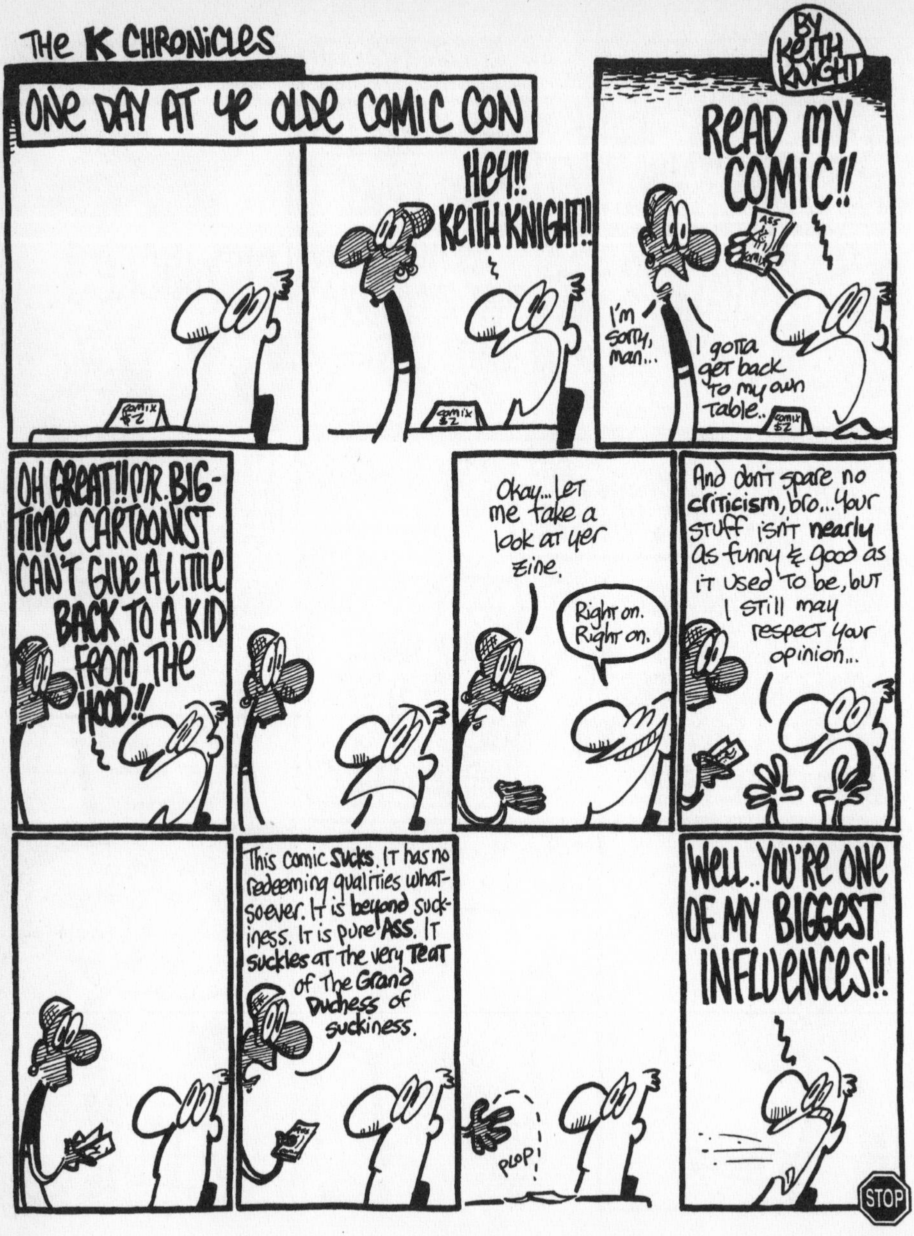
THE K CHRONICLES
BY KEITH KNIGHT
ONE DAY AT YE OLDE COMIC CON
COMIX $2
HEY!! KEITH KNIGHT!!
READ MY COMIC!!
I'm sorry, man...
I gotta get back to my own Table..
OH GREAT!! MR. BIG-TIME CARTOONIST CAN'T GIVE A LITTLE BACK TO A KID FROM THE HOOD!!
Okay... Let me take a look at yer zine.
Right on. Right on.
And don't spare no criticism, bro... Your stuff isn't nearly as funny & good as it used to be, but I still may respect your opinion...
This comic sucks. It has no redeeming qualities whatsoever. It is beyond suckiness. It is pure ASS. It suckles at the very Teat of the Grand Duchess of suckiness.
PLOP!
WELL.. YOU'RE ONE OF MY BIGGEST INFLUENCES!!
STOP

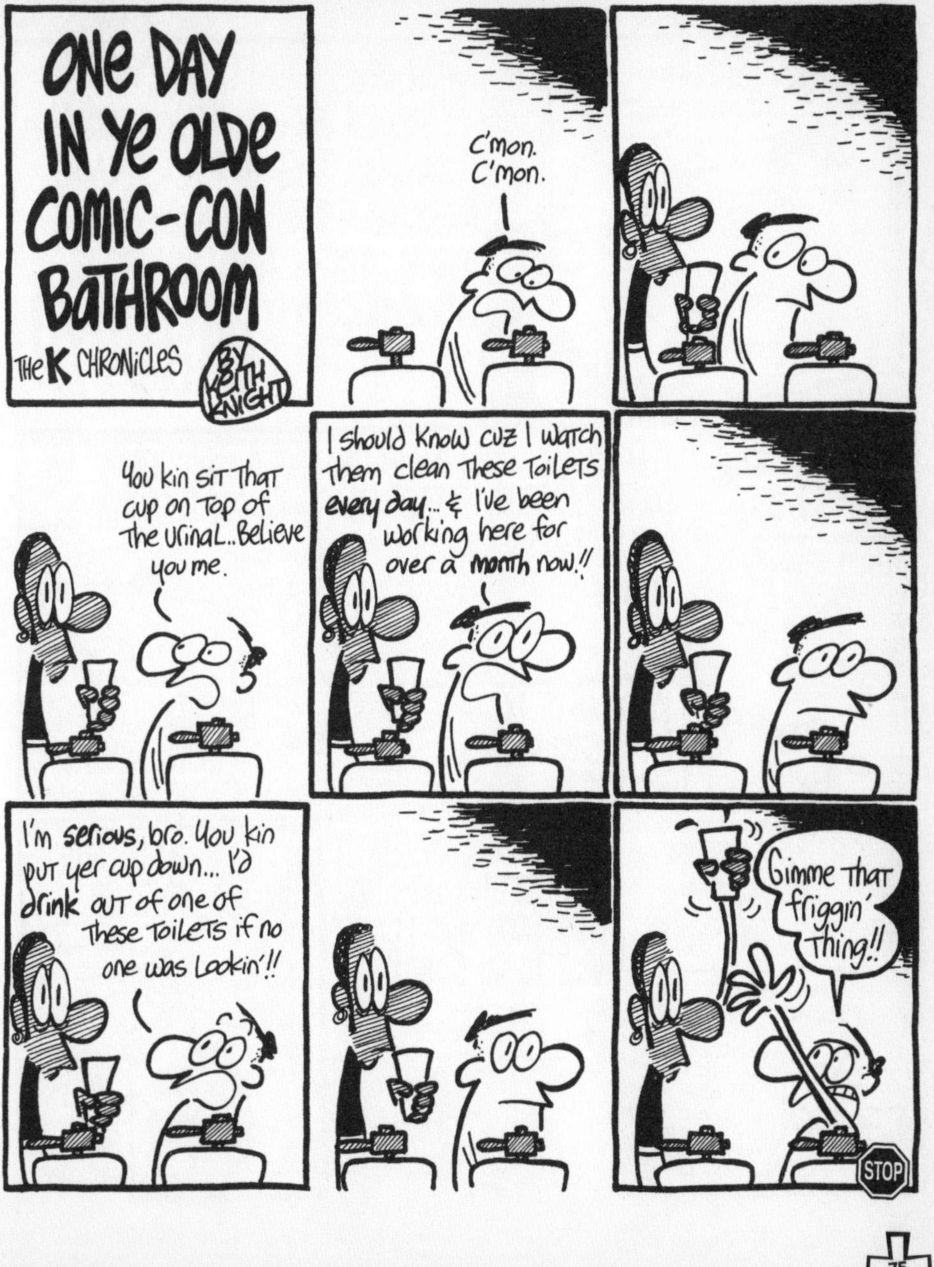

One Day in Ye Olde Comic-Con Bathroom
The K Chronicles
By Keith Knight
C'mon. C'mon.
You kin sit that cup on top of the urinal... Believe you me.
I should know cuz I watch them clean these toilets every day... & I've been working here for over a month now!!
I'm serious, bro. You kin put yer cup down... I'd drink out of one of these toilets if no one was lookin'!!
Gimme that friggin' thing!!
STOP

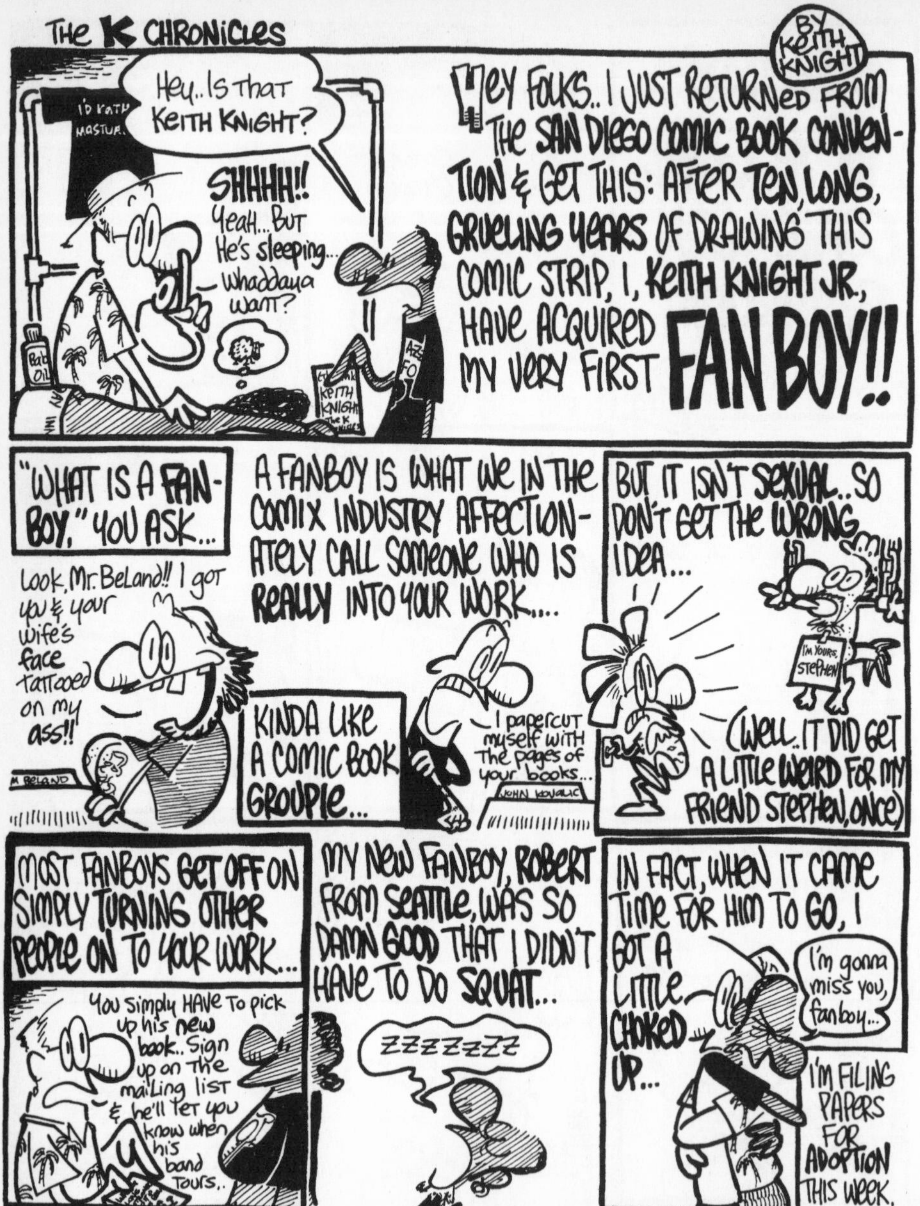
THE K CHRONICLES
BY KEITH KNIGHT
Hey.. Is that Keith Knight?
SHHHH!! Yeah... But He's sleeping... Whaddaya want?
HEY FOLKS.. I JUST RETURNED FROM THE SAN DIEGO COMIC BOOK CONVENTION & GET THIS: AFTER TEN, LONG, GRUELING YEARS OF DRAWING THIS COMIC STRIP, I, KEITH KNIGHT JR., HAVE ACQUIRED MY VERY FIRST FANBOY!!
"WHAT IS A FANBOY," YOU ASK...
Look, Mr. Beland!! I got you & your wife's face tattooed on my ass!!
M BELAND
A FANBOY IS WHAT WE IN THE COMIX INDUSTRY AFFECTIONATELY CALL SOMEONE WHO IS REALLY INTO YOUR WORK....
KINDA LIKE A COMIC BOOK GROUPIE...
I papercut myself with the pages of your books...
JOHN KOVALIC
BUT IT ISN'T SEXUAL.. SO DON'T GET THE WRONG IDEA...
I'M YOURS, STEPHEN
(WELL.. IT DID GET A LITTLE WEIRD FOR MY FRIEND STEPHEN, ONCE)
MOST FANBOYS GET OFF ON SIMPLY TURNING OTHER PEOPLE ON TO YOUR WORK...
You simply HAVE to pick up his new book.. Sign up on the mailing list & he'll let you know when his band tours..
MY NEW FANBOY, ROBERT FROM SEATTLE, WAS SO DAMN GOOD THAT I DIDN'T HAVE TO DO SQUAT...
ZZZZZZZ
IN FACT, WHEN IT CAME TIME FOR HIM TO GO, I GOT A LITTLE CHOKED UP...
I'm gonna miss you, fanboy...
I'M FILING PAPERS FOR ADOPTION THIS WEEK.

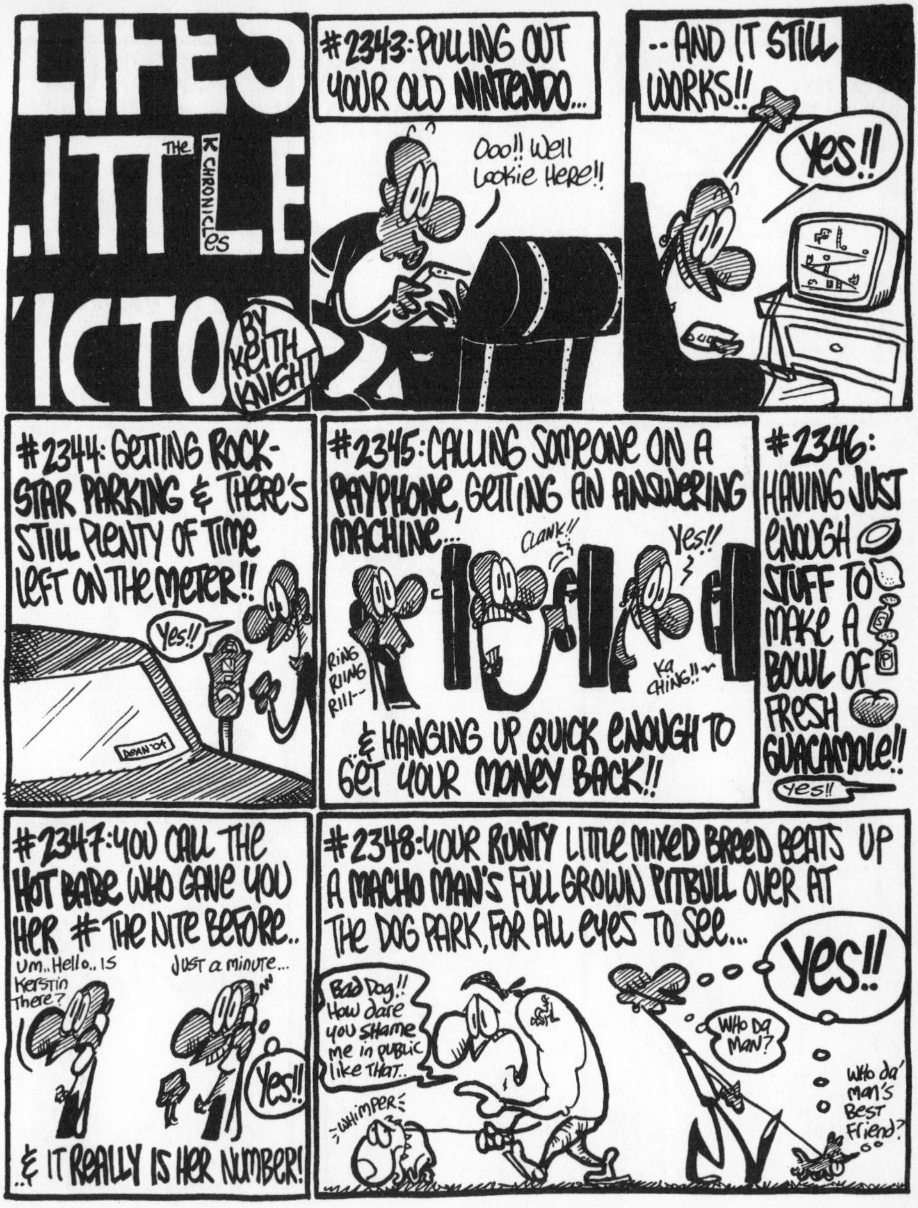

THE K CHRONICLES
BY KEITH KNIGHT
#2343: PULLING OUT YOUR OLD NINTENDO...
Ooo!! Well Lookie Here!!
-- AND IT STILL WORKS!!
YES!!
#2344: GETTING ROCK-STAR PARKING & THERE'S STILL PLENTY OF TIME LEFT ON THE METER!!
Yes!!
DEAN '04
#2345: CALLING SOMEONE ON A PAYPHONE, GETTING AN ANSWERING MACHINE...
RING RING RIII--
CLANK!!
Yes!!
KA CHING!!
...& HANGING UP QUICK ENOUGH TO GET YOUR MONEY BACK!!
#2346: HAVING JUST ENOUGH STUFF TO MAKE A BOWL OF FRESH GUACAMOLE!!..
YES!!
#2347: YOU CALL THE HOT BABE WHO GAVE YOU HER # THE NITE BEFORE..
Um.. Hello.. IS Kerstin There?
JUST a minute...
Yes!!
..& IT REALLY IS HER NUMBER!
#2348: YOUR RUNTY LITTLE MIXED BREED BEATS UP A MACHO MAN'S FULL GROWN PITBULL OVER AT THE DOG PARK, FOR ALL EYES TO SEE...
YES!!
Bad Dog!! How dare you SHAME me in PUBLIC like THAT..
WHIMPER
WHO DA MAN?
Who da' man's Best Friend?

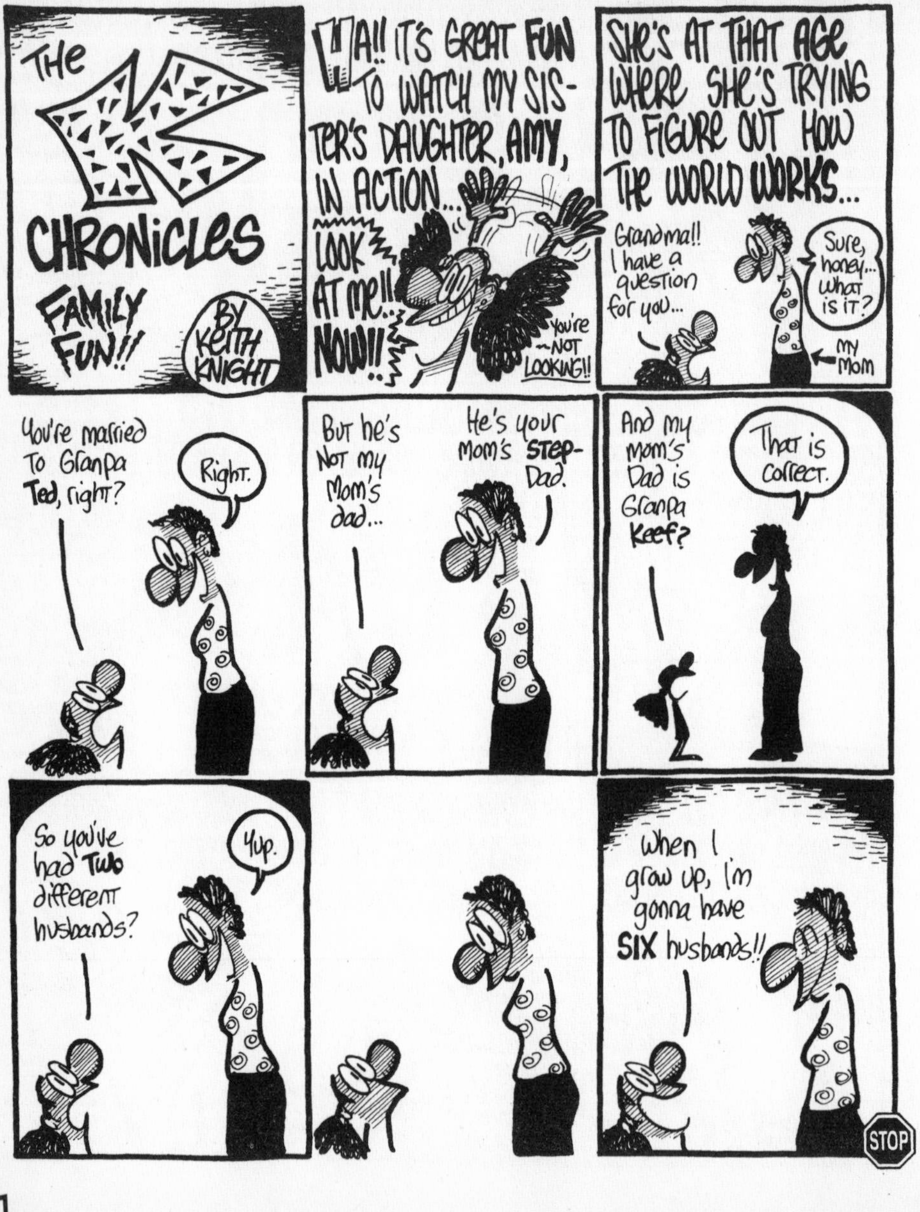

THE K CHRONICLES
FAMILY FUN!!
BY KEITH KNIGHT
HA!! IT'S GREAT FUN TO WATCH MY SISTER'S DAUGHTER, AMY, IN ACTION...
LOOK AT ME!!.. NOW!!..
You're NOT LOOKING!!
SHE'S AT THAT AGE WHERE SHE'S TRYING TO FIGURE OUT HOW THE WORLD WORKS...
Grandma!! I have a question for you...
Sure, honey... what is it?
MY MOM
You're married To Granpa Ted, right?
Right.
But he's NOT my Mom's dad...
He's your Mom's STEP-Dad.
And my mom's Dad is Granpa Keef?
That is correct.
So you've had TWO different husbands?
Yup.
When I grow up, I'm gonna have SIX husbands!!
STOP

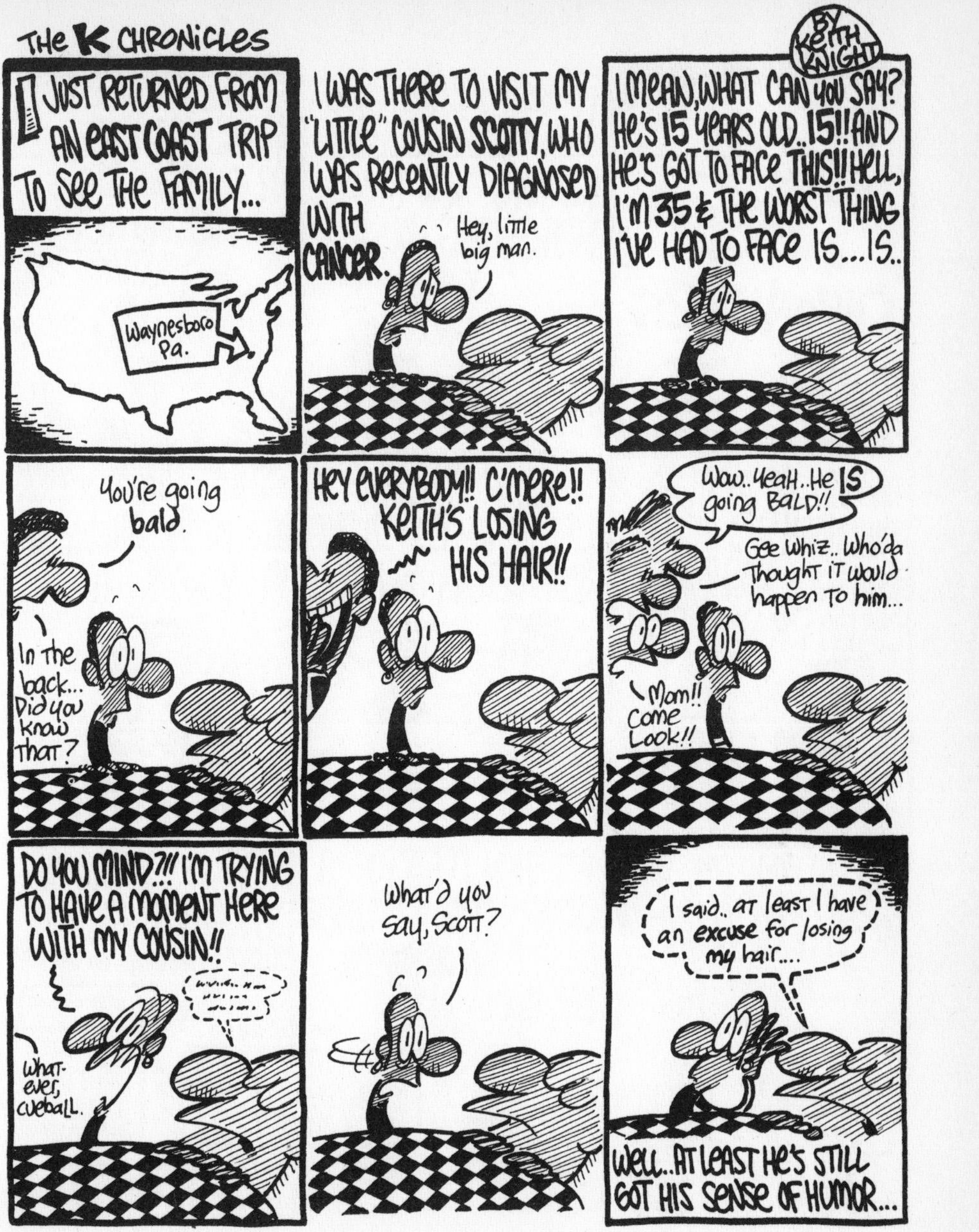
THE K CHRONICLES
BY KEITH KNIGHT
I JUST RETURNED FROM AN EAST COAST TRIP TO SEE THE FAMILY...
Waynesboro Pa.
I WAS THERE TO VISIT MY "LITTLE" COUSIN SCOTTY, WHO WAS RECENTLY DIAGNOSED WITH CANCER.
Hey, little big man.
I MEAN, WHAT CAN YOU SAY? HE'S 15 YEARS OLD.. 15!! AND HE'S GOT TO FACE THIS!! HELL, I'M 35 & THE WORST THING I'VE HAD TO FACE IS...IS..
You're going bald.
In the back... Did you know that?
HEY EVERYBODY!! C'MERE!! KEITH'S LOSING HIS HAIR!!
Wow.. Yeah.. He IS going BALD!!
Gee whiz.. Who'da thought it would happen to him...
Mom!! Come Look!!
DO YOU MIND?!!! I'M TRYING TO HAVE A MOMENT HERE WITH MY COUSIN!!
What-ever, cueball.
What'd you say, Scott?
I said.. at least I have an excuse for losing my hair....
WELL...AT LEAST HE'S STILL GOT HIS SENSE OF HUMOR...

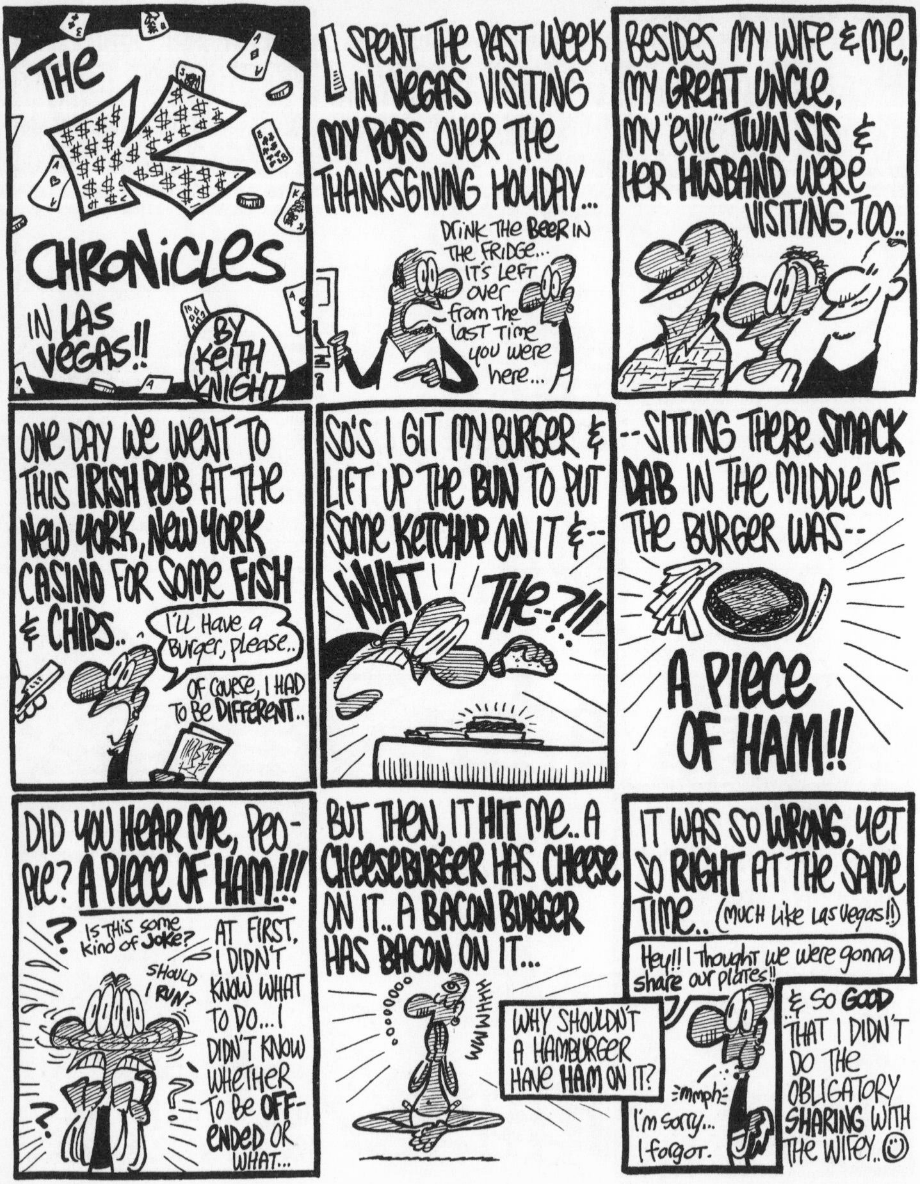

THE K CHRONICLES
IN LAS VEGAS!!
BY KEITH KNIGHT
I SPENT THE PAST WEEK IN VEGAS VISITING MY POPS OVER THE THANKSGIVING HOLIDAY...
DRINK THE BEER IN THE FRIDGE... IT'S LEFT OVER FROM THE LAST TIME YOU WERE HERE...
BESIDES MY WIFE & ME, MY GREAT UNCLE, MY "EVIL" TWIN SIS & HER HUSBAND WERE VISITING, TOO..
ONE DAY WE WENT TO THIS IRISH PUB AT THE NEW YORK, NEW YORK CASINO FOR SOME FISH & CHIPS..
I'LL HAVE A BURGER, PLEASE..
OF COURSE, I HAD TO BE DIFFERENT..
SO'S I GIT MY BURGER & LIFT UP THE BUN TO PUT SOME KETCHUP ON IT &--
WHAT THE--?!!
--SITTING THERE SMACK DAB IN THE MIDDLE OF THE BURGER WAS--
A PIECE OF HAM!!
DID YOU HEAR ME, PEOPLE? A PIECE OF HAM!!!
IS THIS SOME KIND OF JOKE?
SHOULD I RUN?
AT FIRST, I DIDN'T KNOW WHAT TO DO... I DIDN'T KNOW WHETHER TO BE OFFENDED OR WHAT...
BUT THEN, IT HIT ME.. A CHEESEBURGER HAS CHEESE ON IT.. A BACON BURGER HAS BACON ON IT...
HMMMM
WHY SHOULDN'T A HAMBURGER HAVE HAM ON IT?
IT WAS SO WRONG, YET SO RIGHT AT THE SAME TIME.. (MUCH LIKE LAS VEGAS!!)
HEY!! I THOUGHT WE WERE GONNA SHARE OUR PLATES!!
MMPH
I'M SORRY... I FORGOT.
& SO GOOD THAT I DIDN'T DO THE OBLIGATORY SHARING WITH THE WIFEY.. ☺

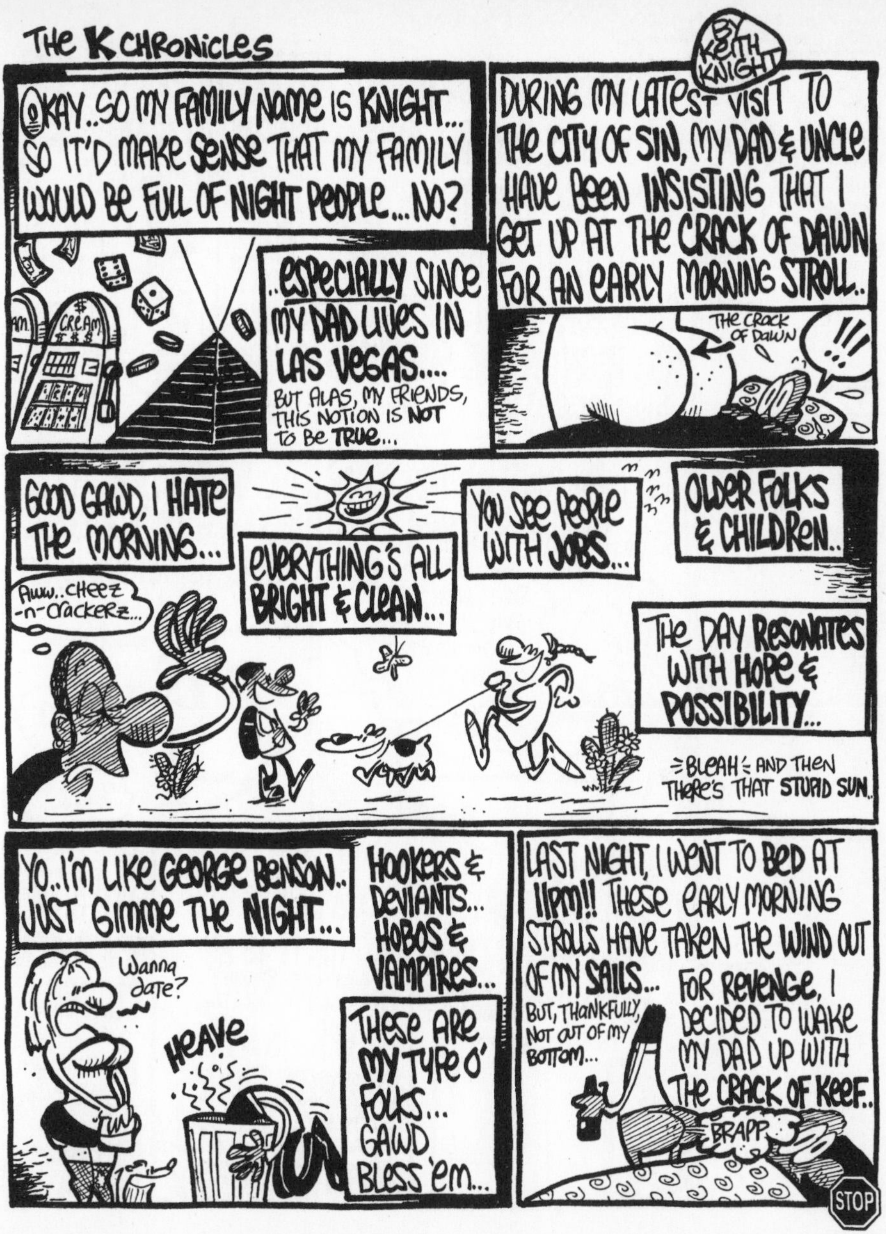
THE K CHRONICLES
BY KEITH KNIGHT
OKAY..SO MY FAMILY NAME IS KNIGHT... SO IT'D MAKE SENSE THAT MY FAMILY WOULD BE FULL OF NIGHT PEOPLE... NO?
..ESPECIALLY SINCE MY DAD LIVES IN LAS VEGAS....
BUT ALAS, MY FRIENDS, THIS NOTION IS NOT TO BE TRUE...
CREAM
DURING MY LATEST VISIT TO THE CITY OF SIN, MY DAD & UNCLE HAVE BEEN INSISTING THAT I GET UP AT THE CRACK OF DAWN FOR AN EARLY MORNING STROLL..
THE CRACK OF DAWN
!!!
GOOD GAWD, I HATE THE MORNING...
EVERYTHING'S ALL BRIGHT & CLEAN...
YOU SEE PEOPLE WITH JOBS...
OLDER FOLKS & CHILDREN..
Aww..CHEEZ -n- CRACKERZ...
THE DAY RESONATES WITH HOPE & POSSIBILITY...
BLEAH AND THEN THERE'S THAT STUPID SUN..
YO..I'M LIKE GEORGE BENSON.. JUST GIMME THE NIGHT...
HOOKERS & DEVIANTS... HOBOS & VAMPIRES...
Wanna date?
HEAVE
THESE ARE MY TYPE O' FOLKS... GAWD BLESS 'EM...
LAST NIGHT, I WENT TO BED AT 11PM!! THESE EARLY MORNING STROLLS HAVE TAKEN THE WIND OUT OF MY SAILS...
BUT, THANKFULLY, NOT OUT OF MY BOTTOM...
FOR REVENGE, I DECIDED TO WAKE MY DAD UP WITH THE CRACK OF KEEF..
BRAPP
STOP

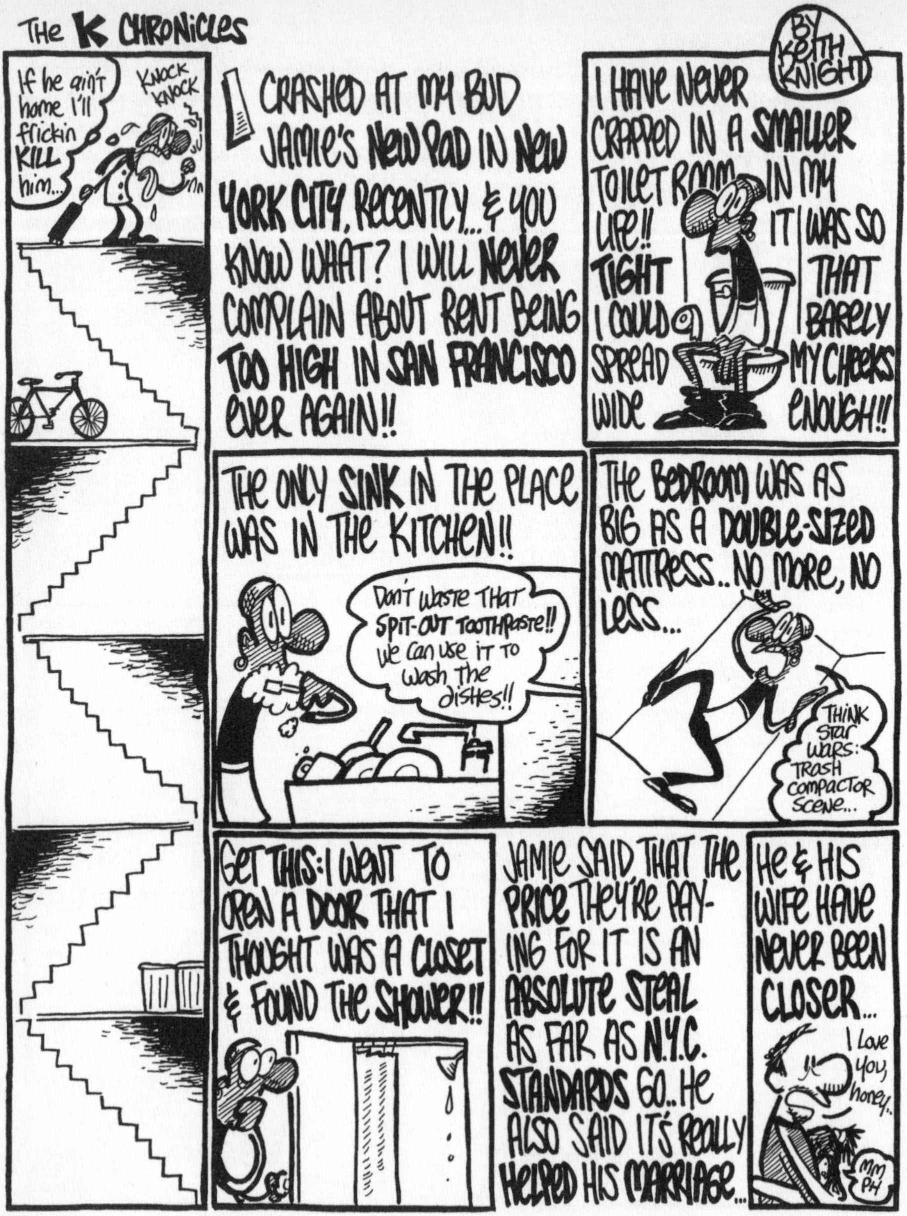
The K Chronicles
By Keith Knight
If he ain't home I'll frickin KILL him...
KNOCK KNOCK
I CRASHED AT MY BUD JAMIE'S NEW PAD IN NEW YORK CITY, RECENTLY... & YOU KNOW WHAT? I WILL NEVER COMPLAIN ABOUT RENT BEING TOO HIGH IN SAN FRANCISCO EVER AGAIN!!
I HAVE NEVER CRAPPED IN A SMALLER TOILET ROOM IN MY LIFE!! IT WAS SO TIGHT THAT I COULD BARELY SPREAD MY CHEEKS WIDE ENOUGH!!
THE ONLY SINK IN THE PLACE WAS IN THE KITCHEN!!
Don't waste that spit-out toothpaste!! We can use it to wash the dishes!!
THE BEDROOM WAS AS BIG AS A DOUBLE-SIZED MATTRESS.. NO MORE, NO LESS...
THINK STAR WARS: TRASH COMPACTOR SCENE...
GET THIS: I WENT TO OPEN A DOOR THAT I THOUGHT WAS A CLOSET & FOUND THE SHOWER!!
JAMIE SAID THAT THE PRICE THEY'RE PAYING FOR IT IS AN ABSOLUTE STEAL AS FAR AS N.Y.C. STANDARDS GO.. HE ALSO SAID IT'S REALLY HELPED HIS MARRIAGE...
HE & HIS WIFE HAVE NEVER BEEN CLOSER...
I love you, honey..
MMPH

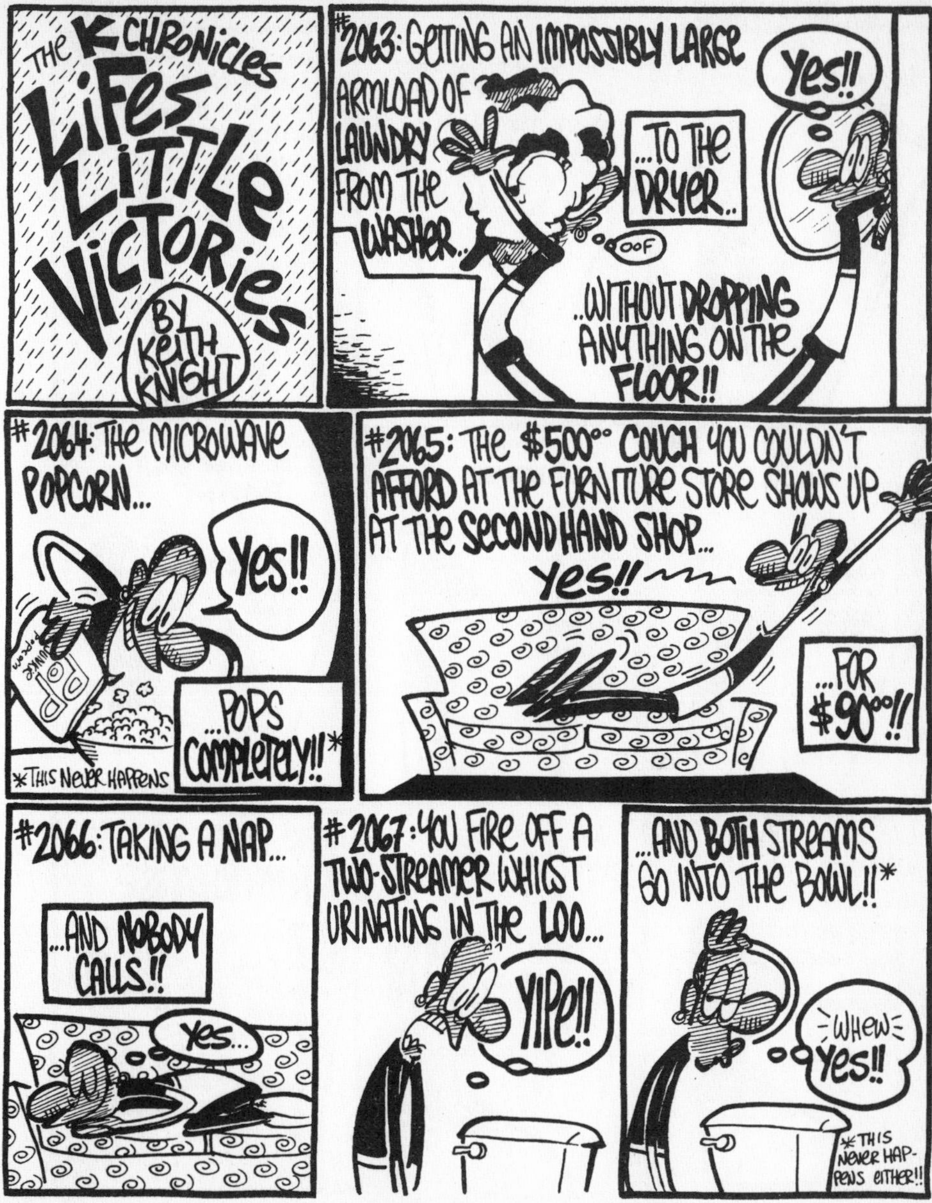
THE K CHRONICLES
LIFES LITTLE VICTORIES
BY KEITH KNIGHT
#2063: GETTING AN IMPOSSIBLY LARGE ARMLOAD OF LAUNDRY FROM THE WASHER..
...TO THE DRYER..
OOF
YES!!
..WITHOUT DROPPING ANYTHING ON THE FLOOR!!
#2064: THE MICROWAVE POPCORN...
YES!!
POP
...POPS COMPLETELY!!*
*THIS NEVER HAPPENS
#2065: THE $500°° COUCH YOU COULDN'T AFFORD AT THE FURNITURE STORE SHOWS UP AT THE SECOND HAND SHOP...
YES!!
...FOR $90°°!!
#2066: TAKING A NAP...
...AND NOBODY CALLS!!
YES...
#2067: YOU FIRE OFF A TWO-STREAMER WHILST URINATING IN THE LOO...
YIPE!!
...AND BOTH STREAMS GO INTO THE BOWL!!*
WHEW
YES!!
*THIS NEVER HAPPENS EITHER!!

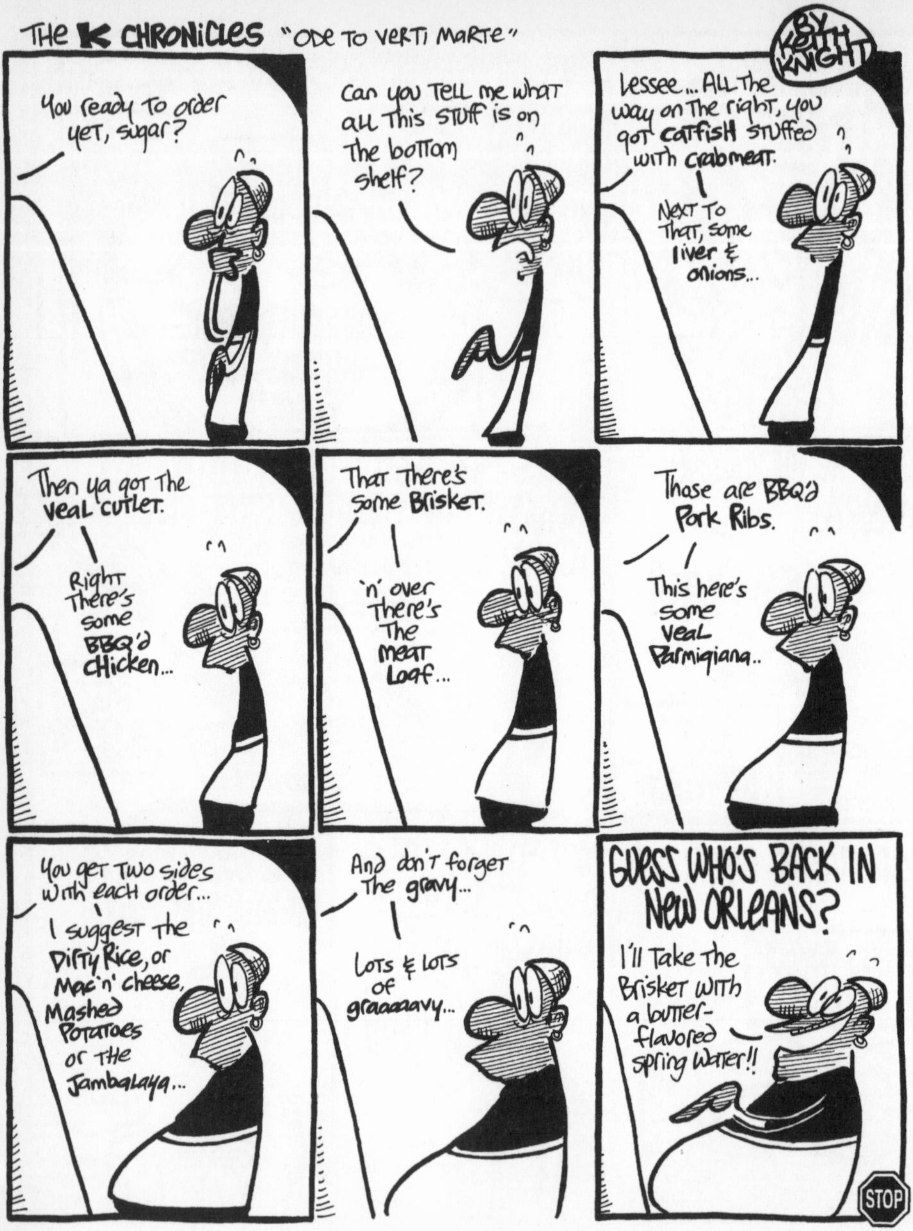
THE K CHRONICLES "ODE TO VERTI MARTE"
BY KEITH KNIGHT
You ready to order yet, sugar?
Can you TELL me what all This STUFF is on The bottom shelf?
Lessee... All The way on The right, you got CATFISH STUFFed with crabmeat.
Next to That, some liver & onions...
Then ya got The veal cutlet.
Right There's some BBQ'd CHicken...
That There's some Brisket.
'n' over There's The meat loaf...
Those are BBQ'd Pork Ribs.
This here's some Veal Parmigiana..
You get Two sides with each order...
I suggest The Dirty Rice, or Mac 'n' cheese, Mashed Potatoes or The Jambalaya...
And don't forget The gravy...
Lots & lots of graaaaavy...
GUESS WHO'S BACK IN NEW ORLEANS?
I'll Take The Brisket with a butter-flavored spring water!!
STOP

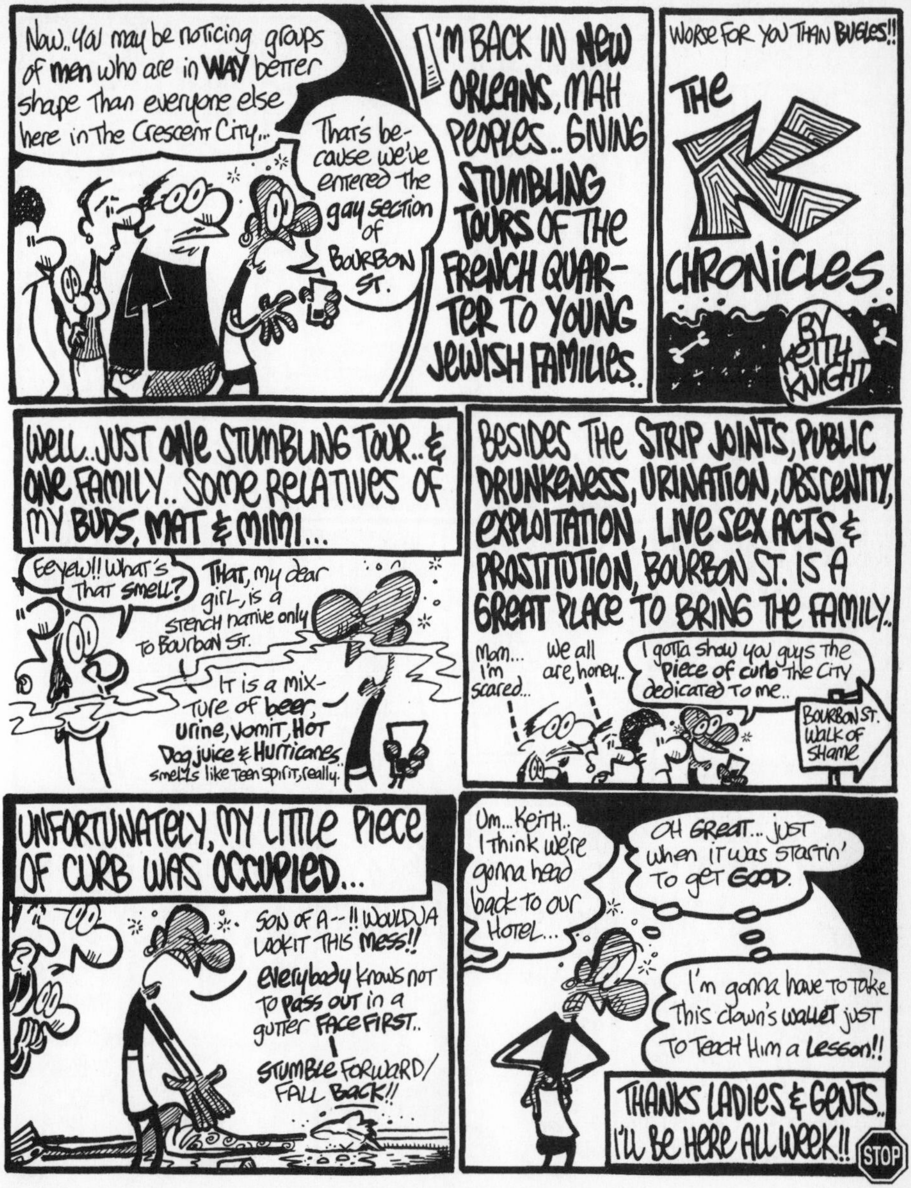
Now.. You may be noticing groups of men who are in WAY better shape than everyone else here in the Crescent City...
That's because we've entered the gay section of Bourbon St.
I'M BACK IN NEW ORLEANS, MAH PEOPLES.. GIVING STUMBLING TOURS OF THE FRENCH QUARTER TO YOUNG JEWISH FAMILIES..
WORSE FOR YOU THAN BUGLES!!
THE K CHRONICLES.
BY KEITH KNIGHT
WELL.. JUST ONE STUMBLING TOUR.. & ONE FAMILY.. SOME RELATIVES OF MY BUDS, MAT & MIMI...
Eeyew!! What's That smell?
THAT, my dear girl, is a stench native only to Bourbon St.
It is a mixture of beer, Urine, Vomit, Hot Dog juice & Hurricanes
smells like Teen spirit, really.
BESIDES THE STRIP JOINTS, PUBLIC DRUNKENESS, URINATION, OBSCENITY, EXPLOITATION, LIVE SEX ACTS & PROSTITUTION, BOURBON ST. IS A GREAT PLACE TO BRING THE FAMILY..
Mom... I'm scared...
We all are, honey..
I gotta show you guys the piece of curb the City dedicated to me..
BOURBON ST. WALK OF SHAME
UNFORTUNATELY, MY LITTLE PIECE OF CURB WAS OCCUPIED...
SON OF A--!! WOULDJA LOOKIT THIS MESS!!
Everybody knows not to pass out in a gutter FACE FIRST..
STUMBLE FORWARD/ FALL BACK!!
Um... Keith.. I think we're gonna head back to our Hotel...
OH GREAT... JUST when IT was startin' To get GOOD.
I'm gonna have to take This clown's wallet just to teach him a lesson!!
THANKS LADIES & GENTS.. I'LL BE HERE ALL WEEK!!
STOP

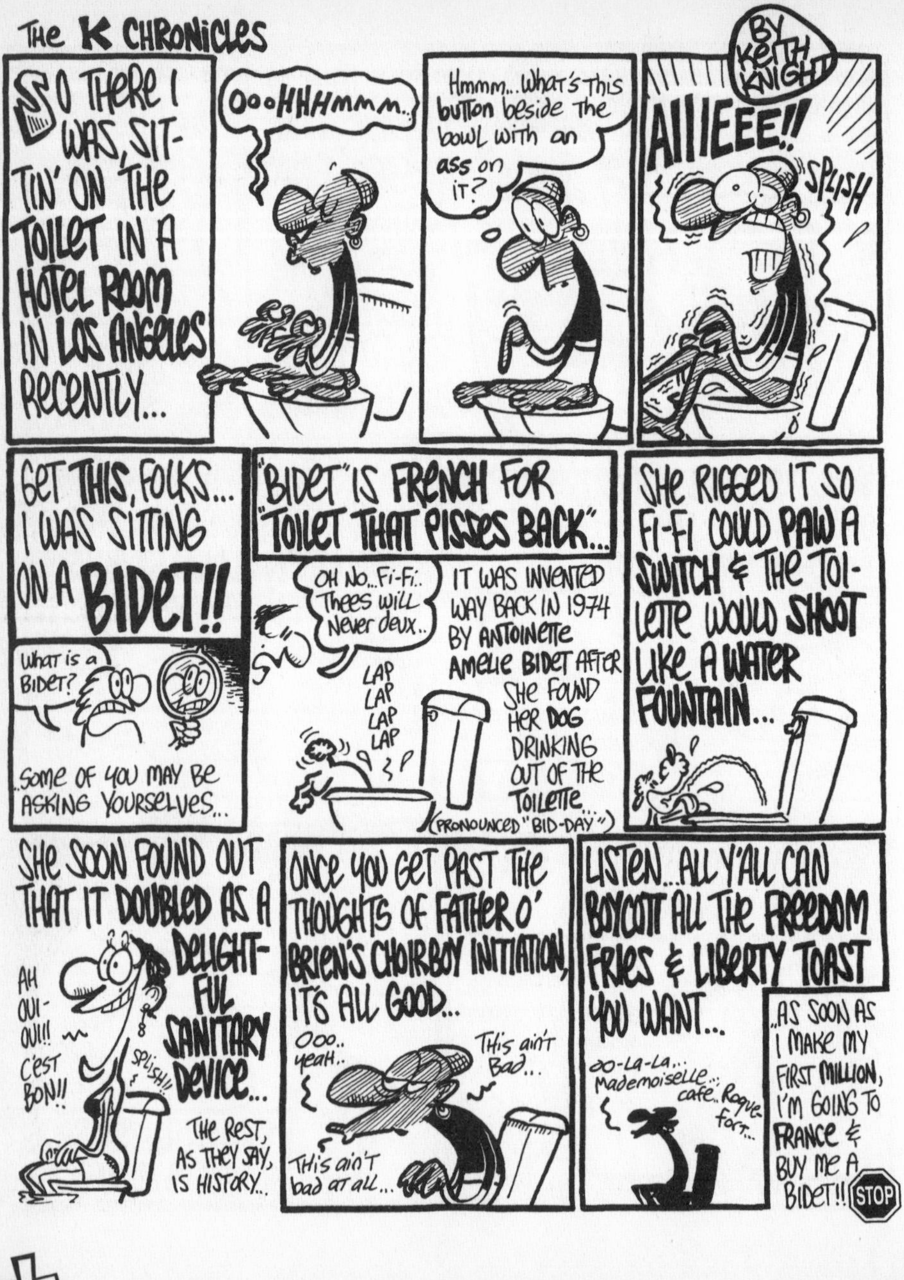

THE K CHRONICLES
BY KEITH KNIGHT
SO THERE I WAS, SITTIN' ON THE TOILET IN A HOTEL ROOM IN LOS ANGELES RECENTLY...
OooHHHmmm...
Hmmm... What's this button beside the bowl with an ass on it?
AIIIEEE!!
SPLISH
GET THIS, FOLKS... I WAS SITTING ON A BIDET!!
What is a bidet?
..SOME OF YOU MAY BE ASKING YOURSELVES...
"BIDET" IS FRENCH FOR "TOILET THAT PISSES BACK"...
OH No... Fi-Fi.. Thees will never deux..
IT WAS INVENTED WAY BACK IN 1974 BY ANTOINETTE AMELIE BIDET AFTER SHE FOUND HER DOG DRINKING OUT OF THE TOILETTE...
LAP LAP LAP LAP LAP
(PRONOUNCED "BID-DAY")
SHE RIGGED IT SO FI-FI COULD PAW A SWITCH & THE TOILETTE WOULD SHOOT LIKE A WATER FOUNTAIN...
SHE SOON FOUND OUT THAT IT DOUBLED AS A DELIGHTFUL SANITARY DEVICE...
AH OUI-OUI!! C'EST BON!!
SPLISH!!
THE REST, AS THEY SAY, IS HISTORY...
ONCE YOU GET PAST THE THOUGHTS OF FATHER O'BRIEN'S CHOIRBOY INITIATION, IT'S ALL GOOD...
Ooo.. yeah..
This ain't bad...
This ain't bad at all...
LISTEN...ALL Y'ALL CAN BOYCOTT ALL THE FREEDOM FRIES & LIBERTY TOAST YOU WANT...
oo-la-la... mademoiselle... café.. Roquefort...
..AS SOON AS I MAKE MY FIRST MILLION, I'M GOING TO FRANCE & BUY ME A BIDET!!
STOP

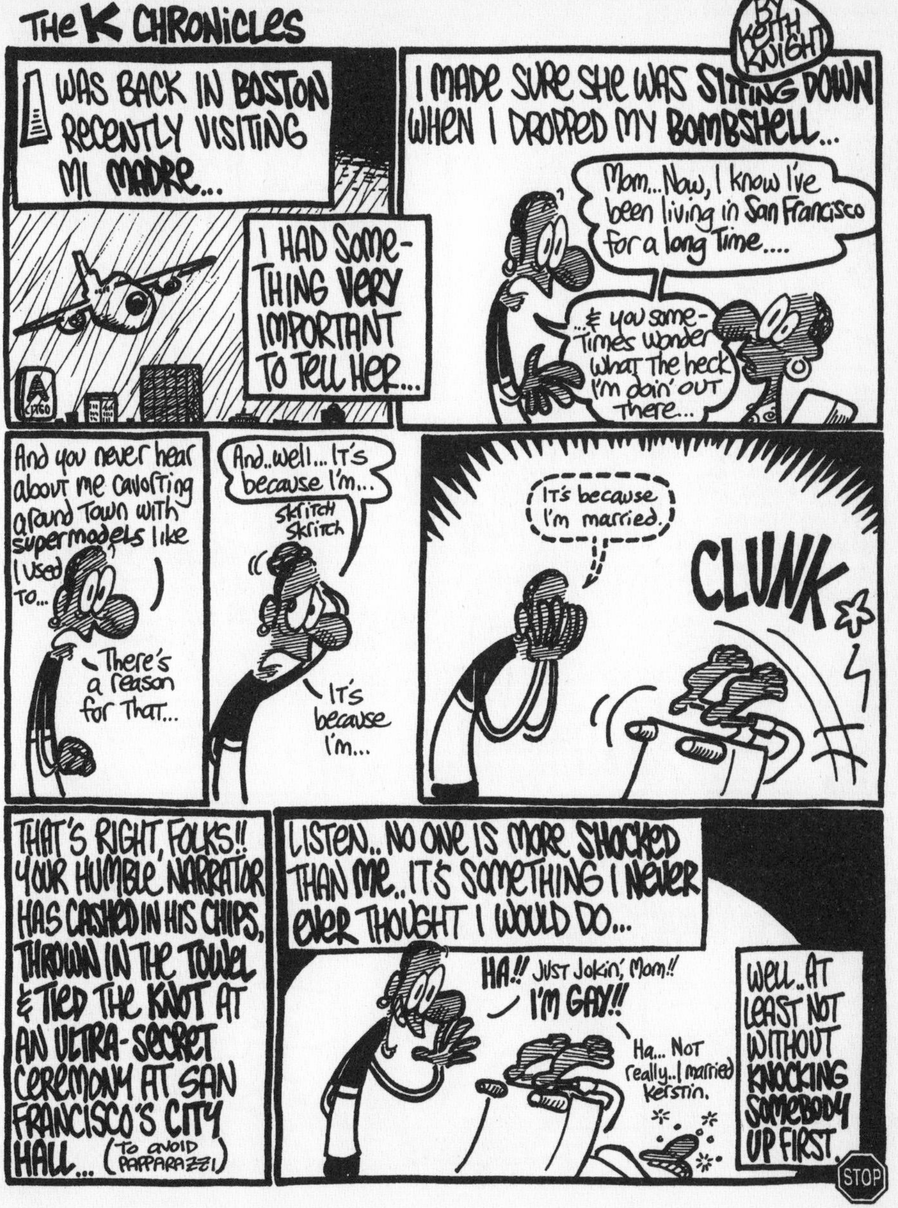
THE K CHRONICLES
BY KEITH KNIGHT
I WAS BACK IN BOSTON RECENTLY VISITING MI MADRE...
I HAD SOMETHING VERY IMPORTANT TO TELL HER...
I MADE SURE SHE WAS SITTING DOWN WHEN I DROPPED MY BOMBSHELL...
Mom... Now, I know I've been living in San Francisco for a long Time....
...& you some-Times wonder what The heck I'm doin' out There...
And you never hear about me cavorting around Town with supermodels like I used To...
There's a reason for That...
And.. well... IT's because I'm...
SKRITCH SKRITCH
IT's because I'm...
IT's because I'm married.
CLUNK
THAT'S RIGHT, FOLKS!! YOUR HUMBLE NARRATOR HAS CASHED IN HIS CHIPS, THROWN IN THE TOWEL & TIED THE KNOT AT AN ULTRA-SECRET CEREMONY AT SAN FRANCISCO'S CITY HALL... (TO AVOID PAPPARAZZI)
LISTEN.. NO ONE IS MORE SHOCKED THAN ME.. IT'S SOMETHING I NEVER EVER THOUGHT I WOULD DO...
HA!! JUST JOKIN', MOM!! I'M GAY!!
Ha... NOT really..I married Kerstin.
WELL.. AT LEAST NOT WITHOUT KNOCKING SOMEBODY UP FIRST.
STOP

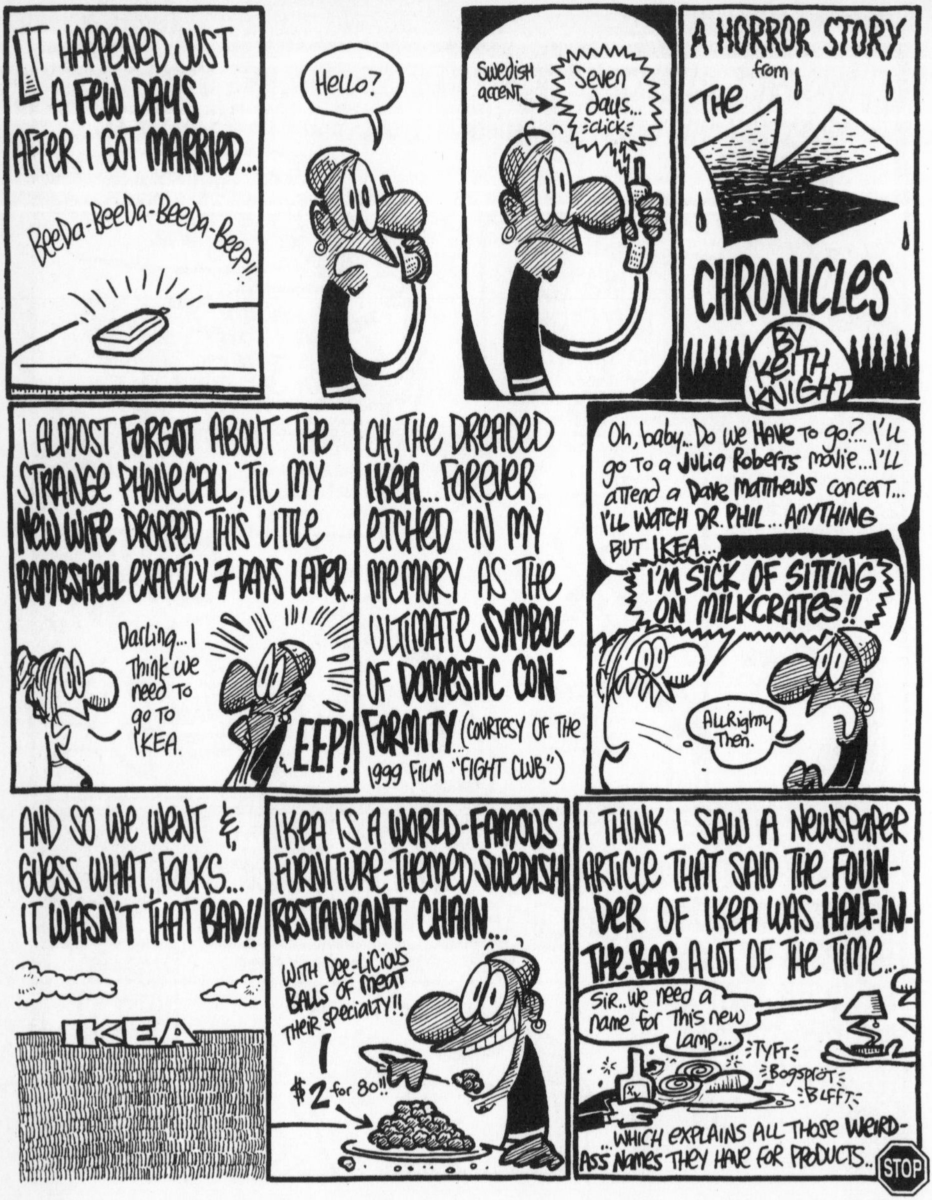
IT HAPPENED JUST A FEW DAYS AFTER I GOT MARRIED...
BeeDa-BeeDa-BeeDa-Beep!!
Hello?
Swedish accent
Seven days... click
A HORROR STORY from THE K CHRONICLES
BY KEITH KNIGHT
I ALMOST FORGOT ABOUT THE STRANGE PHONECALL, 'TIL MY NEW WIFE DROPPED THIS LITTLE BOMBSHELL EXACTLY 7 DAYS LATER...
Darling... I Think we need To go To IKEA.
EEP!
OH, THE DREADED IKEA... FOREVER ETCHED IN MY MEMORY AS THE ULTIMATE SYMBOL OF DOMESTIC CON-FORMITY... (COURTESY OF THE 1999 FILM "FIGHT CLUB")
Oh, baby... Do we HAVE To go?... I'll go to a Julia Roberts movie... I'll attend a Dave Matthews concert... I'll WATCH DR. PHIL... ANYTHING BUT IKEA...
I'M SICK OF SITTING ON MILKCRATES!!
AllRighty Then.
AND SO WE WENT &, GUESS WHAT, FOLKS... IT WASN'T THAT BAD!!
IKEA
IKEA IS A WORLD-FAMOUS FURNITURE-THEMED SWEDISH RESTAURANT CHAIN...
WITH DEE-LICIOUS BALLS OF MEAT THEIR SPECIALTY!!
$2 for 80!!
I THINK I SAW A NEWSPAPER ARTICLE THAT SAID THE FOUN-DER OF IKEA WAS HALF-IN-THE-BAG A LOT OF THE TIME...
Sir.. we need a name for This new lamp...
TYFT
Bogspröt
BLFFT
...WHICH EXPLAINS ALL THOSE WEIRD-ASS NAMES THEY HAVE FOR PRODUCTS..
STOP

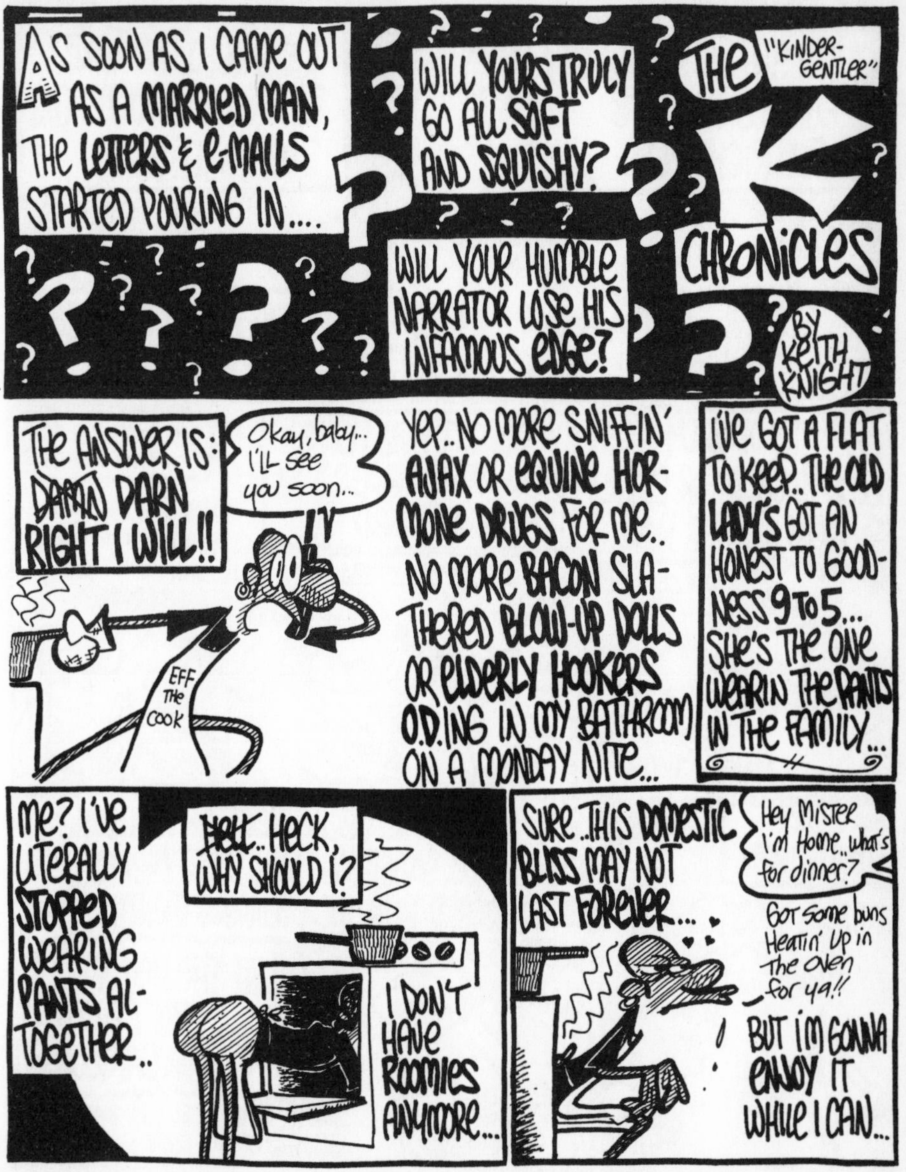
AS SOON AS I CAME OUT AS A MARRIED MAN, THE LETTERS & E-MAILS STARTED POURING IN....
WILL YOURS TRULY GO ALL SOFT AND SQUISHY?
WILL YOUR HUMBLE NARRATOR LOSE HIS INFAMOUS EDGE?
THE "KINDER-GENTLER" K CHRONICLES
BY KEITH KNIGHT
THE ANSWER IS: DAMN DARN RIGHT I WILL!!
Okay, baby... I'll see you soon...
EFF THE COOK
YEP.. NO MORE SNIFFIN' AJAX OR EQUINE HOR-MONE DRUGS FOR ME.. NO MORE BACON SLA-THERED BLOW-UP DOLLS OR ELDERLY HOOKERS O.D.ING IN MY BATHROOM ON A MONDAY NITE...
I'VE GOT A FLAT TO KEEP.. THE OLD LADY'S GOT AN HONEST TO GOOD-NESS 9 TO 5... SHE'S THE ONE WEARIN THE PANTS IN THE FAMILY...
ME? I'VE LITERALLY STOPPED WEARING PANTS AL-TOGETHER..
HELL.. HECK, WHY SHOULD I?
I DON'T HAVE ROOMIES ANYMORE...
SURE.. THIS DOMESTIC BLISS MAY NOT LAST FOREVER...
Hey Mister I'm Home.. what's for dinner?
Got some buns Heatin' Up in The Oven for ya!!
BUT I'M GONNA ENJOY IT WHILE I CAN...

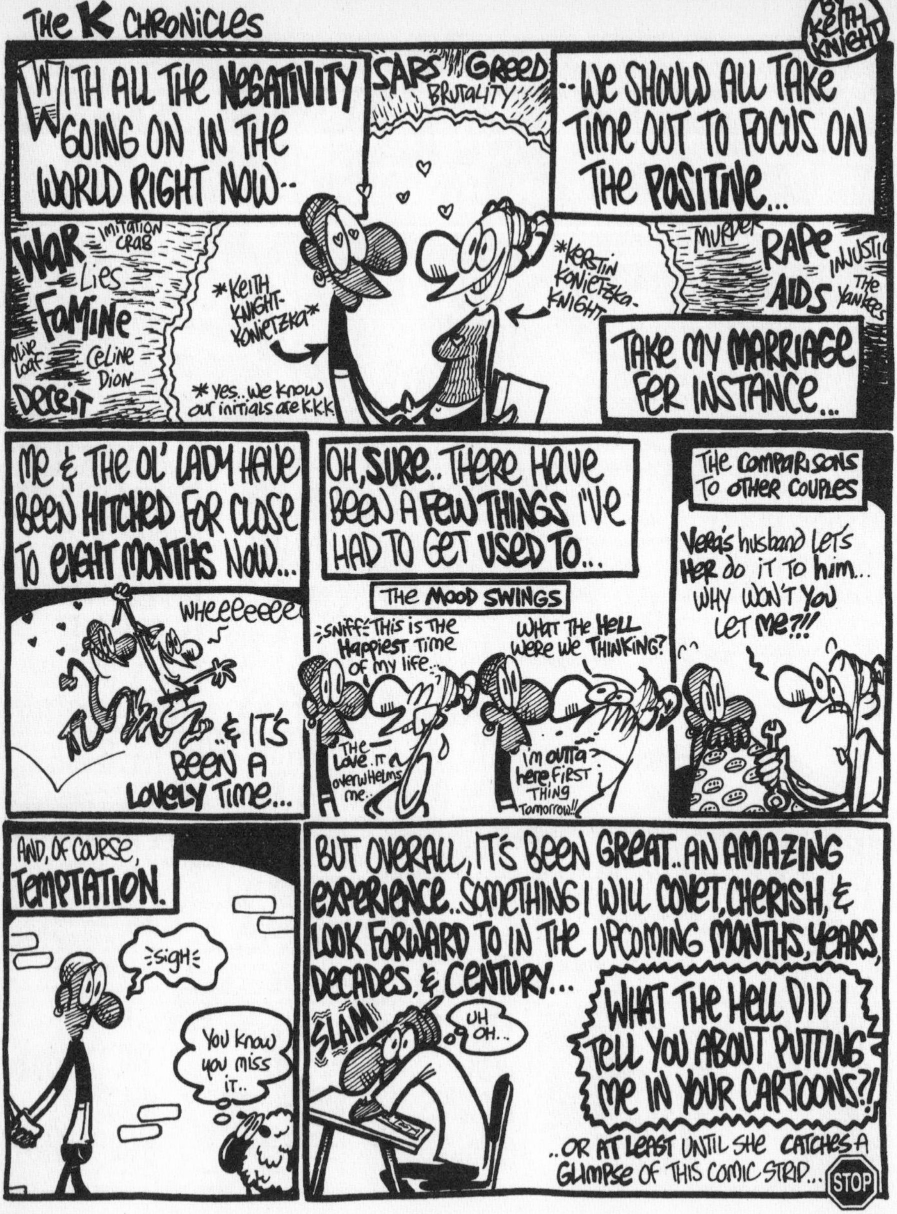

THE K CHRONICLES
BY KEITH KNIGHT
WITH ALL THE NEGATIVITY GOING ON IN THE WORLD RIGHT NOW..
SARS GREED BRUTALITY
..WE SHOULD ALL TAKE TIME OUT TO FOCUS ON THE POSITIVE...
WAR IMITATION CRAB LIES FAMINE OLIVE LOAF CELINE DION DECEIT
KEITH KNIGHT-KONIETZKA
*KERSTIN KONIETZKA-KNIGHT
*YES..WE KNOW OUR INITIALS ARE K.K.K.
MURDER RAPE INJUSTIC AIDS THE YANKEES
TAKE MY MARRIAGE FER INSTANCE...
ME & THE OL' LADY HAVE BEEN HITCHED FOR CLOSE TO EIGHT MONTHS NOW...
WHEEEEEEE
..& IT'S BEEN A LOVELY TIME...
OH, SURE.. THERE HAVE BEEN A FEW THINGS I'VE HAD TO GET USED TO...
THE MOOD SWINGS
SNIFF THIS IS THE HAPPIEST TIME OF MY LIFE..
THE LOVE..IT OVERWHELMS ME..
WHAT THE HELL WERE WE THINKING?
I'M OUTTA HERE FIRST THING TOMORROW!!
THE COMPARISONS TO OTHER COUPLES
VERA'S HUSBAND LET'S HER DO IT TO HIM... WHY WON'T YOU LET ME?!!
AND, OF COURSE, TEMPTATION.
SIGH
YOU KNOW YOU MISS IT..
BUT OVERALL, IT'S BEEN GREAT..AN AMAZING EXPERIENCE..SOMETHING I WILL COVET, CHERISH, & LOOK FORWARD TO IN THE UPCOMING MONTHS, YEARS, DECADES, & CENTURY...
SLAM
UH OH...
WHAT THE HELL DID I TELL YOU ABOUT PUTTING ME IN YOUR CARTOONS?!
..OR AT LEAST UNTIL SHE CATCHES A GLIMPSE OF THIS COMIC STRIP...
STOP

The K CHRONICLES

NEW YORK CITY OF D THANG IN NEW YORK AIN'T ALWAYS IT...ALMIGHTY

CITY IS BUT EVER DATS COOLED DOWN THE ROOM

BY KEITH KNIGHT

ME & THE WIFEY HAVE BEEN STAYING IN NEW YORK CITY FOR THE WEEK....

WELL..HOBOKEN, ACTUALLY.. A FRIEND OF KERSTIN'S LET US CRASH AT HIS PAD...

HOBOKEN?!!!

OOOO I'M DYIN'!!!

WITH MAP IN HAND, WE HAD A LOOSE GAME PLAN OF HOW WE'D BE TACK-LING SAID WEEK...

Okay...so we stay here 'til Monday morn..

And we move to Here starting Monday.. & Then move here Tuesday afternoon.

LET'S GO!!

BUT LIKE ALL SEASONED TRAVELERS, WE WERE PREPARED FOR MANY CHANGES IN OUR PLANS...

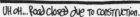
UH OH... Road closed due to construction..

We'll head over here.

...& THE EXORBITANT FEES ASSOCIATED WITH A VISIT TO THE BIG APPLE..

He said $37.00

WHAT?!! No way. Forget it.

OUR FIRST DAY IN N.Y.C. WAS ALL AT ONCE DAUNTING, CHALLENGING, FRUSTRATING & WET...

Mutta-Frickin'

& ALL WE WERE DOING WAS TRYING TO FIND A SPOT TO PUT OUR RENT-A-CAR FOR THE NIGHT...

KEITH...The sign sez Residential permit parking only...

!@%#!!

STOP

91

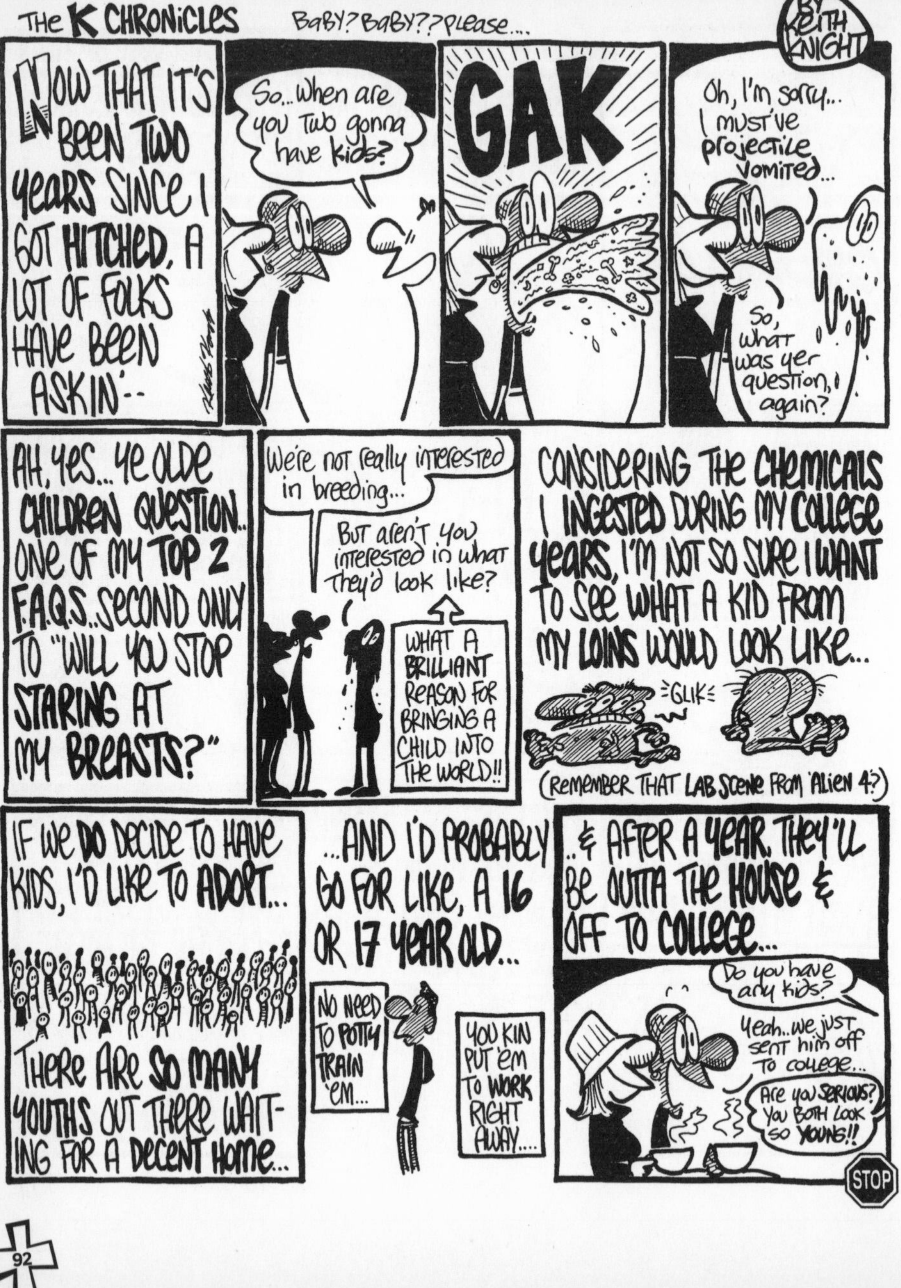
THE K CHRONICLES
BaBY? BaBY?? PLease....
BY KEITH KNIGHT
NOW THAT IT'S BEEN TWO YEARS SINCE I GOT HITCHED, A LOT OF FOLKS HAVE BEEN ASKIN'--
So... When are you Two gonna have kids?
GAK
Oh, I'm sorry... I must've projectile vomited...
So, what was yer question, again?
AH, YES... YE OLDE CHILDREN QUESTION.. ONE OF MY TOP 2 F.A.Q.S.. SECOND ONLY TO "WILL YOU STOP STARING AT MY BREASTS?"
We're not really interested in breeding...
But aren't you interested in what They'd look like?
WHAT A BRILLIANT REASON FOR BRINGING A CHILD INTO THE WORLD!!
CONSIDERING THE CHEMICALS I INGESTED DURING MY COLLEGE YEARS, I'M NOT SO SURE I WANT TO SEE WHAT A KID FROM MY LOINS WOULD LOOK LIKE...
GLIK
(REMEMBER THAT LAB SCENE FROM 'ALIEN 4'?)
IF WE DO DECIDE TO HAVE KIDS, I'D LIKE TO ADOPT...
THERE ARE SO MANY YOUTHS OUT THERE WAITING FOR A DECENT HOME...
...AND I'D PROBABLY GO FOR LIKE, A 16 OR 17 YEAR OLD...
NO NEED TO POTTY TRAIN 'EM...
YOU KIN PUT 'EM TO WORK RIGHT AWAY....
..& AFTER A YEAR, THEY'LL BE OUTTA THE HOUSE & OFF TO COLLEGE...
Do you have any kids?
Yeah.. we just sent him off To college...
Are you serious? You BOTH LOOK so YOUNG!!
STOP

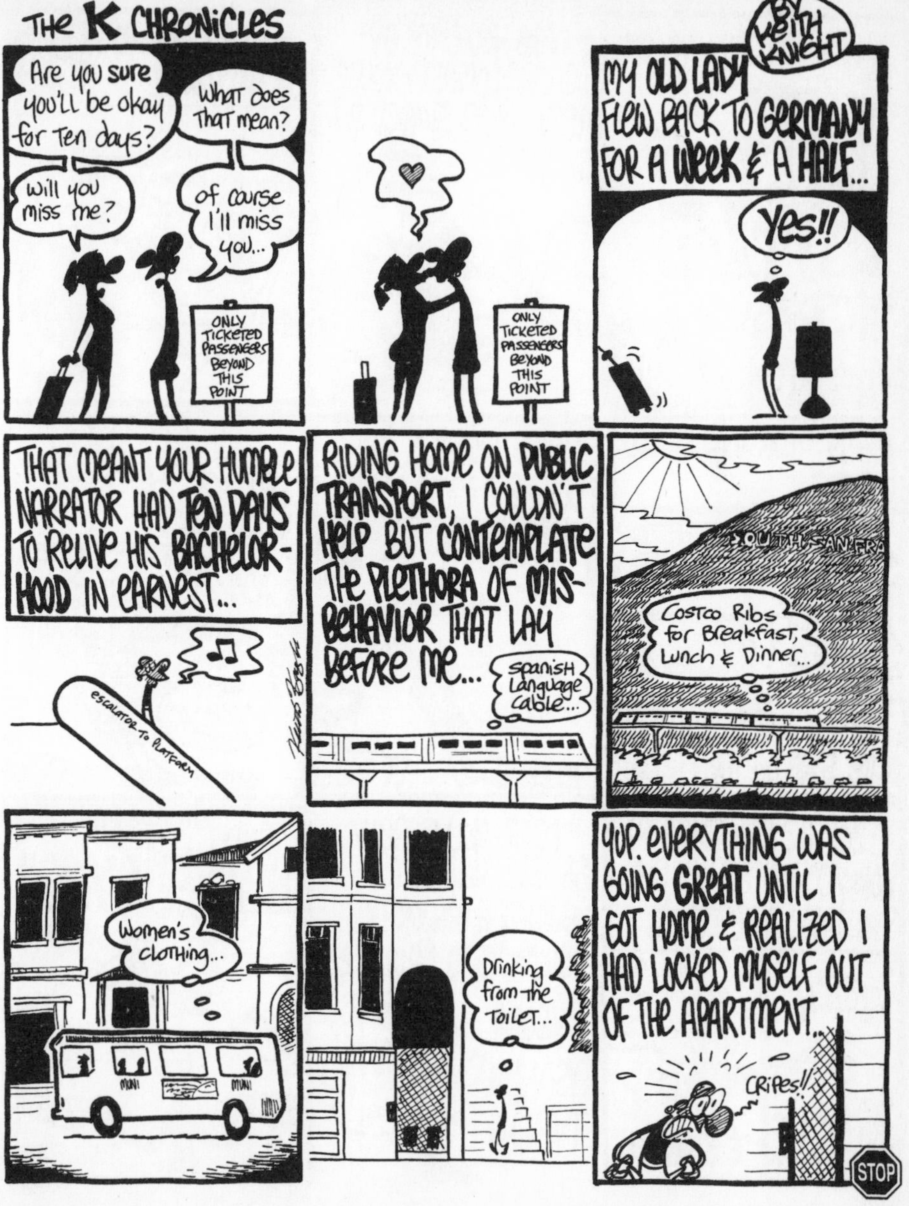
THE K CHRONICLES
BY KEITH KNIGHT
Are you sure you'll be okay for ten days?
What does that mean?
Will you miss me?
Of course I'll miss you...
ONLY TICKETED PASSENGERS BEYOND THIS POINT
ONLY TICKETED PASSENGERS BEYOND THIS POINT
MY OLD LADY FLEW BACK TO GERMANY FOR A WEEK & A HALF...
Yes!!
THAT MEANT YOUR HUMBLE NARRATOR HAD TEN DAYS TO RELIVE HIS BACHELORHOOD IN EARNEST...
ESCALATOR TO PLATFORM
RIDING HOME ON PUBLIC TRANSPORT, I COULDN'T HELP BUT CONTEMPLATE THE PLETHORA OF MISBEHAVIOR THAT LAY BEFORE ME...
Spanish Language Cable...
SOUTH SAN FRA
Costco Ribs for Breakfast, Lunch & Dinner...
Women's clothing...
MUNI
MUNI
Drinking from the Toilet...
YUP. EVERYTHING WAS GOING GREAT UNTIL I GOT HOME & REALIZED I HAD LOCKED MYSELF OUT OF THE APARTMENT...
CRIPES!!
STOP

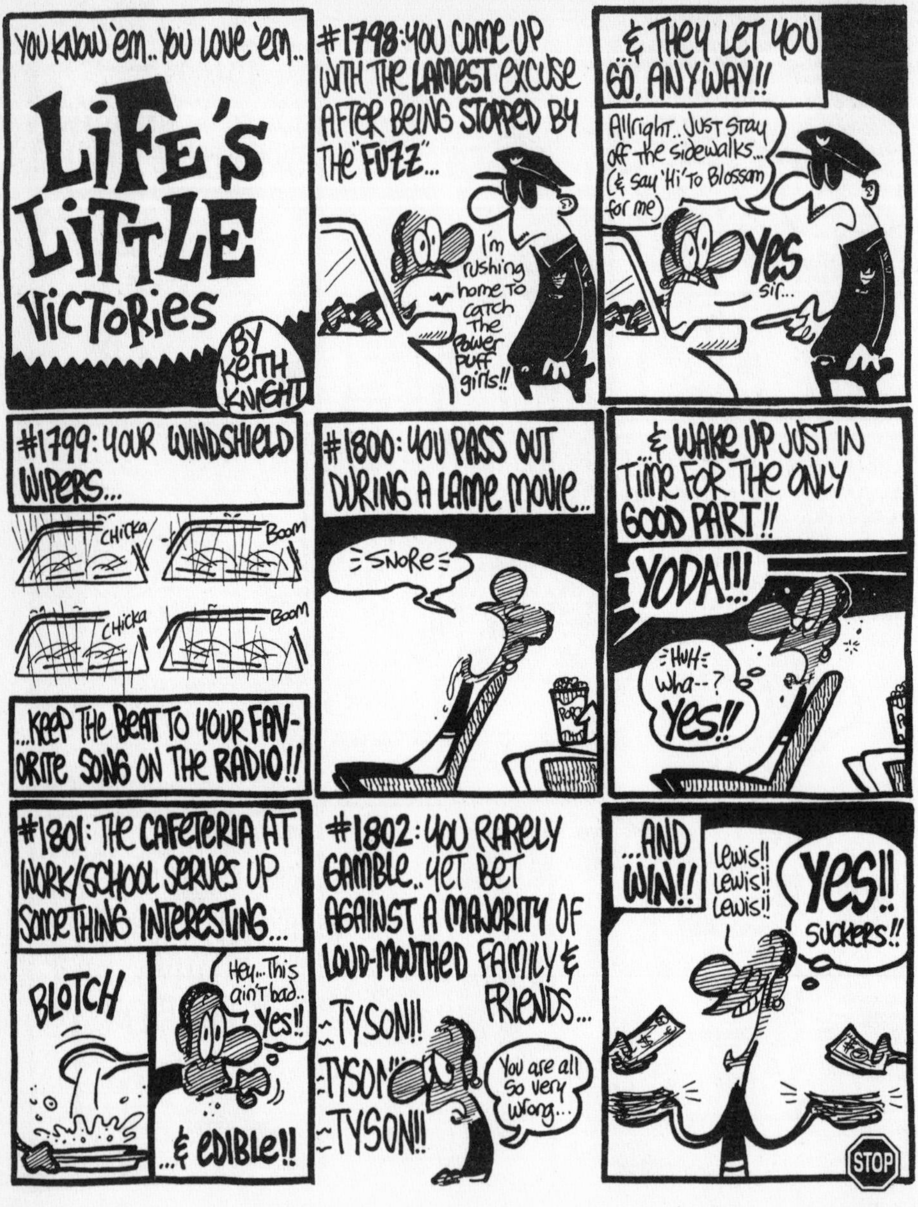
YOU KNOW 'EM.. YOU LOVE 'EM..
LIFE'S LITTLE VICTORIES
BY KEITH KNIGHT
#1798: YOU COME UP WITH THE LAMEST EXCUSE AFTER BEING STOPPED BY THE "FUZZ"...
I'm rushing home to catch The Power Puff girls!!
...& THEY LET YOU GO, ANYWAY!!
Allright.. Just stay off the sidewalks... (& say 'Hi' to Blossom for me)
YES sir...
#1799: YOUR WINDSHIELD WIPERS...
CHICKA
Boom
CHICKA
Boom
...KEEP THE BEAT TO YOUR FAVORITE SONG ON THE RADIO!!
#1800: YOU PASS OUT DURING A LAME MOVIE...
SNORE
...& WAKE UP JUST IN TIME FOR THE ONLY GOOD PART!!
YODA!!!
HUH Wha--? YES!!
#1801: THE CAFETERIA AT WORK/SCHOOL SERVES UP SOMETHING INTERESTING...
BLOTCH
Hey...This ain't bad.. Yes!!
...& EDIBLE!!
#1802: YOU RARELY GAMBLE.. YET BET AGAINST A MAJORITY OF LOUD-MOUTHED FAMILY & FRIENDS...
TYSON!!
TYSON!!
TYSON!!
You are all so very wrong...
...AND WIN!!
Lewis!! Lewis!! Lewis!!
YES!! SUCKERS!!
STOP

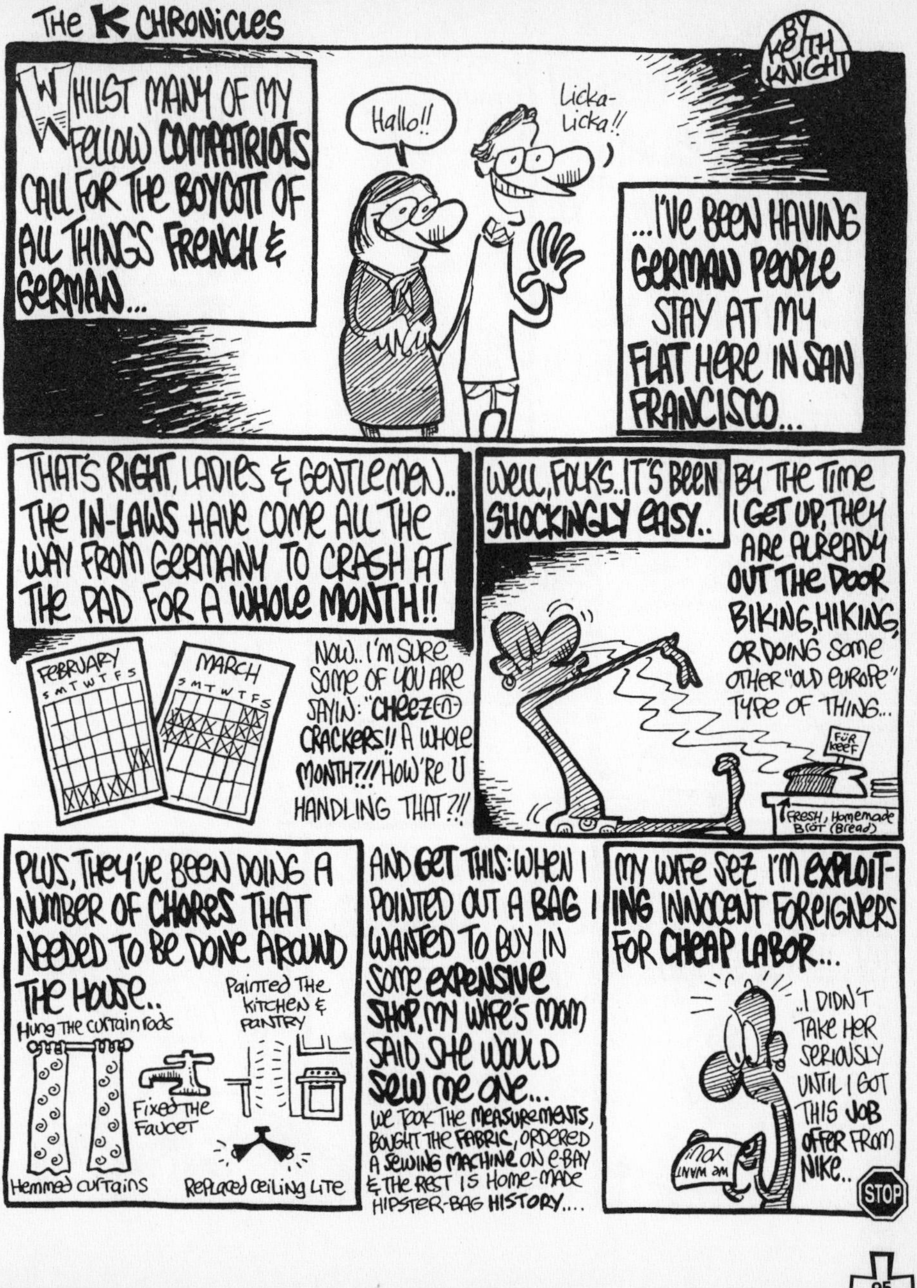
The K Chronicles
By Keith Knight
Whilst many of my fellow compatriots call for the boycott of all things French & German...
Hallo!!
Licka-Licka!!
...I've been having German people stay at my flat here in San Francisco...
That's right, ladies & gentlemen.. The in-laws have come all the way from Germany to crash at the pad for a whole month!!
February
S M T W T F S
March
S M T W T F S
Now.. I'm sure some of you are sayin: "Cheez-n-crackers!! A whole month?!! How're U handling that?!!
Well, folks..it's been shockingly easy..
By the time I get up, they are already out the door biking, hiking, or doing some other "Old Europe" type of thing...
Für Keef
Fresh, homemade Brot (Bread)
Plus, they've been doing a number of chores that needed to be done around the house..
Hung the curtain rods
Painted the kitchen & pantry
Fixed the faucet
Hemmed curtains
Replaced ceiling lite
And get this: when I pointed out a bag I wanted to buy in some expensive shop, my wife's mom said she would sew me one...
We took the measurements, bought the fabric, ordered a sewing machine on e-bay & the rest is home-made hipster-bag history....
My wife sez I'm exploiting innocent foreigners for cheap labor...
..I didn't take her seriously until I got this job offer from Nike..
We want you!
STOP

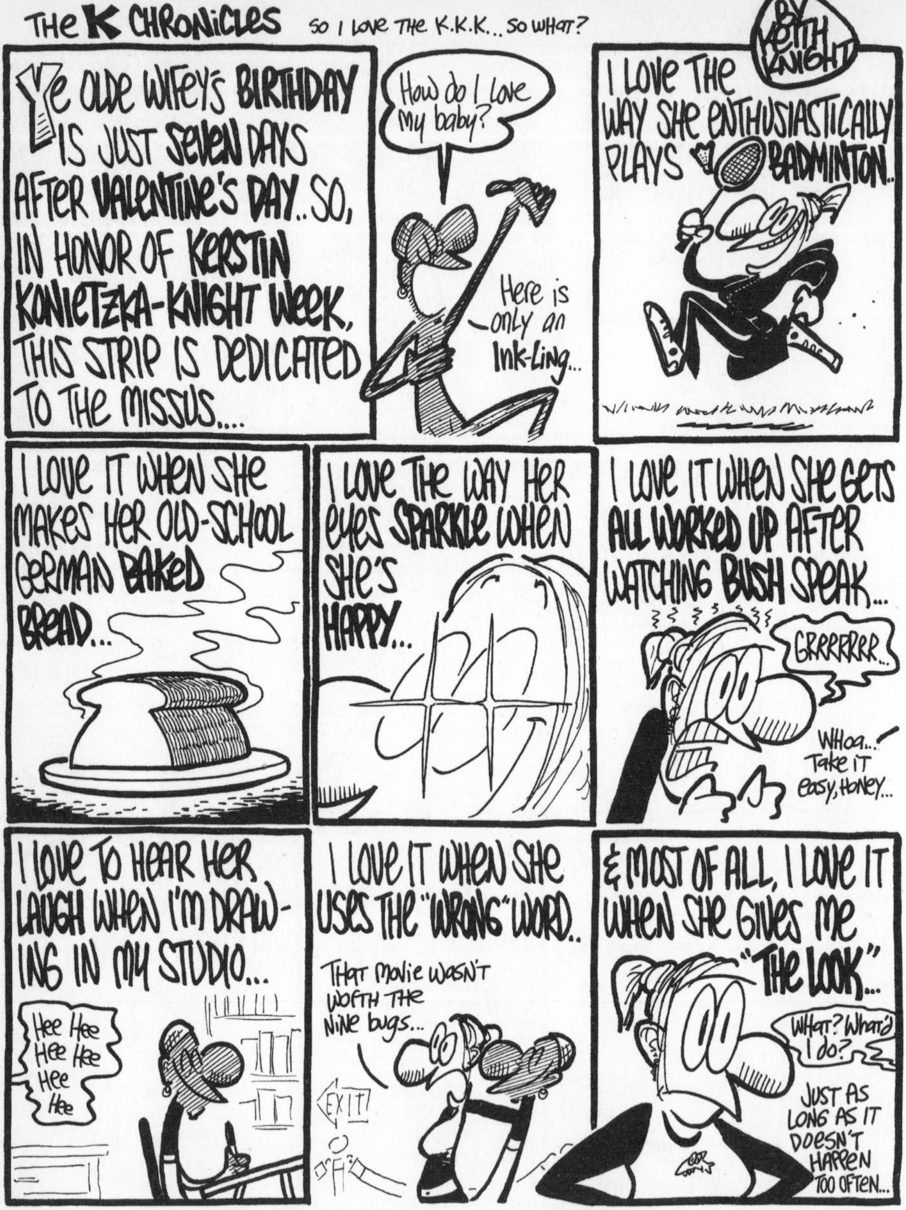
THE K CHRONICLES
SO I LOVE THE K.K.K... SO WHAT?
BY KEITH KNIGHT
YE OLDE WIFEY'S BIRTHDAY IS JUST SEVEN DAYS AFTER VALENTINE'S DAY.. SO, IN HONOR OF KERSTIN KONIETZKA-KNIGHT WEEK, THIS STRIP IS DEDICATED TO THE MISSUS....
How do I love my baby?
Here is only an Ink-Ling...
I LOVE THE WAY SHE ENTHUSIASTICALLY PLAYS BADMINTON..
I LOVE IT WHEN SHE MAKES HER OLD-SCHOOL GERMAN BAKED BREAD...
I LOVE THE WAY HER EYES SPARKLE WHEN SHE'S HAPPY...
I LOVE IT WHEN SHE GETS ALL WORKED UP AFTER WATCHING BUSH SPEAK...
GRRRRRRR...
WHOA...! Take it easy, Honey...
I LOVE TO HEAR HER LAUGH WHEN I'M DRAWING IN MY STUDIO...
Hee Hee Hee Hee Hee Hee
I LOVE IT WHEN SHE USES THE "WRONG" WORD..
THAT MOVIE WASN'T WORTH THE NINE BUGS...
EXIT
& MOST OF ALL, I LOVE IT WHEN SHE GIVES ME "THE LOOK"...
WHAT? WHAT'D I DO?
JUST AS LONG AS IT DOESN'T HAPPEN TOO OFTEN...

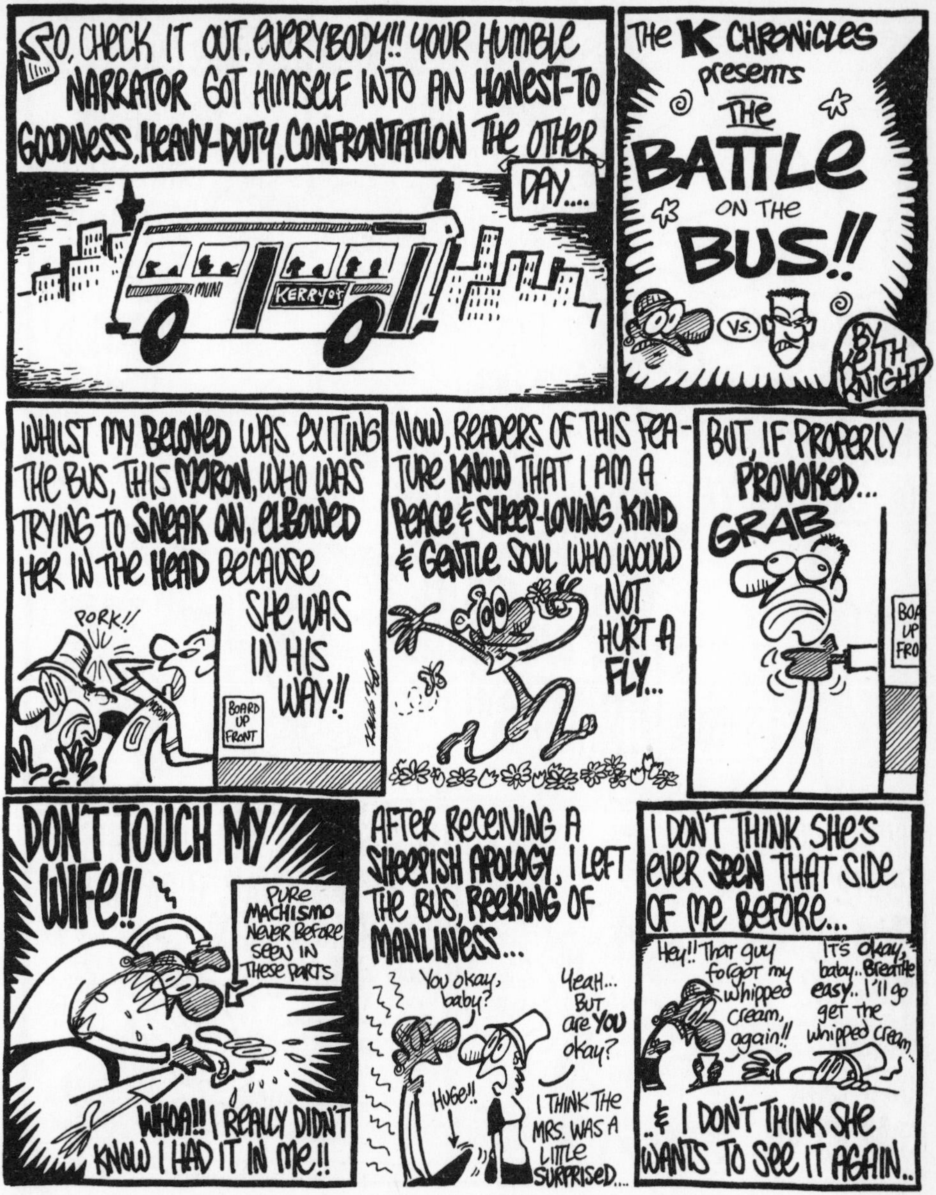
SO, CHECK IT OUT, EVERYBODY!! YOUR HUMBLE NARRATOR GOT HIMSELF INTO AN HONEST-TO GOODNESS, HEAVY-DUTY, CONFRONTATION THE OTHER DAY....
MUNI
KERRY
THE K CHRONICLES presents
THE BATTLE ON THE BUS!!
VS.
BY KEITH KNIGHT
WHILST MY BELOVED WAS EXITING THE BUS, THIS MORON, WHO WAS TRYING TO SNEAK ON, ELBOWED HER IN THE HEAD BECAUSE
PORK!!
MORON
SHE WAS IN HIS WAY!!
BOARD UP FRONT
NOW, READERS OF THIS FEATURE KNOW THAT I AM A PEACE & SHEEP-LOVING, KIND & GENTLE SOUL WHO WOULD
NOT HURT A FLY...
BUT, IF PROPERLY PROVOKED...
GRAB
DON'T TOUCH MY WIFE!!
PURE MACHISMO NEVER BEFORE SEEN IN THESE PARTS
WHOA!! I REALLY DIDN'T KNOW I HAD IT IN ME!!
AFTER RECEIVING A SHEEPISH APOLOGY, I LEFT THE BUS, REEKING OF MANLINESS...
You okay, baby?
Yeah... But are YOU okay?
HUGE!!
I THINK THE MRS. WAS A LITTLE SURPRISED....
I DON'T THINK SHE'S EVER SEEN THAT SIDE OF ME BEFORE...
Hey!! That guy forgot my whipped cream, again!!
It's okay, baby.. Breathe easy.. I'll go get the whipped cream...
..& I DON'T THINK SHE WANTS TO SEE IT AGAIN..

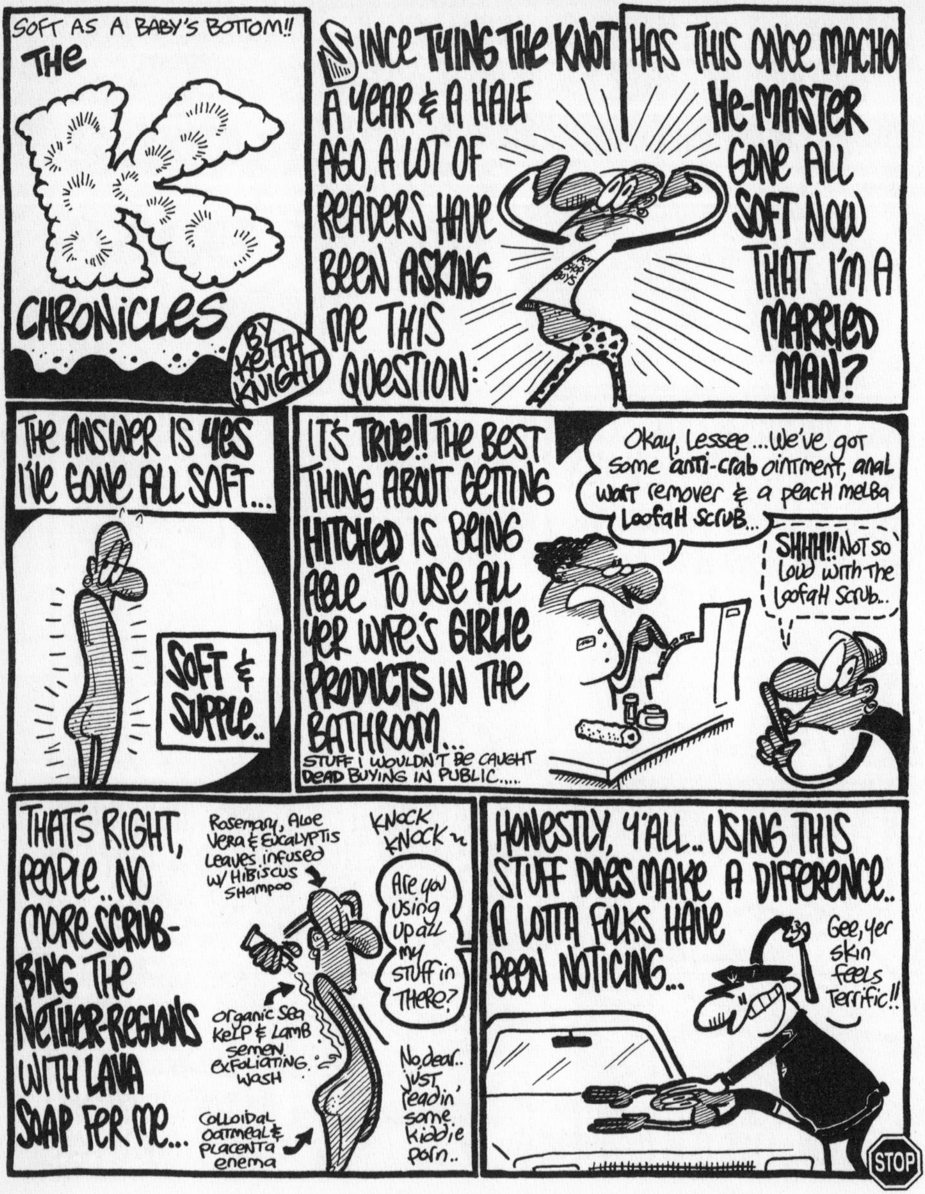
SOFT AS A BABY'S BOTTOM!!
THE K CHRONICLES
BY KEITH KNIGHT
SINCE TYING THE KNOT A YEAR & A HALF AGO, A LOT OF READERS HAVE BEEN ASKING ME THIS QUESTION:
HAS THIS ONCE MACHO HE-MASTER GONE ALL SOFT NOW THAT I'M A MARRIED MAN?
BAD BOYS
THE ANSWER IS YES I'VE GONE ALL SOFT...
SOFT & SUPPLE..
IT'S TRUE!! THE BEST THING ABOUT GETTING HITCHED IS BEING ABLE TO USE ALL YER WIFE'S GIRLIE PRODUCTS IN THE BATHROOM...
STUFF I WOULDN'T BE CAUGHT DEAD BUYING IN PUBLIC....
Okay, Lessee... We've got some anti-crab ointment, anal wart remover & a peach melba Loofah scrub...
SHHH!! Not so loud with the Loofah Scrub..
THAT'S RIGHT, PEOPLE.. NO MORE SCRUB-BING THE NETHER-REGIONS WITH LAVA SOAP FER ME...
Rosemary, Aloe Vera & Eucalyptis Leaves infused w/ Hibiscus Shampoo
KNOCK KNOCK
Are you using up all my stuff in there?
Organic Sea Kelp & Lamb semen exfoliating wash
No, dear.. just readin' some kiddie porn..
Colloidal oatmeal & placenta enema
HONESTLY, Y'ALL.. USING THIS STUFF DOES MAKE A DIFFERENCE.. A LOTTA FOLKS HAVE BEEN NOTICING...
Gee, yer skin feels terrific!!
STOP

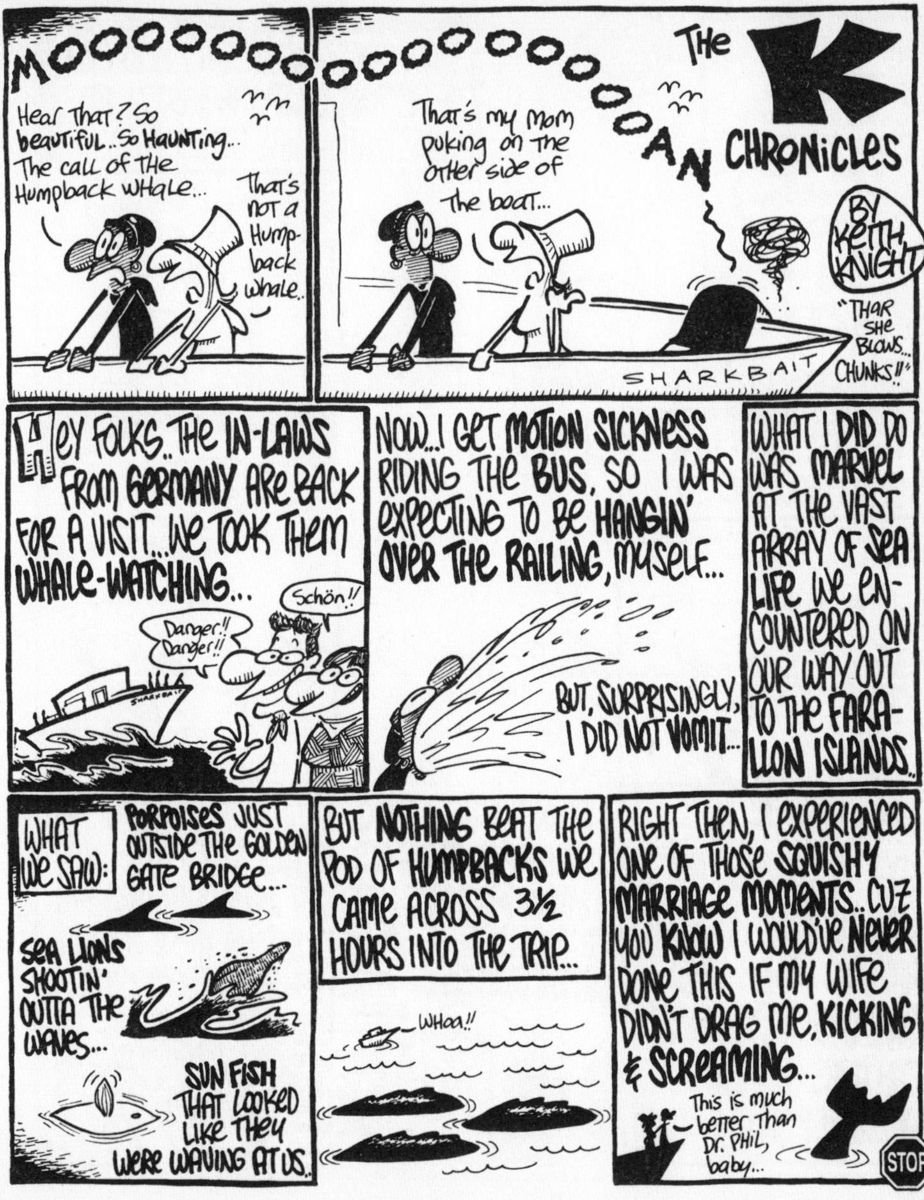
MOOOOOOOOOOOOOOOOAN
Hear that? So beautiful.. So haunting... The call of the Humpback whale...
That's not a Humpback whale..
That's my mom puking on the other side of the boat...
THE K CHRONICLES
BY KEITH KNIGHT
"THAR SHE BLOWS... CHUNKS!!"
SHARKBAIT
Hey folks.. the in-laws from Germany are back for a visit... we took them whale-watching...
Schön!!
Danger!! Danger!!
Now... I get motion sickness riding the bus, so I was expecting to be hangin' over the railing, myself...
But, surprisingly, I did not vomit...
What I did do was marvel at the vast array of sea life we encountered on our way out to the Farallon Islands..
What we saw:
Porpoises just outside the Golden Gate Bridge...
Sea lions shootin' outta the waves...
Sun fish that looked like they were waving at us..
But nothing beat the pod of humpbacks we came across 3½ hours into the trip...
Whoa!!
Right then, I experienced one of those squishy marriage moments.. cuz you know I would've never done this if my wife didn't drag me, kicking & screaming...
This is much better than Dr. Phil, baby...
STOP

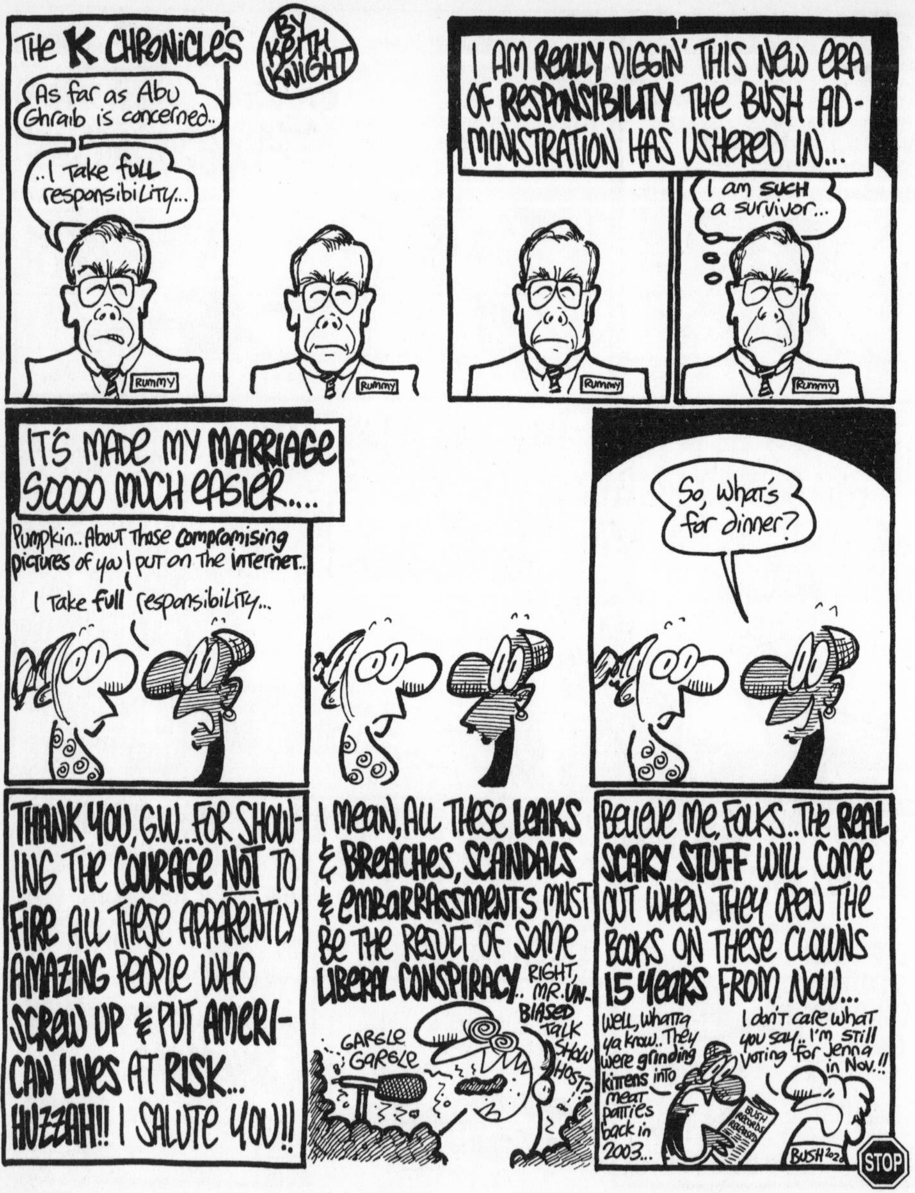
THE K CHRONICLES
BY KEITH KNIGHT
As far as Abu Ghraib is concerned..
..I take full responsibility...
RUMMY
RUMMY
I AM REALLY DIGGIN' THIS NEW ERA OF RESPONSIBILITY THE BUSH ADMINISTRATION HAS USHERED IN...
RUMMY
I am SUCH a survivor...
RUMMY
IT'S MADE MY MARRIAGE SOOOO MUCH EASIER.....
Pumpkin.. About those compromising pictures of you I put on the internet..
I take full responsibility...
So, what's for dinner?
THANK YOU, G.W...FOR SHOWING THE COURAGE NOT TO FIRE ALL THESE APPARENTLY AMAZING PEOPLE WHO SCREW UP & PUT AMERICAN LIVES AT RISK... HUZZAH!! I SALUTE YOU!!
I MEAN, ALL THESE LEAKS & BREACHES, SCANDALS & EMBARRASSMENTS MUST BE THE RESULT OF SOME LIBERAL CONSPIRACY..
RIGHT, MR. UNBIASED TALK SHOW HOST?
GARGLE GARGLE
BELIEVE ME, FOLKS..THE REAL SCARY STUFF WILL COME OUT WHEN THEY OPEN THE BOOKS ON THESE CLOWNS 15 YEARS FROM NOW...
Well, whatta ya know.. They were grinding kittens into meat patties back in 2003...
BUSH RECORDS RELEASED
I don't care what you say.. I'm still voting for Jenna in Nov.!!
BUSH 2020
STOP

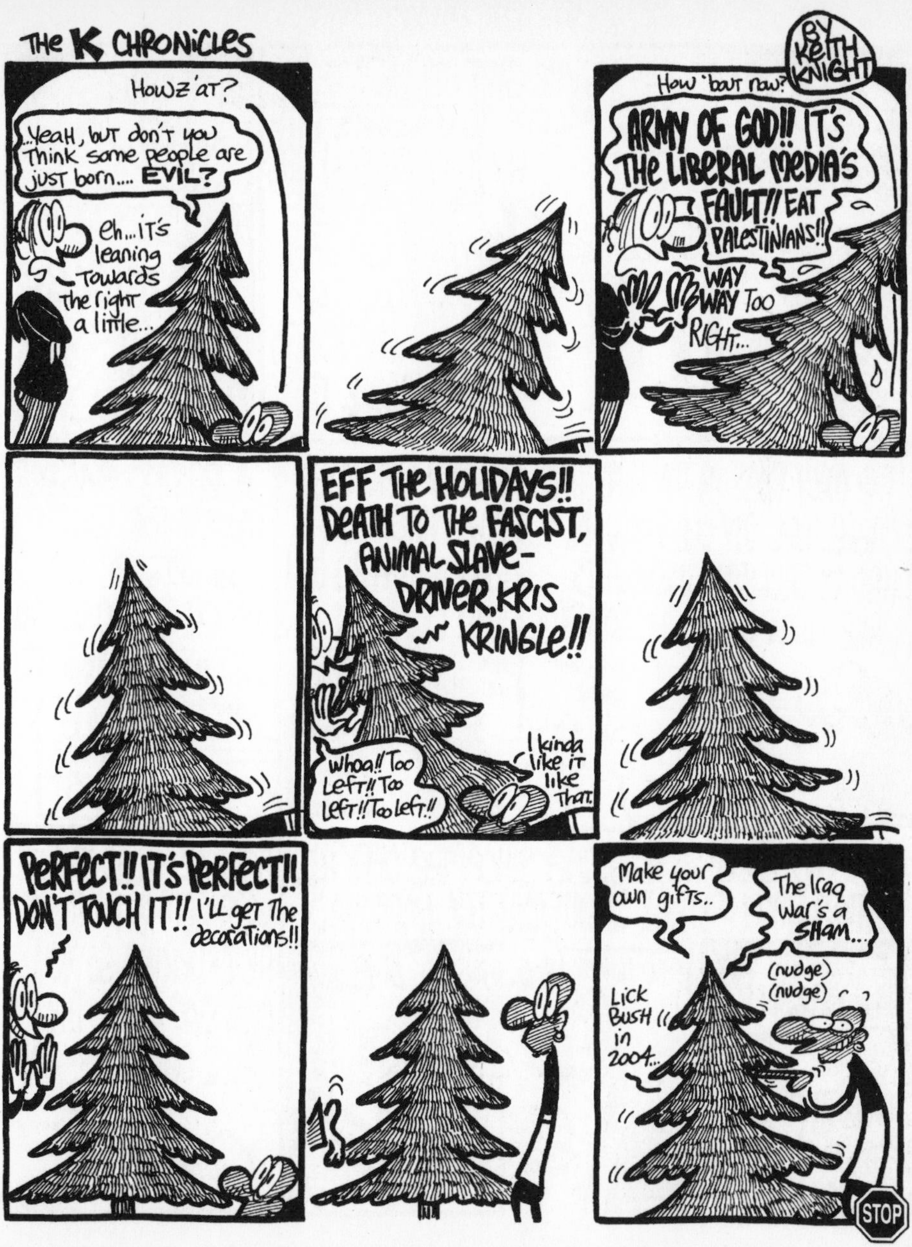
THE K CHRONICLES
BY KEITH KNIGHT
HOWZ'AT?
...YeaH, but don't you Think some people are just born.... EVIL?
eh...IT'S leaning Towards The right a little...
How 'bout now?
ARMY OF GOD!! IT'S THE LIBERAL MEDIA'S FAULT!! EAT PALESTINIANS!!
WAY WAY TOO RIGHT...
EFF THE HOLIDAYS!! DEATH TO THE FASCIST, ANIMAL SLAVE-DRIVER, KRIS KRINGLE!!
Whoa!! Too Left!! Too Left!! Too Left!!
I kinda like it like That.
PERFECT!! IT'S PERFECT!! DON'T TOUCH IT!! I'LL get The decorations!!
Make your own gifts..
The Iraq war's a SHAM...
(nudge) (nudge)
Lick BUSH in 2004...
STOP

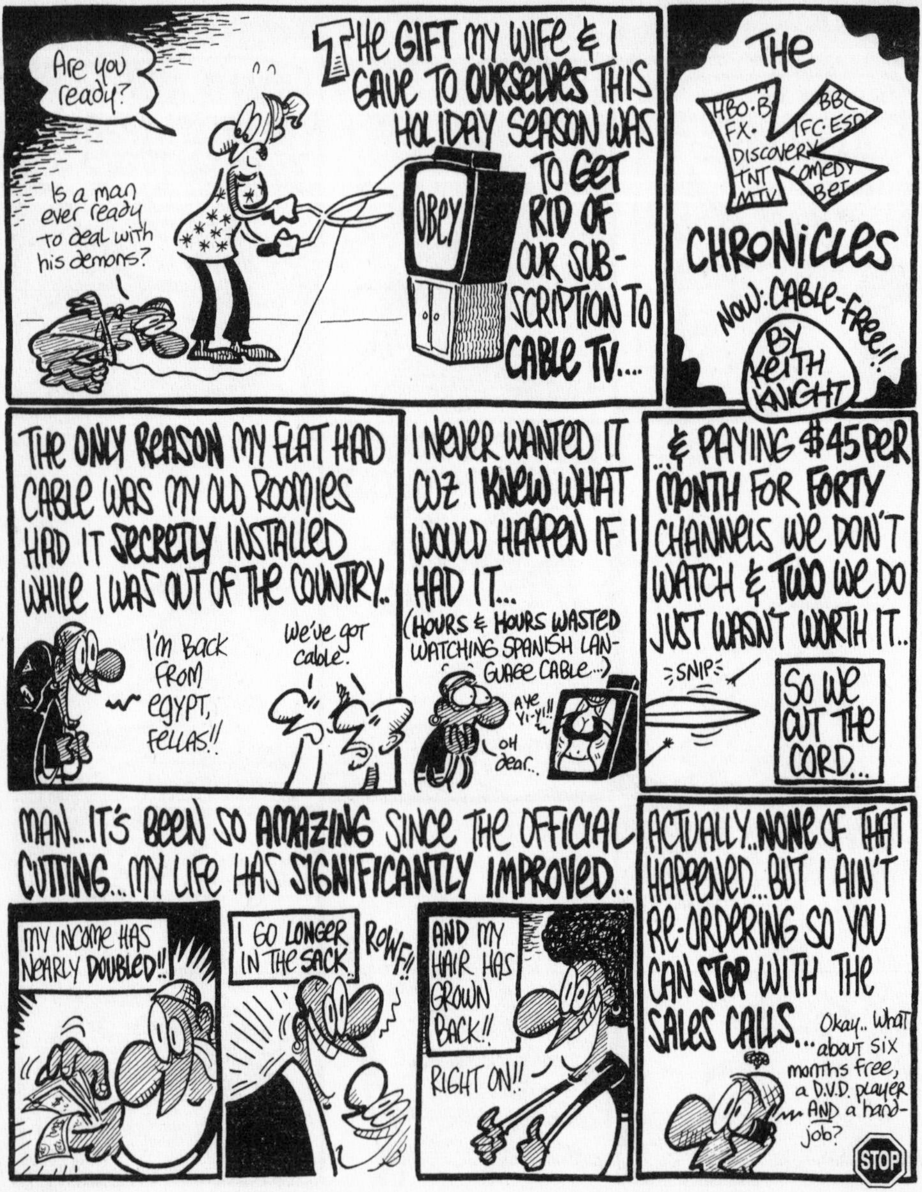
THE K CHRONICLES
HBO • BBC • FX • IFC • ESP • DISCOVERY • TNT • COMEDY • MTV • BET
NOW: CABLE-FREE!!
BY KEITH KNIGHT
THE GIFT MY WIFE & I GAVE TO OURSELVES THIS HOLIDAY SEASON WAS TO GET RID OF OUR SUB-SCRIPTION TO CABLE TV....
Are you ready?
Is a man ever ready to deal with his demons?
OBEY
THE ONLY REASON MY FLAT HAD CABLE WAS MY OLD ROOMIES HAD IT SECRETLY INSTALLED WHILE I WAS OUT OF THE COUNTRY..
I'm Back FROM egypt, fellas!!
We've got cable.
I NEVER WANTED IT CUZ I KNEW WHAT WOULD HAPPEN IF I HAD IT...
(HOURS & HOURS WASTED WATCHING SPANISH LAN-GUAGE CABLE...)
AYE YI-YI!!
OH dear..
...& PAYING $45 PER MONTH FOR FORTY CHANNELS WE DON'T WATCH & TWO WE DO JUST WASN'T WORTH IT..
SNIP
So we CUT THE CORD...
MAN...IT'S BEEN SO AMAZING SINCE THE OFFICIAL CUTTING...MY LIFE HAS SIGNIFICANTLY IMPROVED...
MY INCOME HAS NEARLY DOUBLED!!
I GO LONGER IN THE SACK.
ROWF!!
AND MY HAIR HAS GROWN BACK!!
RIGHT ON!!
ACTUALLY..NONE OF THAT HAPPENED...BUT I AIN'T RE-ORDERING SO YOU CAN STOP WITH THE SALES CALLS...
Okay.. What about six months free, a D.V.D. player AND a hand-job?
STOP

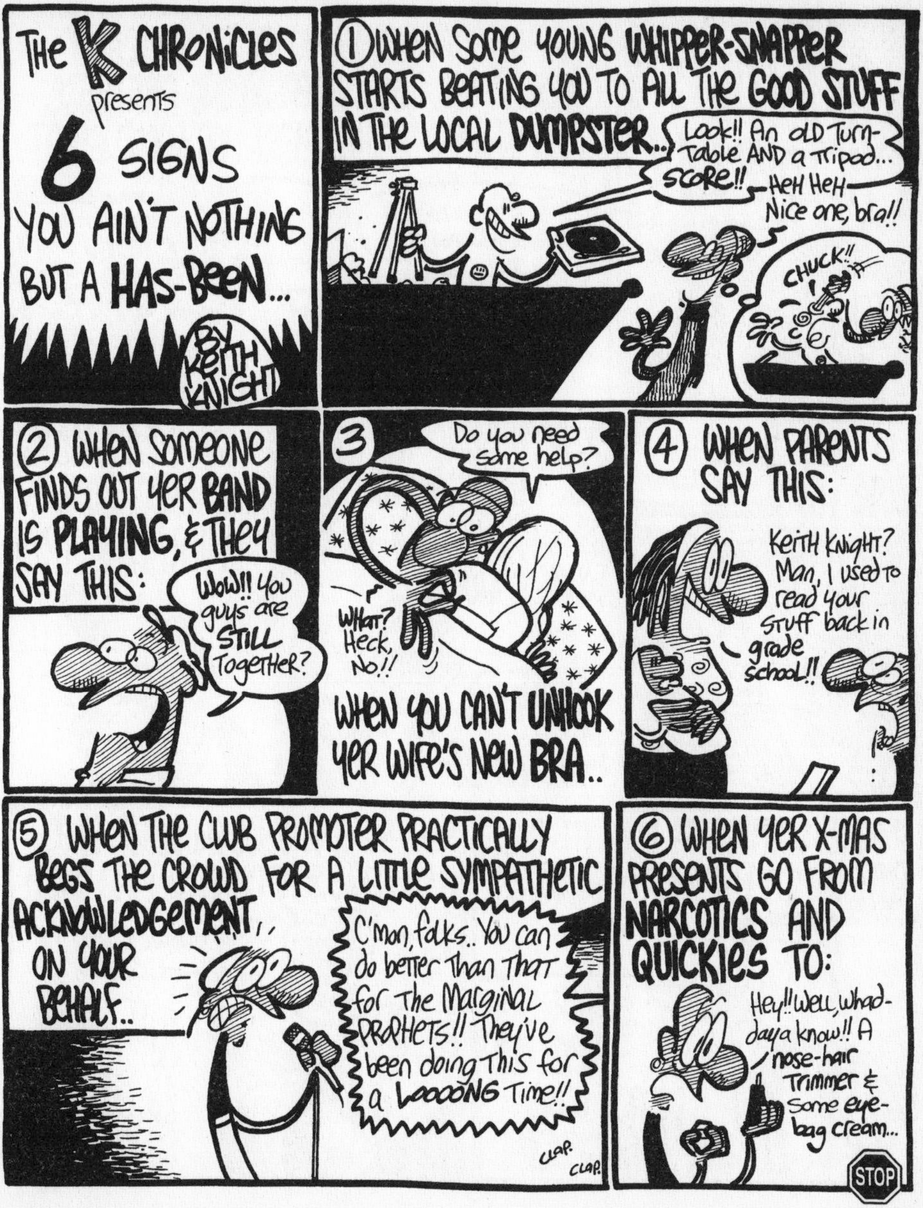
The K Chronicles
presents
6 SIGNS
YOU AIN'T NOTHING
BUT A HAS-BEEN...
BY KEITH KNIGHT
① WHEN SOME YOUNG WHIPPER-SNAPPER STARTS BEATING YOU TO ALL THE GOOD STUFF IN THE LOCAL DUMPSTER..
Look!! An old Turn-Table AND a Tripod... SCORE!!
Heh Heh Nice one, bra!!
CHUCK!!
② WHEN SOMEONE FINDS OUT YER BAND IS PLAYING, & THEY SAY THIS:
WOW!! You guys are STILL Together?
③
Do you need some help?
WHAT? Heck, No!!
WHEN YOU CAN'T UNHOOK YER WIFE'S NEW BRA..
④ WHEN PARENTS SAY THIS:
Keith Knight? Man, I used to read your stuff back in grade school!!
⑤ WHEN THE CLUB PROMOTER PRACTICALLY BEGS THE CROWD FOR A LITTLE SYMPATHETIC ACKNOWLEDGEMENT, ON YOUR BEHALF..
C'mon, folks.. You can do better than that for The Marginal Prophets!! They've been doing this for a LOOOONG Time!!
CLAP. CLAP.
⑥ WHEN YER X-MAS PRESENTS GO FROM NARCOTICS AND QUICKIES TO:
Hey!! Well, whad-daya know!! A nose-hair Trimmer & some eye-bag cream...
STOP

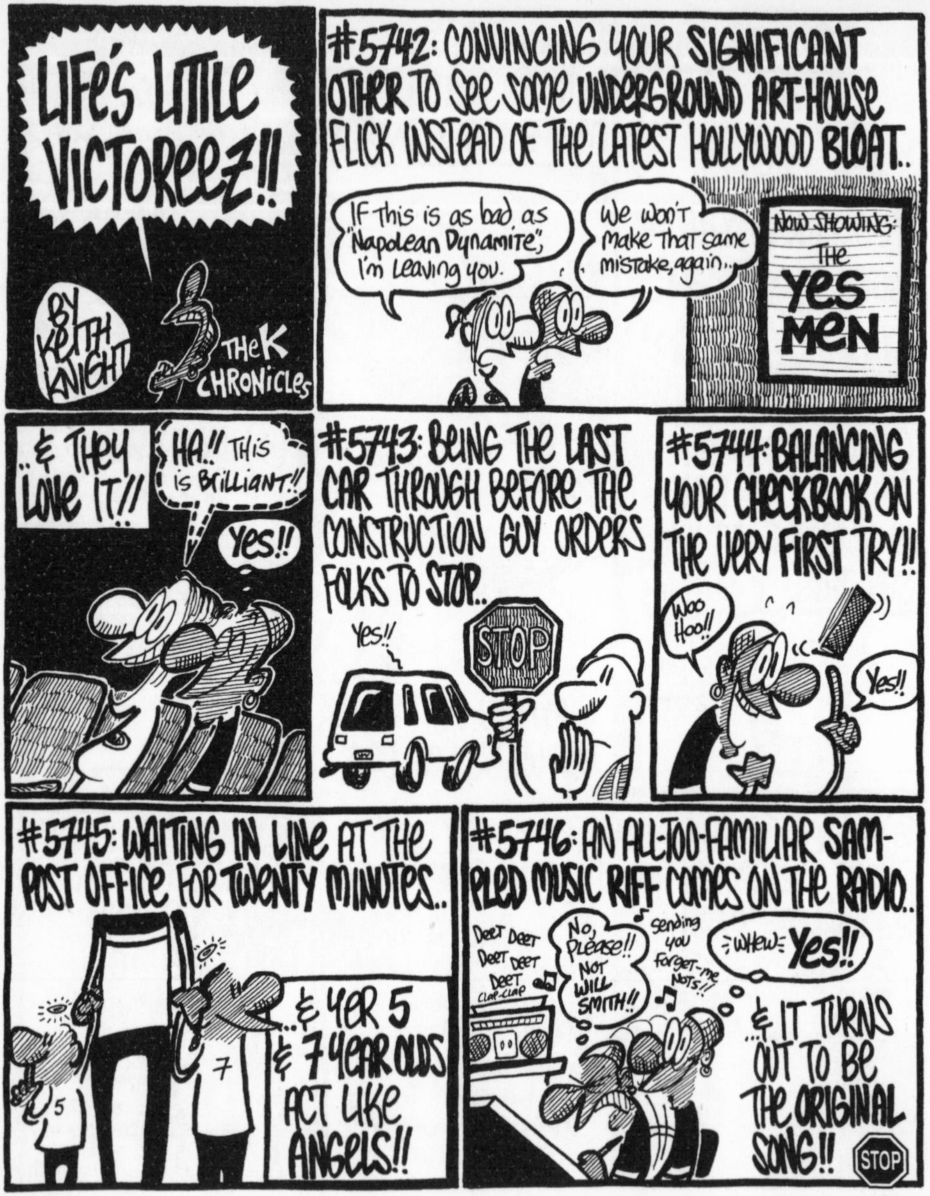
LIFE'S LITTLE VICTOREEZ!!
BY KEITH KNIGHT
THE K CHRONICLES
#5742: CONVINCING YOUR SIGNIFICANT OTHER TO SEE SOME UNDERGROUND ART-HOUSE FLICK INSTEAD OF THE LATEST HOLLYWOOD BLOAT..
If this is as bad as "Napolean Dynamite", I'm leaving you.
We won't make that same mistake, again...
NOW SHOWING: THE YES MEN
..& THEY LOVE IT!!
HA..!! THIS is Brilliant!!
Yes!!
#5743: BEING THE LAST CAR THROUGH BEFORE THE CONSTRUCTION GUY ORDERS FOLKS TO STOP..
Yes!!
STOP
#5744: BALANCING YOUR CHECKBOOK ON THE VERY FIRST TRY!!
Woo Hoo!!
Yes!!
#5745: WAITING IN LINE AT THE POST OFFICE FOR TWENTY MINUTES..
..& YER 5 & 7 YEAR OLDS ACT LIKE ANGELS!!
#5746: AN ALL-TOO-FAMILIAR SAMPLED MUSIC RIFF COMES ON THE RADIO..
DEET DEET DEET DEET DEET CLAP-CLAP
No, PLEASE!! NOT WILL SMITH!!
sending you forget-me nots!!
WHEW Yes!!
..& IT TURNS OUT TO BE THE ORIGINAL SONG!!
STOP

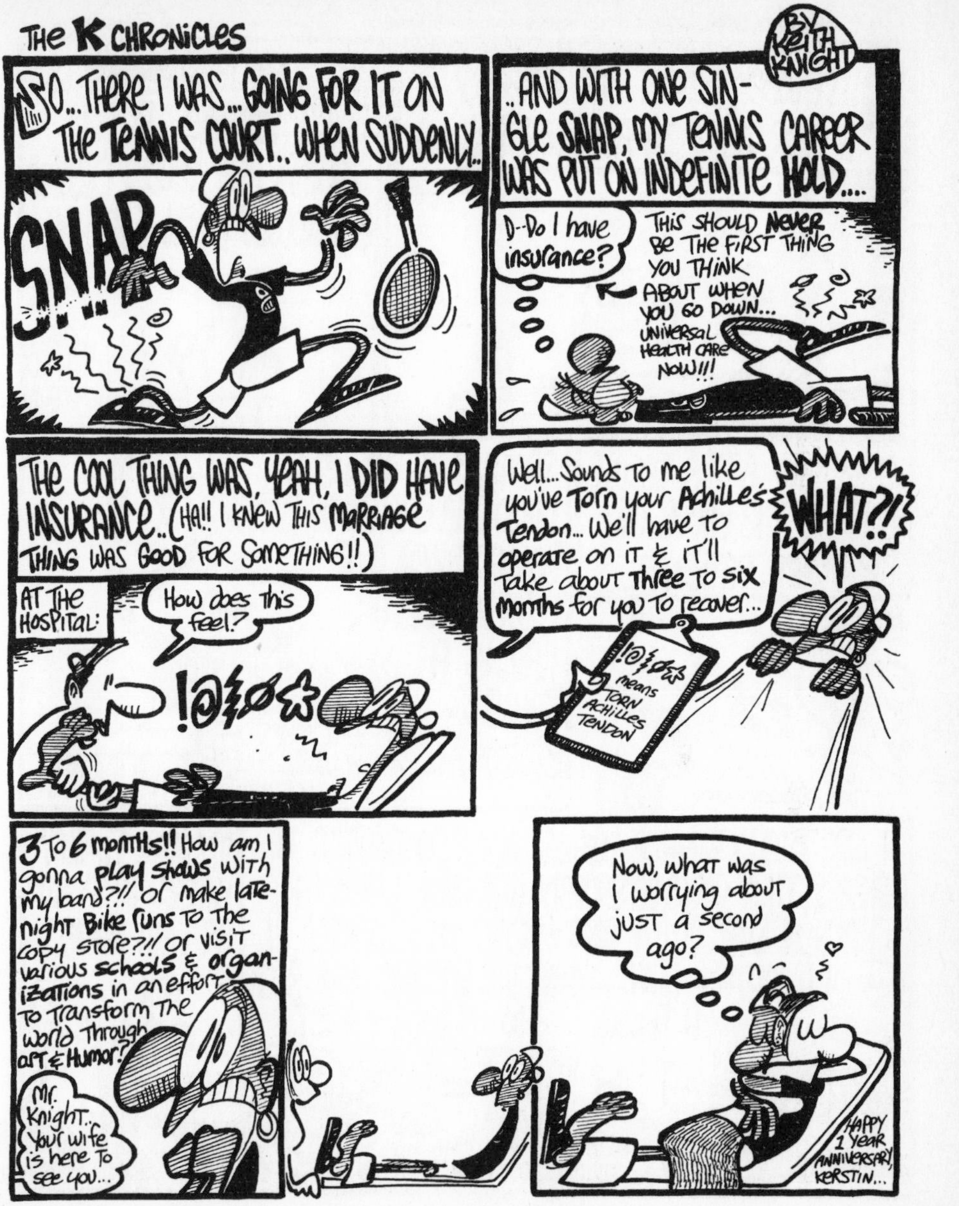
THE K CHRONICLES
BY KEITH KNIGHT
SO... THERE I WAS... GOING FOR IT ON THE TENNIS COURT.. WHEN SUDDENLY..
SNAP
..AND WITH ONE SINGLE SNAP, MY TENNIS CAREER WAS PUT ON INDEFINITE HOLD....
D--Do I have insurance?
THIS SHOULD NEVER BE THE FIRST THING YOU THINK ABOUT WHEN YOU GO DOWN... UNIVERSAL HEALTH CARE NOW!!!
THE COOL THING WAS, YEAH, I DID HAVE INSURANCE..(HA!! I KNEW THIS MARRIAGE THING WAS GOOD FOR SOMETHING!!)
AT THE HOSPITAL:
How does this feel?
!@ϟø✲
Well... Sounds to me like you've Torn your Achilles Tendon... We'll have to operate on it & it'll Take about Three to six months for you to recover...
WHAT?!
!@ϟø✲ means TORN Achilles TENDON
3 To 6 months!! How am I gonna play shows with my band?!! or make late-night Bike runs to the copy store?!! or visit various schools & organizations in an effort to Transform The world Through art & Humor?
Mr. Knight... Your wife is here To see you...
Now, what was I worrying about just a second ago?
HAPPY 1 YEAR ANNIVERSARY, KERSTIN...

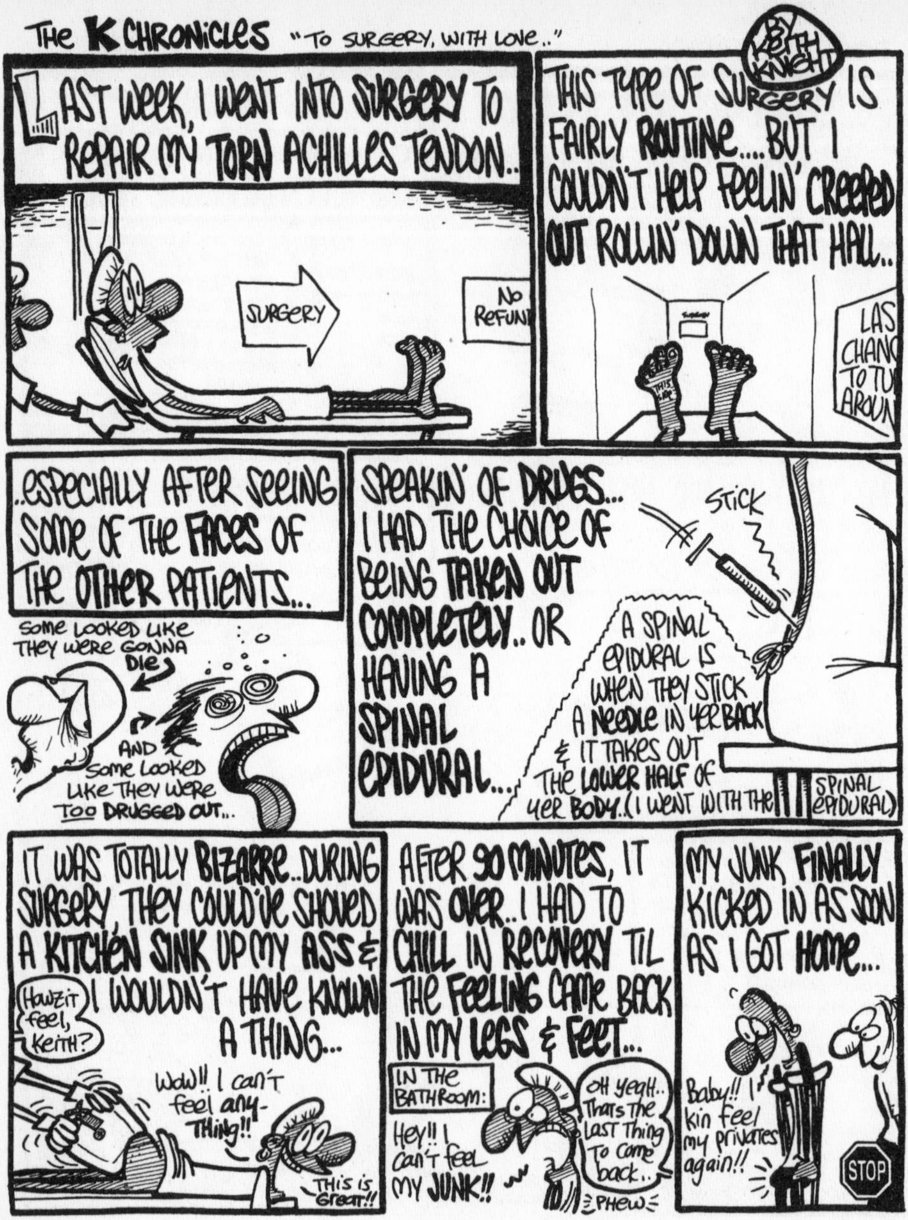
The K Chronicles
"To surgery, with love.."
By Keith Knight
Last week, I went into surgery to repair my torn Achilles tendon..
SURGERY
No Refun
This type of surgery is fairly routine.... but I couldn't help feelin' creeped out rollin' down that hall..
LAS CHANC TO TU AROUN
..especially after seeing some of the faces of the other patients...
Some looked like they were gonna die
And some looked like they were too drugged out...
Speakin' of drugs... I had the choice of being taken out completely.. or having a spinal epidural...
STICK
A spinal epidural is when they stick a needle in yer back & it takes out the lower half of yer body..(I went with the spinal epidural)
It was totally bizarre..during surgery, they could've shoved a kitchen sink up my ass & I wouldn't have known a thing...
Howz it feel, Keith?
Wow!! I can't feel any-thing!!
This is great!!
After 90 minutes, it was over.. I had to chill in recovery til the feeling came back in my legs & feet...
In the bathroom:
Hey!! I can't feel my junk!!
Oh yeah.. Thats the last thing to come back..
PHEW
My junk finally kicked in as soon as I got home...
Baby!! I kin feel my privates again!!
STOP

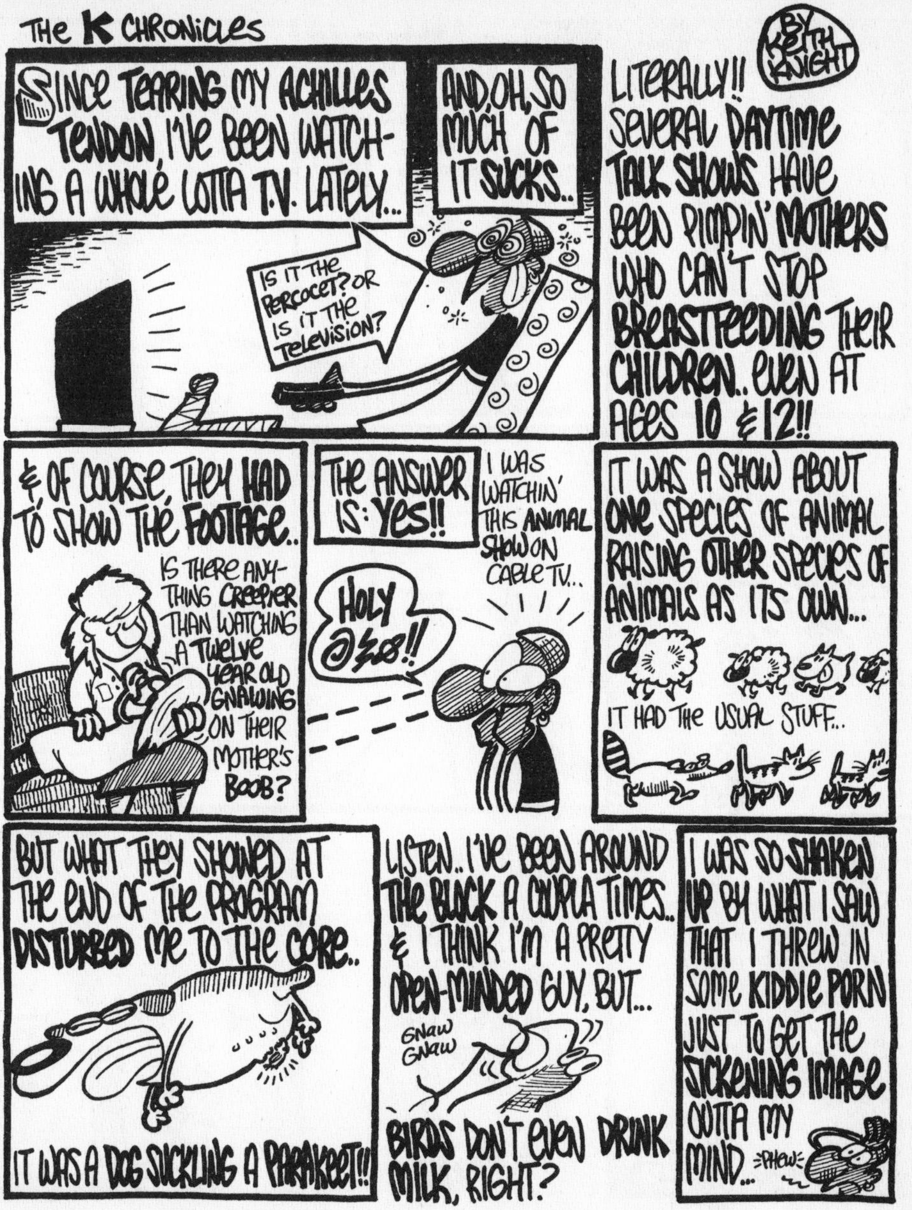
THE K CHRONICLES
BY KEITH KNIGHT
SINCE TEARING MY ACHILLES TENDON, I'VE BEEN WATCHING A WHOLE LOTTA T.V. LATELY...
AND, OH, SO MUCH OF IT SUCKS..
IS IT THE PERCOCET? OR IS IT THE TELEVISION?
LITERALLY!! SEVERAL DAYTIME TALK SHOWS HAVE BEEN PIMPIN' MOTHERS WHO CAN'T STOP BREASTFEEDING THEIR CHILDREN.. EVEN AT AGES 10 & 12!!
& OF COURSE, THEY HAD TO SHOW THE FOOTAGE..
IS THERE ANYTHING CREEPIER THAN WATCHING A TWELVE YEAR OLD GNAWING ON THEIR MOTHER'S BOOB?
THE ANSWER IS: YES!!
I WAS WATCHIN' THIS ANIMAL SHOW ON CABLE TV...
HOLY @*&!!
IT WAS A SHOW ABOUT ONE SPECIES OF ANIMAL RAISING OTHER SPECIES OF ANIMALS AS ITS OWN...
IT HAD THE USUAL STUFF...
BUT WHAT THEY SHOWED AT THE END OF THE PROGRAM DISTURBED ME TO THE CORE..
IT WAS A DOG SUCKLING A PARAKEET!!!
LISTEN.. I'VE BEEN AROUND THE BLOCK A COUPLA TIMES.. & I THINK I'M A PRETTY OPEN-MINDED GUY, BUT...
GNAW GNAW
BIRDS DON'T EVEN DRINK MILK, RIGHT?
I WAS SO SHAKEN UP BY WHAT I SAW THAT I THREW IN SOME KIDDIE PORN JUST TO GET THE SICKENING IMAGE OUTTA MY MIND...
PHEW

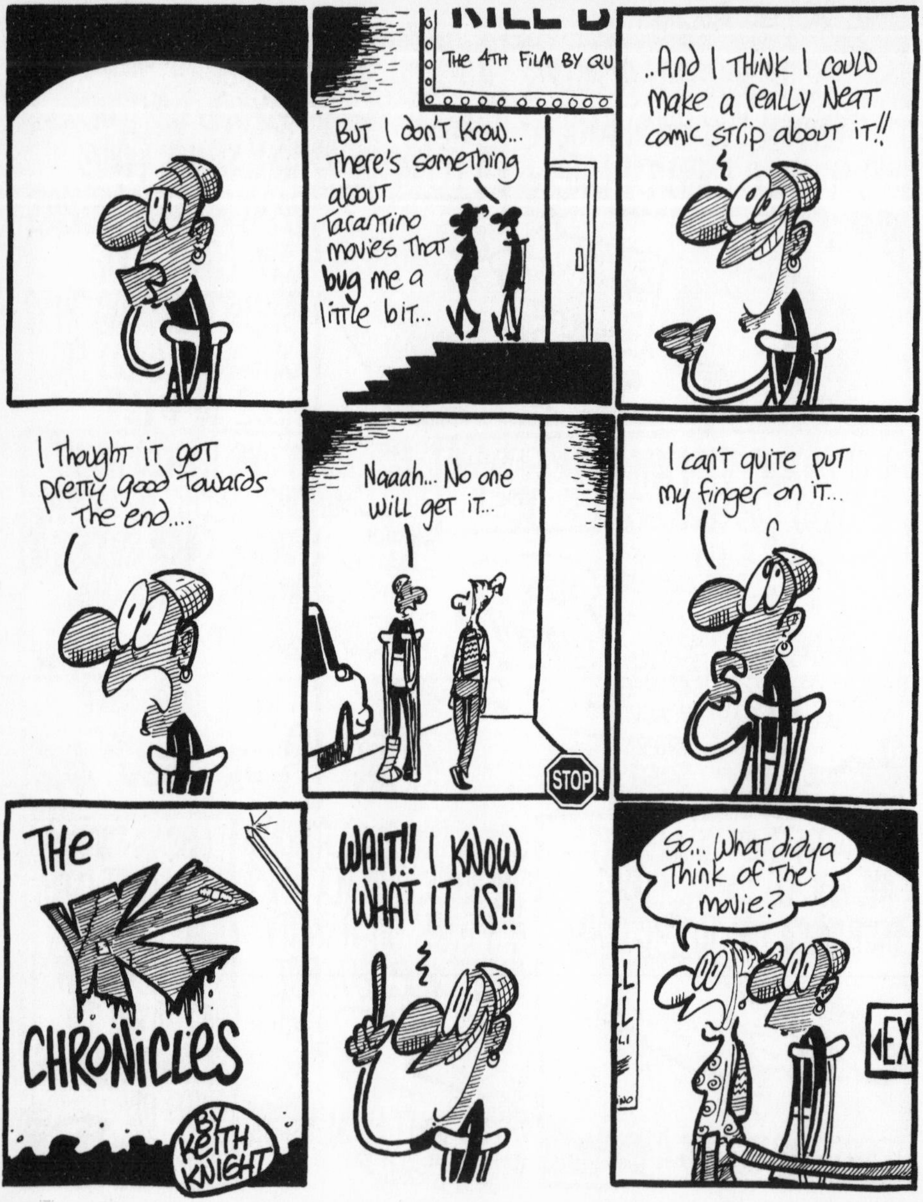

THE 4TH FILM BY QU
BUT I don't know... There's something about Tarantino movies That bug me a little bit...
..And I THINK I COULD make a really NEAT comic strip about it!!
I Thought it got pretty good Towards The end....
Naaah... No one will get it...
STOP
I can't quite put my finger on it...
THE K CHRONICLES
BY KEITH KNIGHT
WAIT!! I KNOW WHAT IT IS!!
So... What didya Think of The movie?
EX

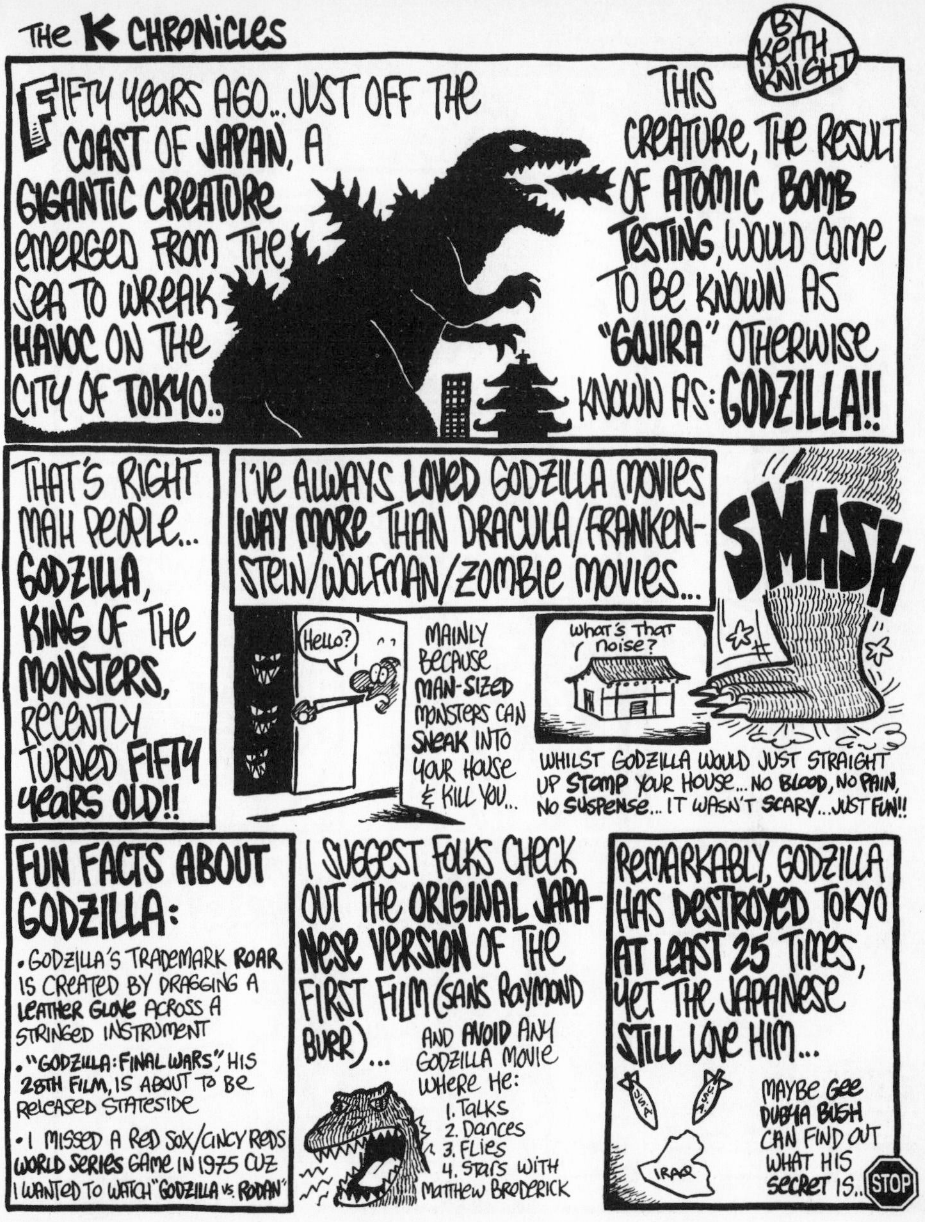
The K Chronicles
By Keith Knight
Fifty years ago... just off the coast of Japan, a gigantic creature emerged from the sea to wreak havoc on the city of Tokyo..
This creature, the result of atomic bomb testing, would come to be known as "Gojira" otherwise known as: Godzilla!!
That's right mah people... Godzilla, King of the Monsters, recently turned fifty years old!!
I've always loved Godzilla movies way more than Dracula/Franken-stein/Wolfman/Zombie movies...
Hello?
Mainly because man-sized monsters can sneak into your house & kill you...
What's that noise?
SMASH
Whilst Godzilla would just straight up stamp your house... no blood, no pain, no suspense... it wasn't scary... just fun!!
Fun facts about Godzilla:
• Godzilla's trademark roar is created by dragging a leather glove across a stringed instrument
• "Godzilla: Final Wars", his 28th film, is about to be released stateside
• I missed a Red Sox/Cincy Reds World Series game in 1975 cuz I wanted to watch "Godzilla vs. Rodan"
I suggest folks check out the original Japa-nese version of the first film (sans Raymond Burr)...
and avoid any Godzilla movie where he:
1. Talks
2. Dances
3. Flies
4. Stars with Matthew Broderick
Remarkably, Godzilla has destroyed Tokyo at least 25 times, yet the Japanese still love him...
Iraq
Maybe Gee Dubya Bush can find out what his secret is..
STOP

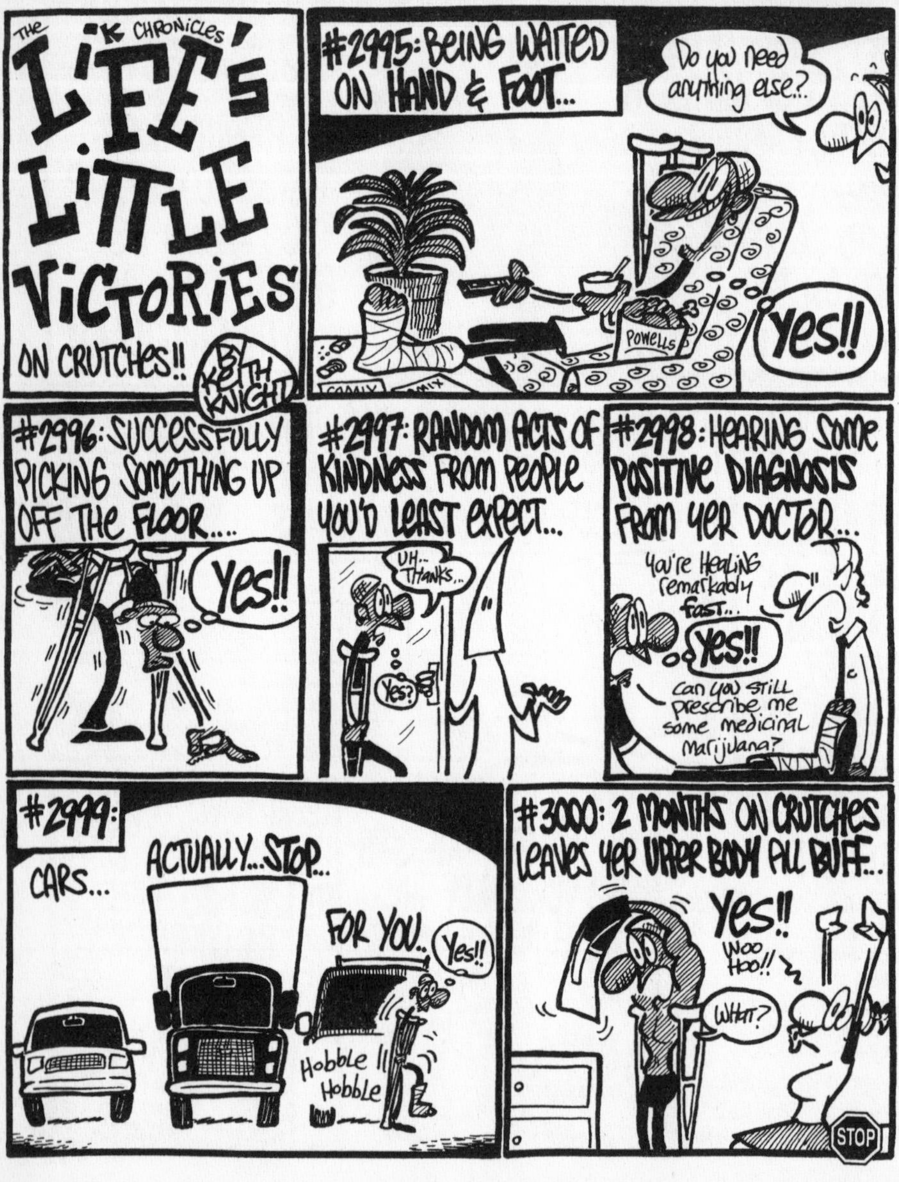
THE "K CHRONICLES"
LIFE'S LITTLE VICTORIES
ON CRUTCHES!!
BY KEITH KNIGHT
#2995: BEING WAITED ON HAND & FOOT...
Do you need anything else?..
POWELLS
Yes!!
#2996: SUCCESSFULLY PICKING SOMETHING UP OFF THE FLOOR....
Yes!!
#2997: RANDOM ACTS OF KINDNESS FROM PEOPLE YOU'D LEAST EXPECT...
UH.. THANKS..
Yes?
#2998: HEARING SOME POSITIVE DIAGNOSIS FROM YER DOCTOR...
You're Healing remarkably fast...
Yes!!
Can you still prescribe me some medicinal Marijuana?
#2999:
CARS...
ACTUALLY...STOP...
FOR YOU...
Yes!!
Hobble Hobble
#3000: 2 MONTHS ON CRUTCHES LEAVES YER UPPER BODY ALL BUFF...
Yes!!
WOO HOO!!
WHAT?
STOP

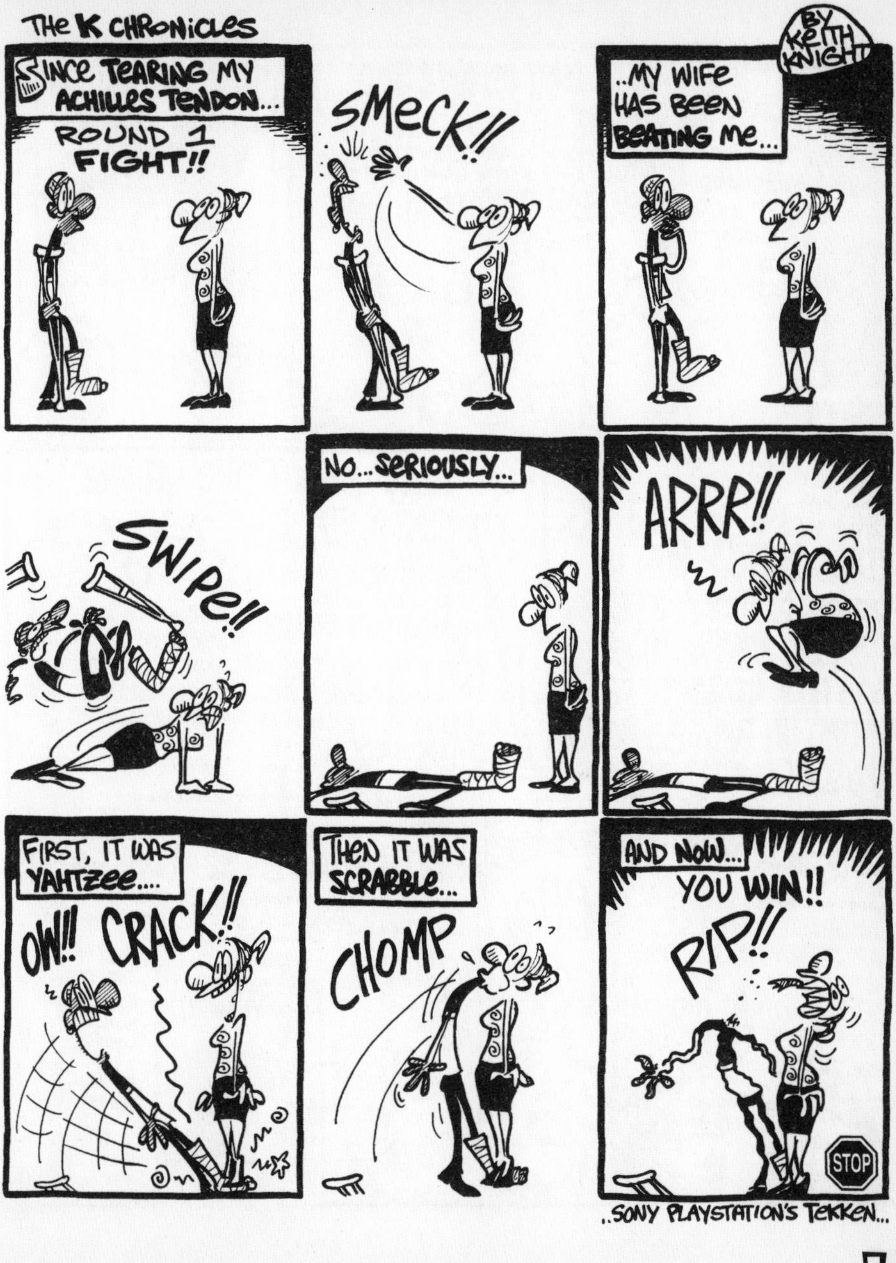
The K Chronicles
By Keith Knight
Since tearing my Achilles tendon...
ROUND 1
FIGHT!!
SMECK!!
..My wife has been beating me...
SWIPE!!
No... seriously...
ARRR!!
First, it was Yahtzee....
OW!!
CRACK!!
Then it was Scrabble...
CHOMP
And now...
YOU WIN!!
RIP!!
STOP
..Sony Playstation's Tekken...

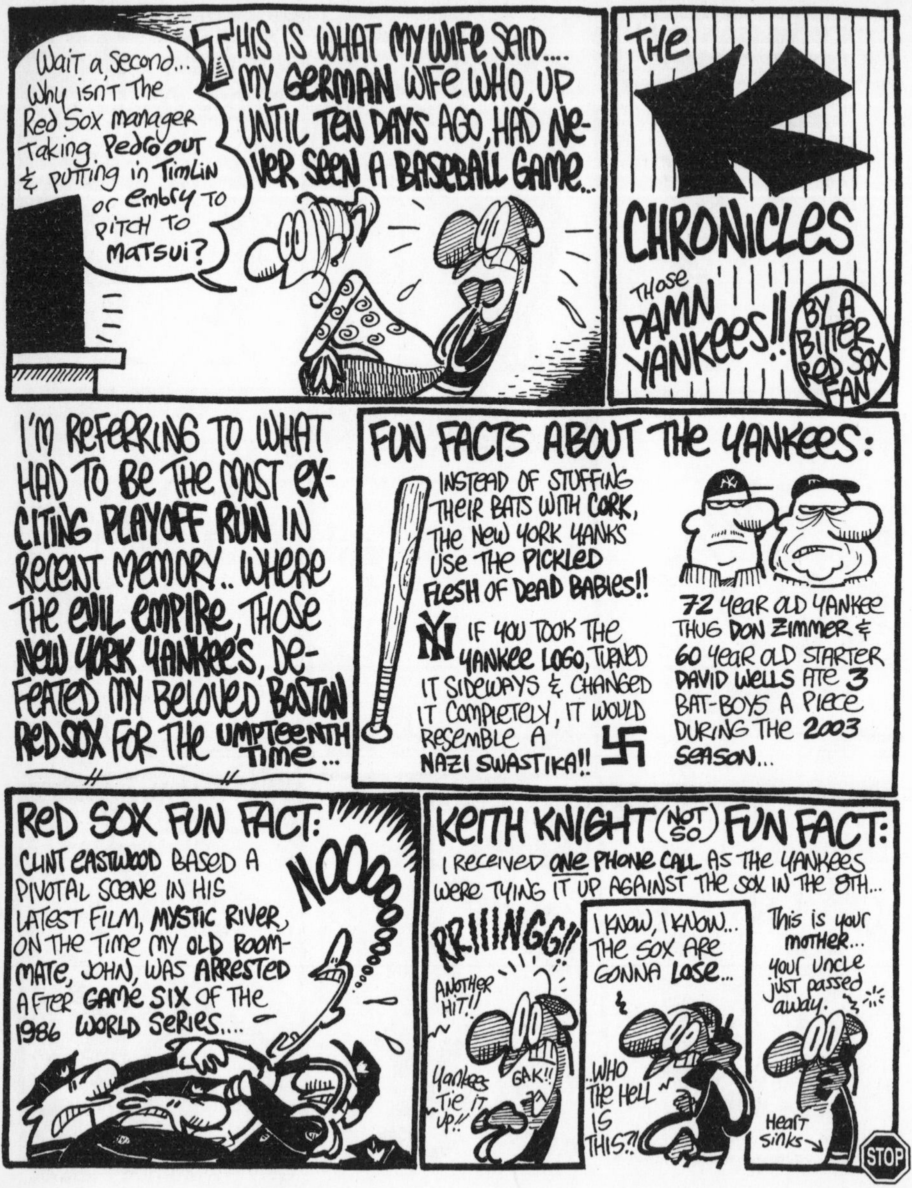
Wait a second... Why isn't The Red Sox manager Taking Pedro out & putting in Timlin or embry to pitch to Matsui?
THIS IS WHAT MY WIFE SAID.... MY GERMAN WIFE WHO, UP UNTIL TEN DAYS AGO, HAD NEVER SEEN A BASEBALL GAME...
THE K CHRONICLES
THOSE DAMN YANKEES!!
BY A BITTER RED SOX FAN
I'M REFERRING TO WHAT HAD TO BE THE MOST EXCITING PLAYOFF RUN IN RECENT MEMORY.. WHERE THE EVIL EMPIRE, THOSE NEW YORK YANKEES, DEFEATED MY BELOVED BOSTON RED SOX FOR THE UMPTEENTH TIME...
FUN FACTS ABOUT THE YANKEES:
INSTEAD OF STUFFING THEIR BATS WITH CORK, THE NEW YORK YANKS USE THE PICKLED FLESH OF DEAD BABIES!!
IF YOU TOOK THE YANKEE LOGO, TURNED IT SIDEWAYS & CHANGED IT COMPLETELY, IT WOULD RESEMBLE A NAZI SWASTIKA!!
72 YEAR OLD YANKEE THUG DON ZIMMER & 60 YEAR OLD STARTER DAVID WELLS ATE 3 BAT-BOYS A PIECE DURING THE 2003 SEASON...
RED SOX FUN FACT:
CLINT EASTWOOD BASED A PIVOTAL SCENE IN HIS LATEST FILM, MYSTIC RIVER, ON THE TIME MY OLD ROOMMATE, JOHN, WAS ARRESTED AFTER GAME SIX OF THE 1986 WORLD SERIES...
NOOOOOOOO
KEITH KNIGHT (NOT SO) FUN FACT:
I RECEIVED ONE PHONE CALL AS THE YANKEES WERE TYING IT UP AGAINST THE SOX IN THE 8TH...
RRIIIINGG!!
ANOTHER HIT!!
Yankees Tie it up!!
GAK!!
I KNOW, I KNOW... THE SOX ARE GONNA LOSE...
..WHO THE HELL IS THIS?!
This is your mother... Your uncle just passed away.
Heart sinks
STOP

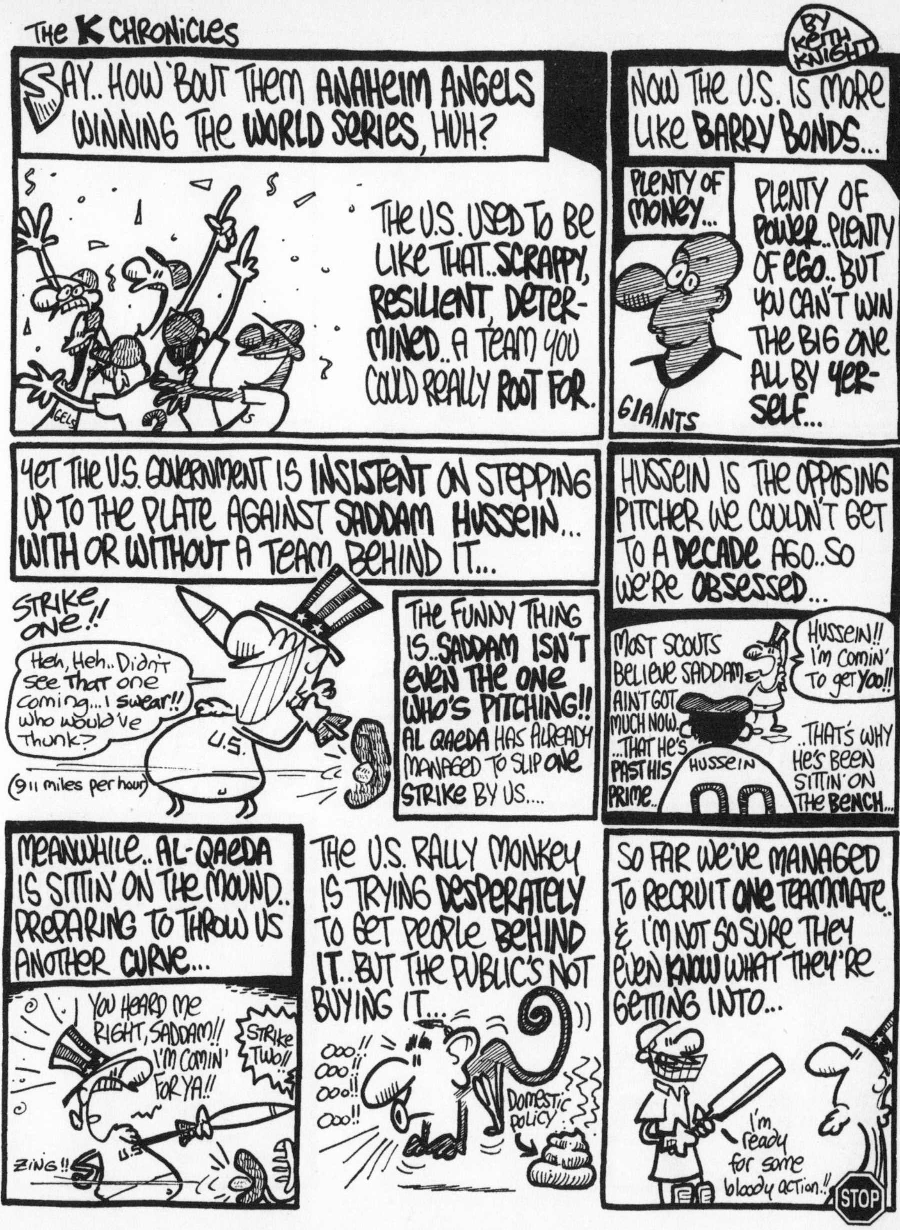

THE K CHRONICLES
BY KEITH KNIGHT
SAY.. HOW 'BOUT THEM ANAHEIM ANGELS WINNING THE WORLD SERIES, HUH?
THE U.S. USED TO BE LIKE THAT.. SCRAPPY, RESILIENT, DETERMINED.. A TEAM YOU COULD REALLY ROOT FOR.
GELS
NOW THE U.S. IS MORE LIKE BARRY BONDS...
PLENTY OF MONEY...
PLENTY OF POWER.. PLENTY OF EGO.. BUT YOU CAN'T WIN THE BIG ONE ALL BY YERSELF...
GIANTS
YET THE U.S. GOVERNMENT IS INSISTENT ON STEPPING UP TO THE PLATE AGAINST SADDAM HUSSEIN... WITH OR WITHOUT A TEAM BEHIND IT...
STRIKE ONE!!
Heh, Heh.. Didn't see that one coming... I swear!! who would've thunk?
U.S.
(911 miles per hour)
THE FUNNY THING IS.. SADDAM ISN'T EVEN THE ONE WHO'S PITCHING!! AL QAEDA HAS ALREADY MANAGED TO SLIP ONE STRIKE BY US....
HUSSEIN IS THE OPPOSING PITCHER WE COULDN'T GET TO A DECADE AGO.. SO WE'RE OBSESSED...
MOST SCOUTS BELIEVE SADDAM AIN'T GOT MUCH NOW. ...THAT HE'S PAST HIS PRIME..
HUSSEIN!! I'm comin' to get yoo!!
HUSSEIN
..THAT'S WHY HE'S BEEN SITTIN' ON THE BENCH...
MEANWHILE.. AL-QAEDA IS SITTIN' ON THE MOUND.. PREPARING TO THROW US ANOTHER CURVE...
YOU HEARD ME RIGHT, SADDAM!! I'M COMIN' FOR YA!!
STRIKE TWO!!
ZING!!
U.S.
THE U.S. RALLY MONKEY IS TRYING DESPERATELY TO GET PEOPLE BEHIND IT.. BUT THE PUBLIC'S NOT BUYING IT...
OOO!! OOO!! OOO!! OOO!! OOO!!
DOMESTIC POLICY
SO FAR WE'VE MANAGED TO RECRUIT ONE TEAMMATE... & I'M NOT SO SURE THEY EVEN KNOW WHAT THEY'RE GETTING INTO...
I'm ready for some bloody action!!
STOP

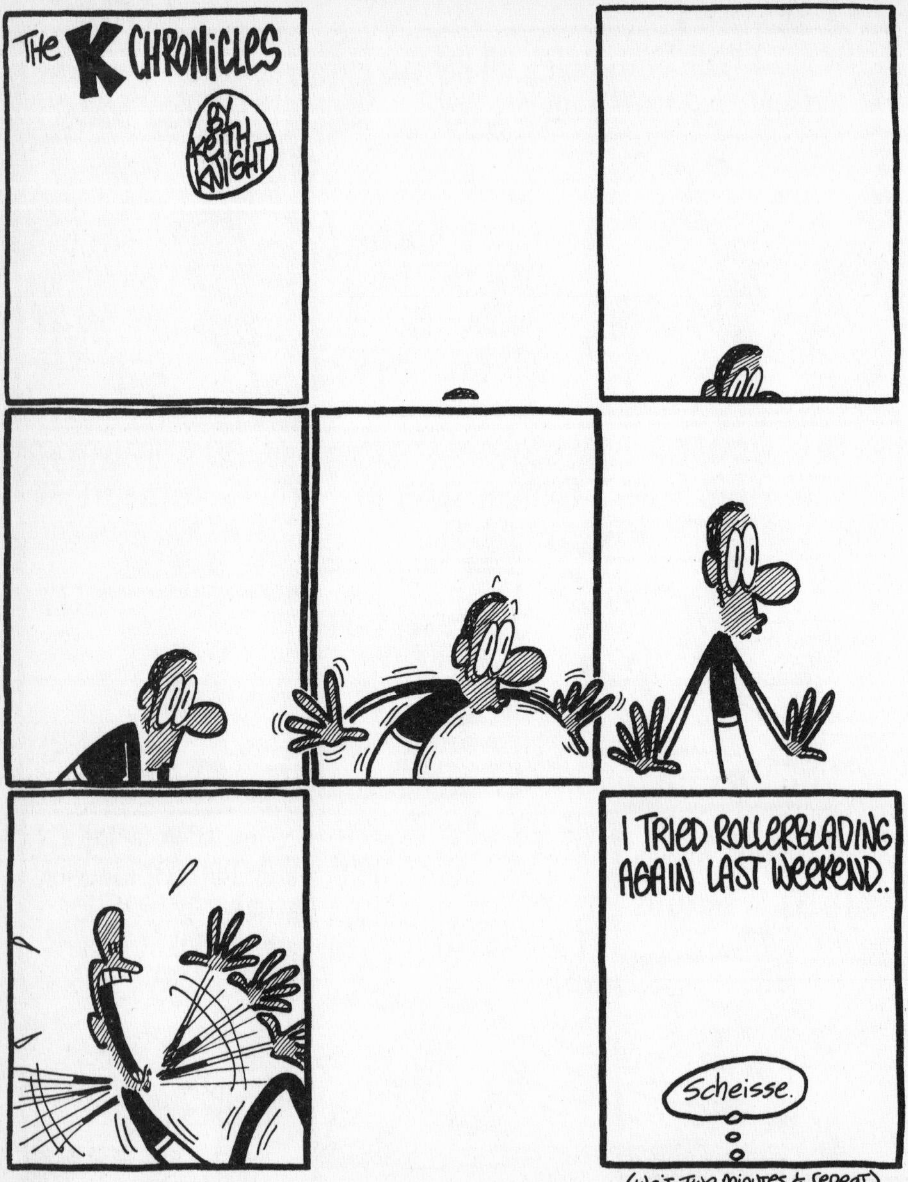
THE K CHRONICLES
BY KEITH KNIGHT
I TRIED ROLLERBLADING AGAIN LAST WEEKEND..
Scheisse.
(wait two minutes & repeat)

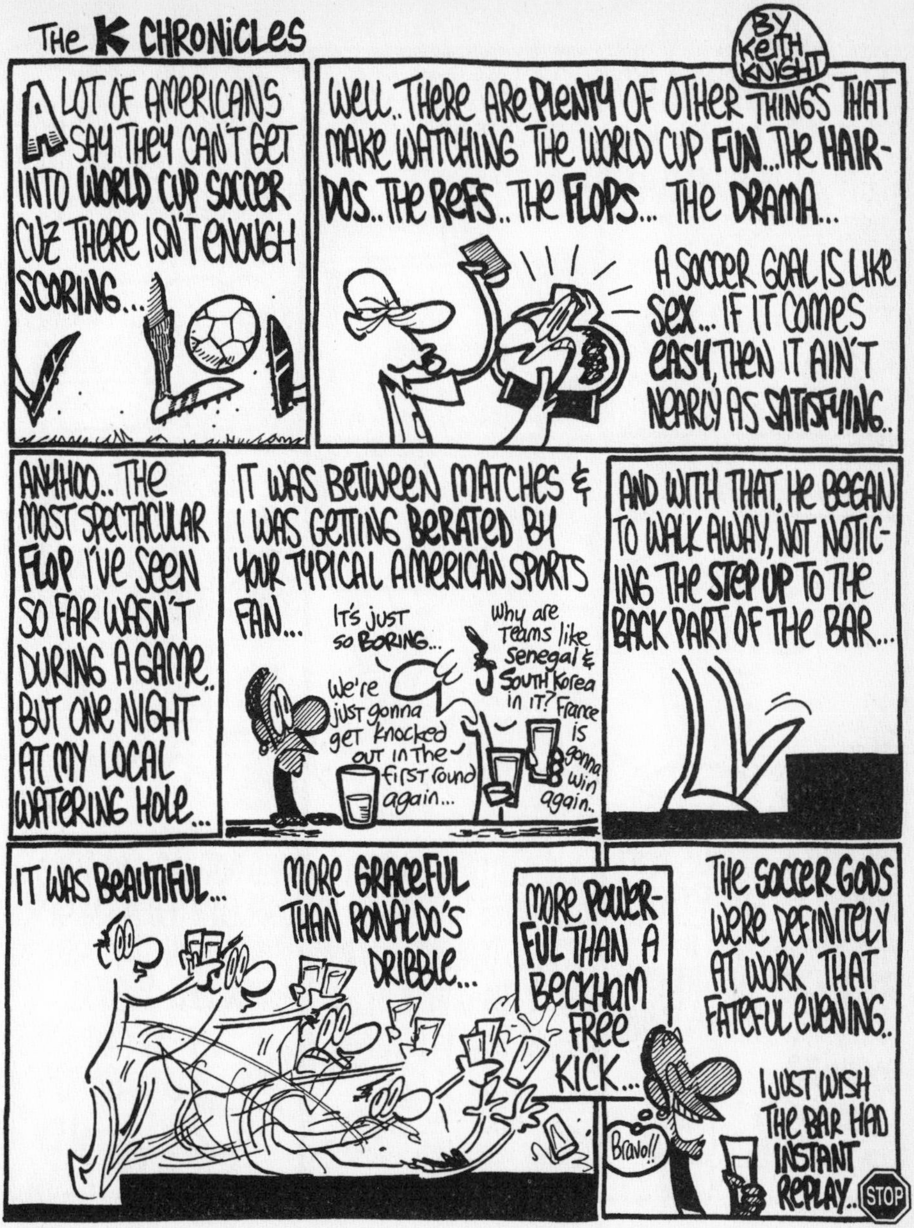
The K Chronicles
By Keith Knight
A lot of Americans say they can't get into World Cup Soccer cuz there isn't enough scoring...
Well.. there are plenty of other things that make watching the World Cup fun... the hair-dos.. the refs.. the flops... the drama...
A soccer goal is like sex... if it comes easy, then it ain't nearly as satisfying..
Anyhoo.. the most spectacular flop I've seen so far wasn't during a game.. but one night at my local watering hole...
It was between matches & I was getting berated by your typical American sports fan...
It's just so boring...
We're just gonna get knocked out in the first round again...
Why are teams like Senegal & South Korea in it?
France is gonna win again..
And with that, he began to walk away, not noticing the step up to the back part of the bar...
It was beautiful...
More graceful than Ronaldo's dribble...
More power-ful than a Beckham free kick...
Bravo!!
The soccer gods were definitely at work that fateful evening..
I just wish the bar had instant replay..
STOP

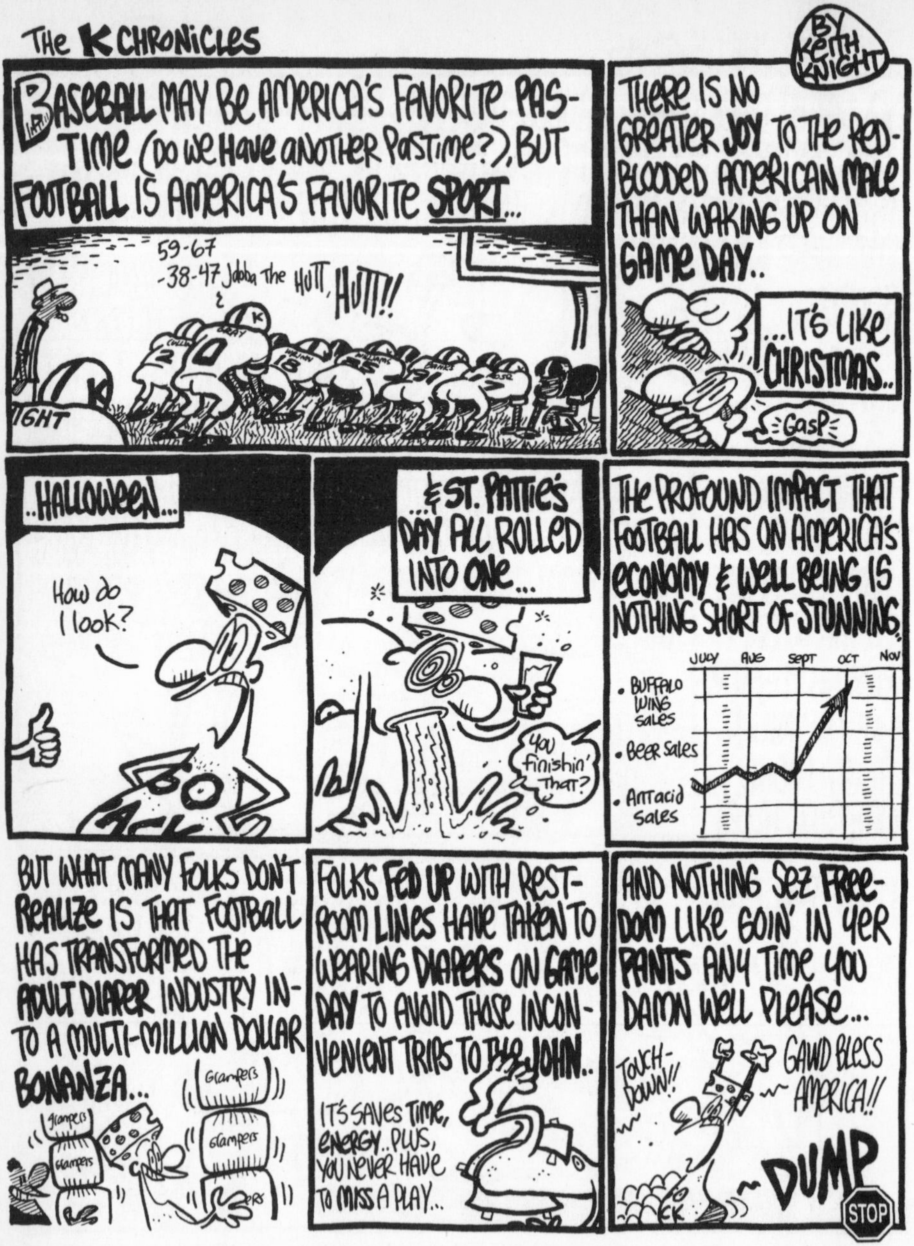
The K CHRONICLES
BY KEITH KNIGHT
BASEBALL MAY BE AMERICA'S FAVORITE PASTIME (DO WE HAVE ANOTHER PASTIME?), BUT FOOTBALL IS AMERICA'S FAVORITE SPORT...
59-67 -38-47 Jabba the HUTT, HUTT!!
THERE IS NO GREATER JOY TO THE RED-BLOODED AMERICAN MALE THAN WAKING UP ON GAME DAY..
...IT'S LIKE CHRISTMAS...
GASP
..HALLOWEEN...
How do I look?
...& ST. PATTIE'S DAY ALL ROLLED INTO ONE...
You finishin' that?
THE PROFOUND IMPACT THAT FOOTBALL HAS ON AMERICA'S ECONOMY & WELL BEING IS NOTHING SHORT OF STUNNING.
JULY
AUG
SEPT
OCT
NOV
• BUFFALO WING SALES
• BEER SALES
• ANTACID SALES
BUT WHAT MANY FOLKS DON'T REALIZE IS THAT FOOTBALL HAS TRANSFORMED THE ADULT DIAPER INDUSTRY INTO A MULTI-MILLION DOLLAR BONANZA...
Grampers
Grampers
Grampers
Grampers
FOLKS FED UP WITH RESTROOM LINES HAVE TAKEN TO WEARING DIAPERS ON GAME DAY TO AVOID THOSE INCONVENIENT TRIPS TO THE JOHN..
IT'S SAVES TIME, ENERGY..PLUS, YOU NEVER HAVE TO MISS A PLAY...
AND NOTHING SEZ FREEDOM LIKE GOIN' IN YER PANTS ANY TIME YOU DAMN WELL PLEASE...
TOUCH-DOWN!!
GAWD BLESS AMERICA!!
DUMP
STOP

YA KNOW... THE CBS TELEVISION NETWORK DESERVES ALL THE FLACK IT GETS.. NOT ONLY FOR WHAT WAS SHOWN DURING ITS 2004 SUPERBOWL BROADCAST...

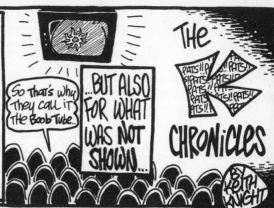

So that's why they call it The Boob Tube..

...BUT ALSO FOR WHAT WAS NOT SHOWN...

THE

CHRONICLES

BY KEITH KNIGHT

FIRST OFF.. THE SPINELESS MORONS WOULDN'T AIR A MOVEON.ORG AD CRITICIZING BUSH'S TRILLION DOLLAR DEFICIT, DURING A COMMERCIAL BREAK..

We don't air controversial ads...
← Their excuse

CBS RAN ADS FEATURING SERIAL KILLERS & NUDISTS THE LAST TIME THEY BROADCAST THE BIG GAME IN 2001..

REMEMBER: THESE ARE THE CLOWNS THAT WERE TOO CHICKEN TO AIR A T.V. MOVIE THAT WAS MILDLY CRITICAL OF EX-U.S. PREZ RONALD REAGAN...

SECONDLY.. AFTER ENDING THE SANCTIONED HALFTIME BLOAT WITH JANET JACKSON'S EXPOSED MAMMARY, CBS REFUSED TO AIR THE MOST AMUSING PART OF THE MID-GAME SPECTACLE:

JUST BEFORE THE 2ND HALF KICKOFF, A "REFEREE" TORE OFF HIS UNIFORM & BEGAN RIVERDANCING IN THE MIDDLE OF THE STADIUM...

IT WAS MARK ROBERTS, AN INFAMOUS BRITISH STREAKER.. CHECK OUT PIX AT: www.THESTREAKER.ORG.UK

CBS.. YOU COWARDLY LITTLE JELLYFISH OF A NETWORK.. IF I WASN'T ON A 7 DAY BINGE OF BOOZE & EPHEDRA, CELEBRATING ANOTHER NEW ENGLAND PATS WIN, I'D ORGANIZE A BOYCOTT...

117

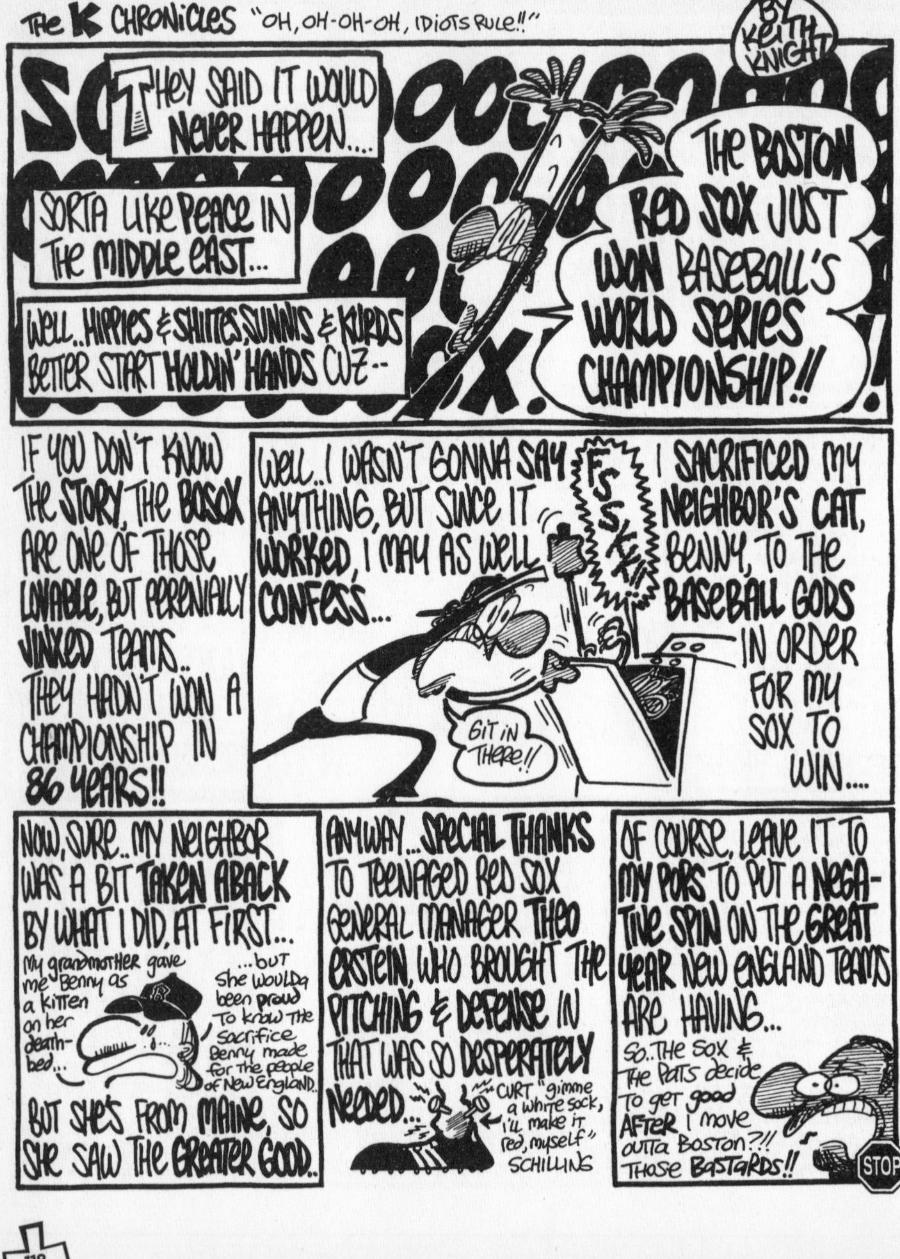
The K Chronicles "Oh, oh-oh-oh, idiots rule!!"
By Keith Knight
They said it would never happen....
Sorta like peace in the middle east...
Well.. hippies & Shiites, Sunnis & Kurds better start holdin' hands cuz--
The Boston Red Sox just won baseball's World Series Championship!!
If you don't know the story, the BoSox are one of those lovable, but perenially jinxed teams.. They hadn't won a championship in 86 years!!
Well.. I wasn't gonna say anything, but since it worked, I may as well confess...
FSSKK!!
I sacrificed my neighbor's cat, Benny, to the baseball gods in order for my Sox to win....
Git in there!!
Now, sure.. my neighbor was a bit taken aback by what I did, at first...
My grandmother gave me Benny as a kitten on her death-bed...
...but she woulda been proud to know the sacrifice Benny made for the people of New England..
But she's from Maine, so she saw the greater good..
Anyway... special thanks to teenaged Red Sox general manager Theo Epstein, who brought the pitching & defense in that was so desperately needed...
Curt "gimme a white sock, i'll make it red, myself" Schilling
Of course, leave it to my pops to put a nega-tive spin on the great year New England teams are having...
So.. the Sox & the Pats decide to get good after I move outta Boston?!! Those bastards!!
STOP

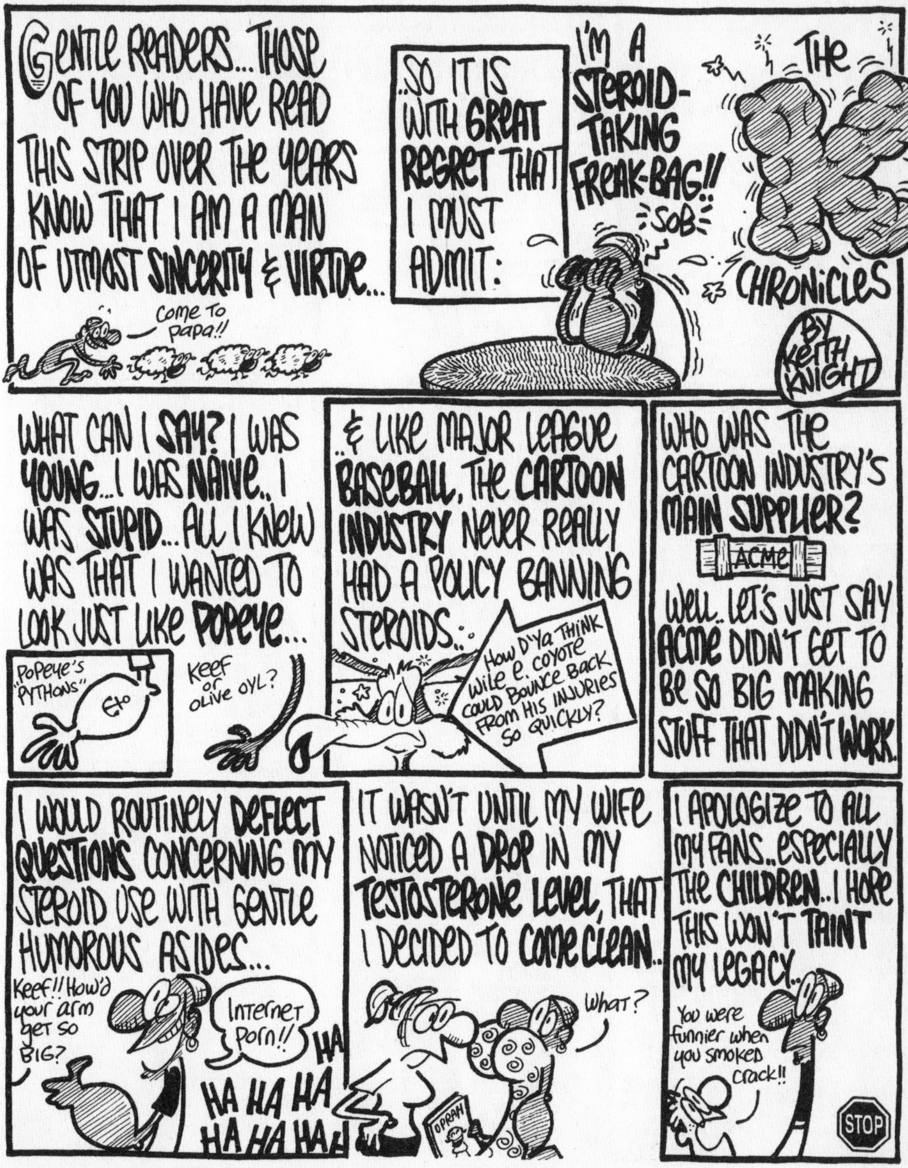
Gentle readers... those of you who have read this strip over the years know that I am a man of utmost sincerity & virtue...
Come to papa!!
...So it is with great regret that I must admit:
I'm a steroid-taking freak-bag!!
SOB
The K Chronicles
By Keith Knight
What can I say? I was young... I was naive... I was stupid... All I knew was that I wanted to look just like Popeye...
"Popeye's Pythons"
Keef or Olive Oyl?
...& like Major League Baseball, the cartoon industry never really had a policy banning steroids...
How d'ya think Wile E. Coyote could bounce back from his injuries so quickly?
Who was the cartoon industry's main supplier?
ACME
Well.. let's just say Acme didn't get to be so big making stuff that didn't work.
I would routinely deflect questions concerning my steroid use with gentle humorous asides...
Keef!! How'd your arm get so big?
Internet porn!!
HA HA HA HA HA HA HA HA
It wasn't until my wife noticed a drop in my testosterone level, that I decided to come clean...
What?
OPRAH
I apologize to all my fans.. especially the children.. I hope this won't taint my legacy...
You were funnier when you smoked crack!!
STOP

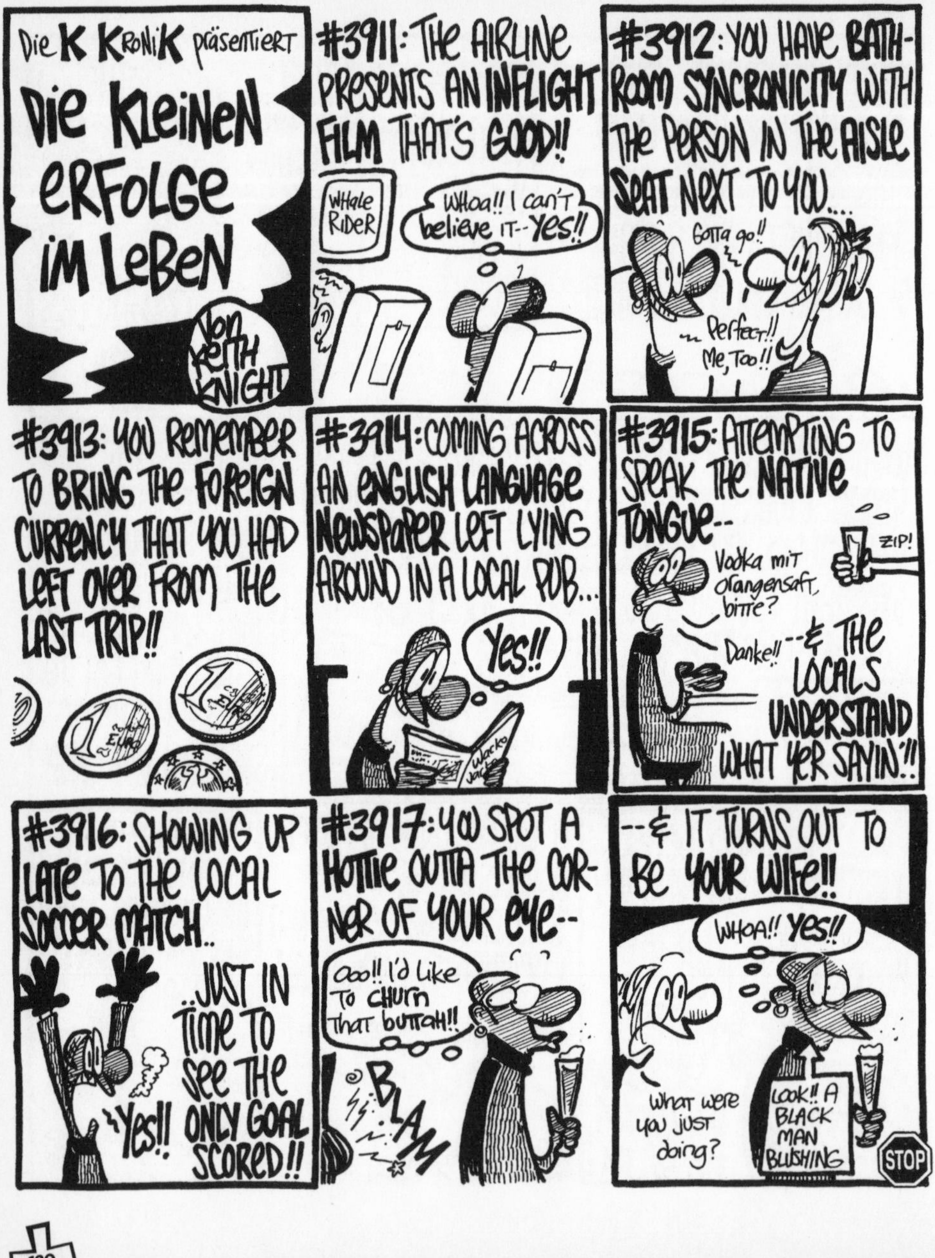

Die K Kronik präsentiert
Die Kleinen Erfolge im Leben
von Keith Knight
#3911: The airline presents an inflight film that's good!!
Whale Rider
Whoa!! I can't believe it--Yes!!
#3912: You have bathroom syncronicity with the person in the aisle seat next to you...
Gotta go!!
Perfect!! Me, Too!!
#3913: You remember to bring the foreign currency that you had left over from the last trip!!
1 Euro
#3914: Coming across an English language newspaper left lying around in a local pub...
Yes!!
#3915: Attempting to speak the native tongue--
Vodka mit Orangensaft, bitte?
Zip!
Danke!!
--& the locals understand what yer sayin'!!
#3916: Showing up late to the local soccer match..
..just in time to see the only goal scored!!
Yes!!
#3917: You spot a hottie outta the corner of your eye--
Ooo!! I'd like to churn that buttah!!
Blam
--& it turns out to be your wife!!
Whoa!! Yes!!
What were you just doing?
Look!! A black man blushing
Stop

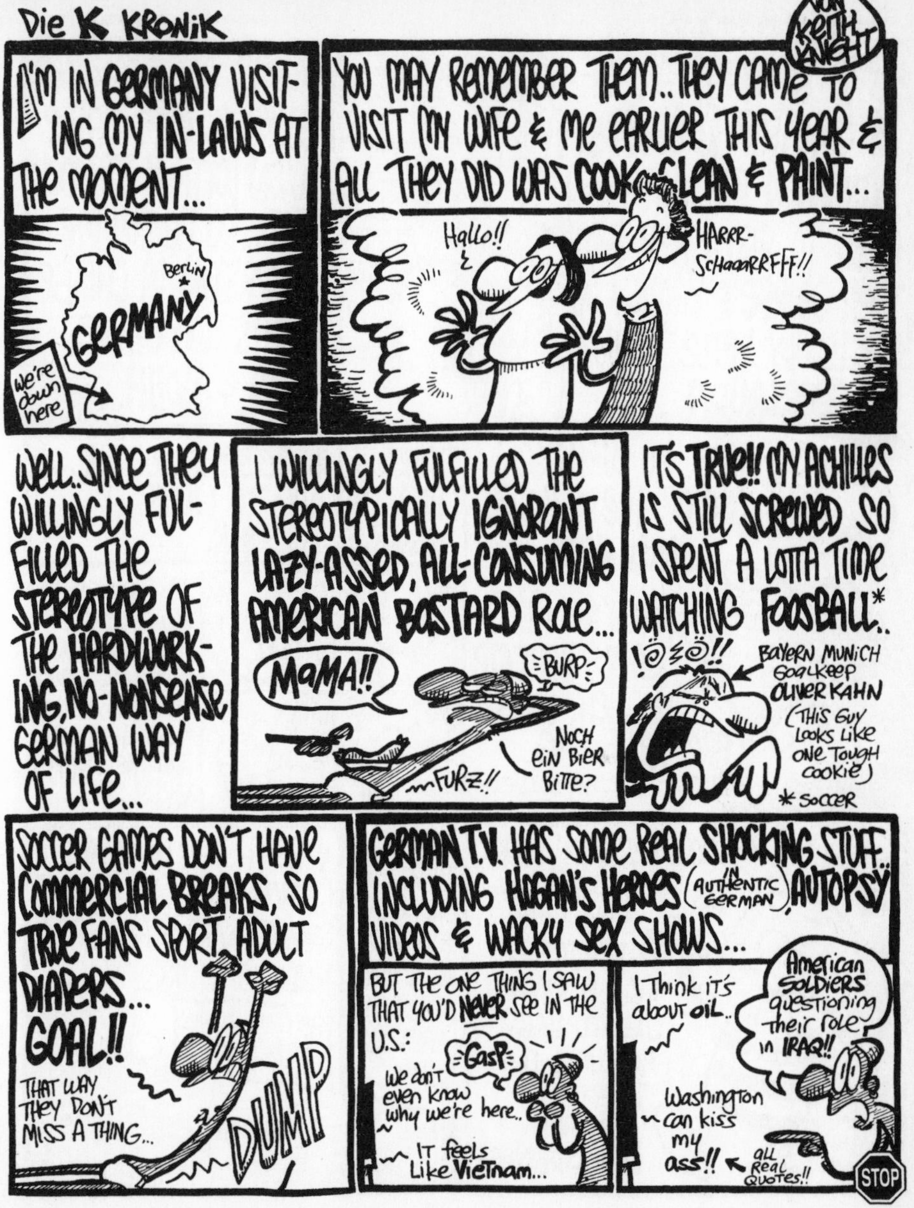

Die K KRONIK
VON KEITH KNIGHT
I'M IN GERMANY VISITING MY IN-LAWS AT THE MOMENT...
BERLIN
GERMANY
We're down here
YOU MAY REMEMBER THEM.. THEY CAME TO VISIT MY WIFE & ME EARLIER THIS YEAR & ALL THEY DID WAS COOK, CLEAN & PAINT...
Hallo!!
HARRR-SCHAAARRFFF!!
WELL.. SINCE THEY WILLINGLY FULFILLED THE STEREOTYPE OF THE HARDWORKING, NO-NONSENSE GERMAN WAY OF LIFE...
I WILLINGLY FULFILLED THE STEREOTYPICALLY IGNORANT LAZY-ASSED, ALL-CONSUMING AMERICAN BASTARD ROLE...
MaMA!!
BURP
NOCH EIN BIER BITTE?
FURZ!!
IT'S TRUE!! MY ACHILLES IS STILL SCREWED SO I SPENT A LOTTA TIME WATCHING FOOSBALL*..
BAYERN MUNICH GOALKEEP OLIVER KAHN
(THIS GUY LOOKS LIKE ONE TOUGH COOKIE)
* SOCCER
SOCCER GAMES DON'T HAVE COMMERCIAL BREAKS, SO TRUE FANS SPORT ADULT DIAPERS...
GOAL!!
THAT WAY THEY DON'T MISS A THING...
DUMP
GERMAN T.V. HAS SOME REAL SHOCKING STUFF.. INCLUDING HOGAN'S HEROES (IN AUTHENTIC GERMAN), AUTOPSY VIDEOS & WACKY SEX SHOWS...
BUT THE ONE THING I SAW THAT YOU'D NEVER SEE IN THE U.S.:
GASP
We don't even know why we're here..
IT feels Like VIETNAM...
I Think it's about OIL..
American SOLDIERS questioning their role in IRAQ!!
Washington can kiss my ass!!
ALL REAL QUOTES!!
STOP

The K Chronicles

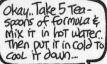
BY KEITH KNIGHT

The TOUGHEST PART OF OUR TRIP TO GERMANY WAS WHEN THE WIFEY & I WENT TO VISIT HER BROTHER GEORGE'S FAMILY IN THE LOVELY LITTLE TOWN OF OBERLAUDA...

Okay.. Take 5 Teaspoons of formula & mix it in hot water. Then put it in cold to cool it down....

OK...5 cold spoons in Hot Tea but no water.

..TURNS OUT GEORGE'S WIFE CAME DOWN WITH A STOMACH VIRUS..SO HE PUT ME & KERSTIN IN CHARGE OF HIS TWO BABIES, FINN & NOAH...

BURP

HAVE YOU EVER SEEN ONE OF THESE BABIES CLOSE-UP?

THEY'RE ALL SOFT & DELICATE & THEIR EYES ARE REAL BIG...

(IT GIVES ME THE WILLIES!!)

PFFT

ANYHOO.. I WAS TERRIFIED OF THE LITTLE TINY ONE SO I WAS ASSIGNED TO FINN...

① ② POP ③ ④ BLEAH

...& THROUGH PAINSTAKINGLY CAREFUL & THOROUGH ANALYSIS, I CAME TO THE CONCLUSION THAT HE HAD THE STOMACH VIRUS, TOO...

gbbLFFT!!

*"Please give me a Hug" in German

NOW I ASK YOU, FOLKS.. IS THERE ANYTHING MORE BEAUTIFUL THAN A VOMIT-COVERED BABY REACHING OUT TO YOU FOR LOVE AND UNDERSTANDING?

We WERE THERE FOR ONLY A DAY & A HALF... BUT I SWEAR I AGED AT LEAST 20 years....

& AS A SIGN OF APPRECIATION, LITTLE FINN GAVE US SOMETHING TO TAKE BACK HOME WITH US....

HE GAVE US HIS STOMACH VIRUS

STOP

122

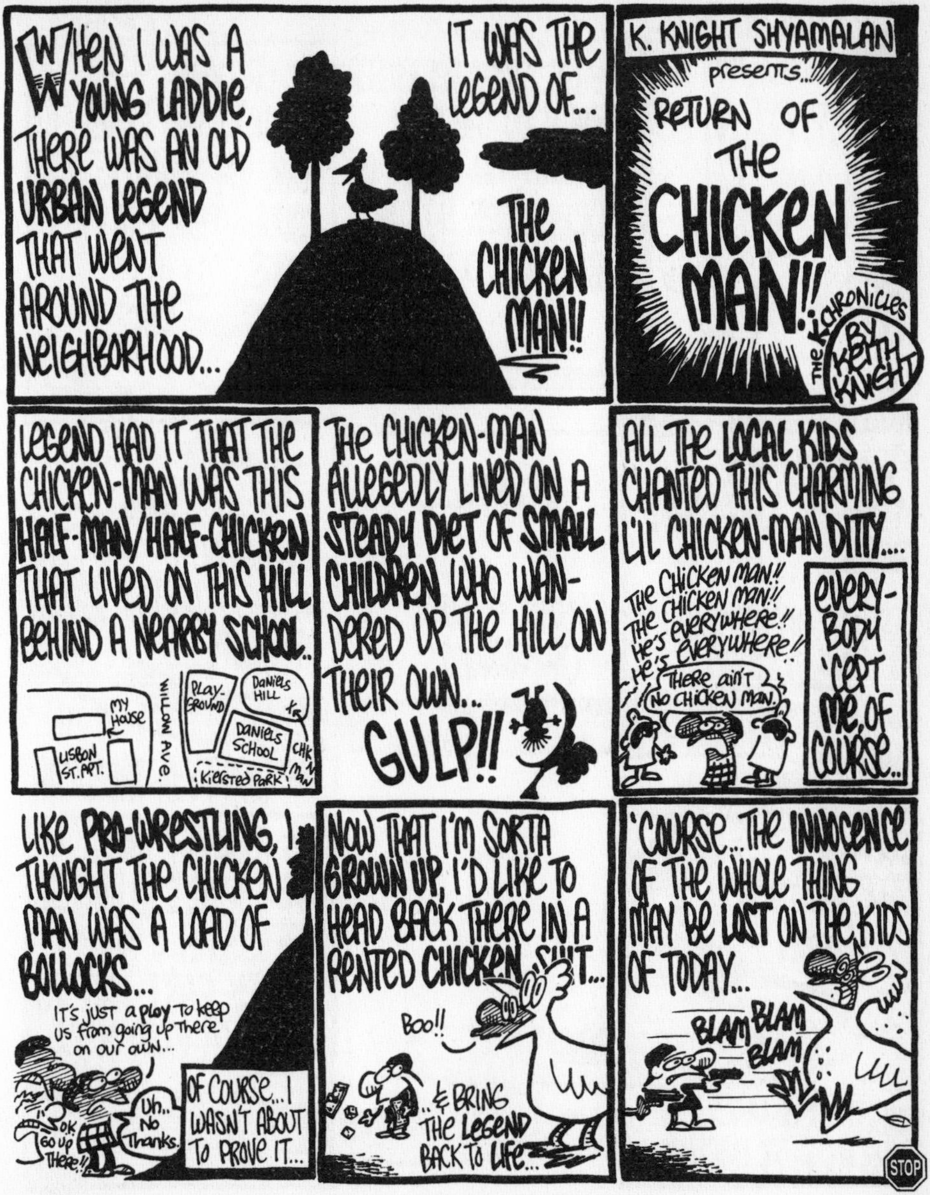
When I was a young laddie, there was an old urban legend that went around the neighborhood...
It was the legend of...
The Chicken Man!!
K. Knight Shyamalan
presents...
Return of the Chicken Man!!
The K Chronicles
By Keith Knight
Legend had it that the Chicken-Man was this half-man/half-chicken that lived on this hill behind a nearby school..
My House
Lisbon St. Apt.
Willow Ave.
Play-ground
Daniels Hill
Daniels School
Kiersted Park
CHK Man
The Chicken-Man allegedly lived on a steady diet of small children who wandered up the hill on their own...
GULP!!
All the local kids chanted this charming li'l Chicken-Man ditty....
The Chicken Man!! The Chicken Man!! He's everywhere!! He's everywhere!!
There ain't no Chicken Man.
Every-body 'cept me, of course...
Like pro-wrestling, I thought the Chicken Man was a load of bollocks...
It's just a ploy to keep us from going up there on our own...
O.K. Go up there!!
Uh... No Thanks.
Of course... I wasn't about to prove it...
Now that I'm sorta grown up, I'd like to head back there in a rented chicken suit...
Boo!!
...& bring the legend back to life...
'Course... the innocence of the whole thing may be lost on the kids of today...
BLAM BLAM BLAM
STOP

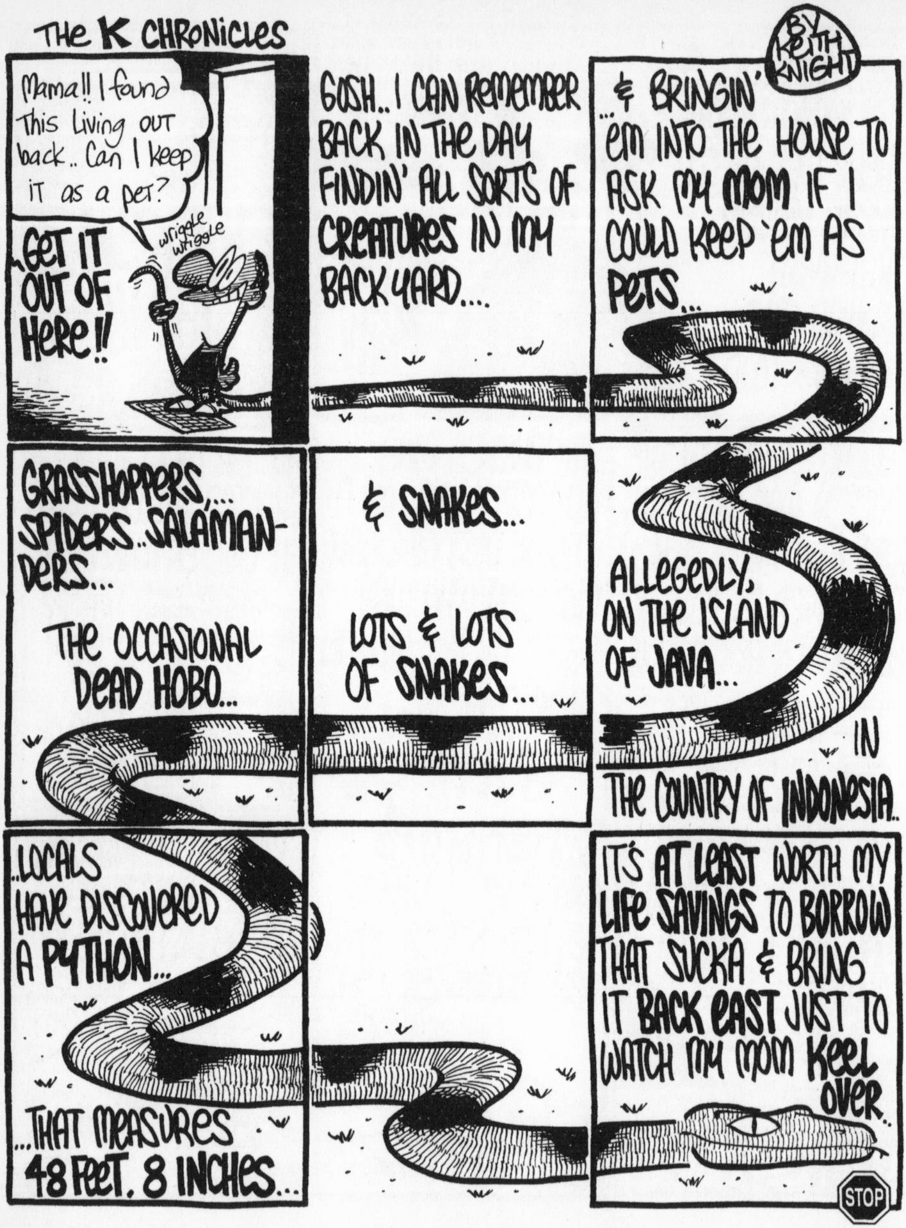

THE K CHRONICLES
BY KEITH KNIGHT
Mama!! I found This Living out back.. Can I keep it as a pet?
wriggle wriggle
..GET IT OUT OF HERE!!
GOSH.. I CAN REMEMBER BACK IN THE DAY FINDIN' ALL SORTS OF CREATURES IN MY BACKYARD....
...& BRINGIN' 'EM INTO THE HOUSE TO ASK MY MOM IF I COULD KEEP 'EM AS PETS...
GRASSHOPPERS,... SPIDERS.. SALAMANDERS...
THE OCCASIONAL DEAD HOBO...
& SNAKES...
LOTS & LOTS OF SNAKES...
ALLEGEDLY, ON THE ISLAND OF JAVA...
IN THE COUNTRY OF INDONESIA..
..LOCALS HAVE DISCOVERED A PYTHON...
...THAT MEASURES 48 FEET, 8 INCHES...
IT'S AT LEAST WORTH MY LIFE SAVINGS TO BORROW THAT SUCKA & BRING IT BACK EAST JUST TO WATCH MY MOM KEEL OVER..
STOP

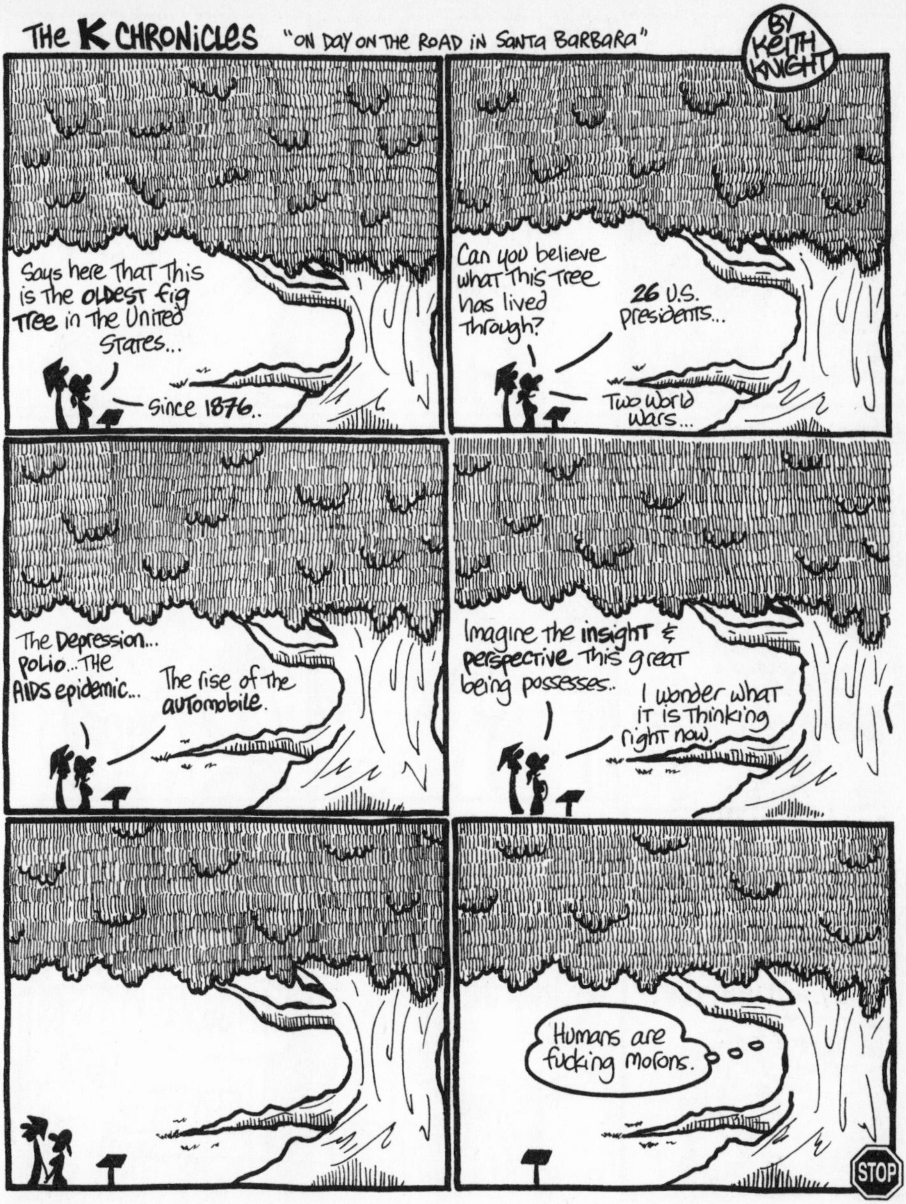
The K Chronicles
"On Day on the Road in Santa Barbara"
By Keith Knight
Says here that this is the oldest fig tree in the United States...
Since 1876..
Can you believe what this tree has lived through?
26 U.S. presidents...
Two World Wars...
The Depression... polio... the AIDS epidemic...
The rise of the automobile.
Imagine the insight & perspective this great being possesses..
I wonder what it is thinking right now.
Humans are fucking morons.
STOP

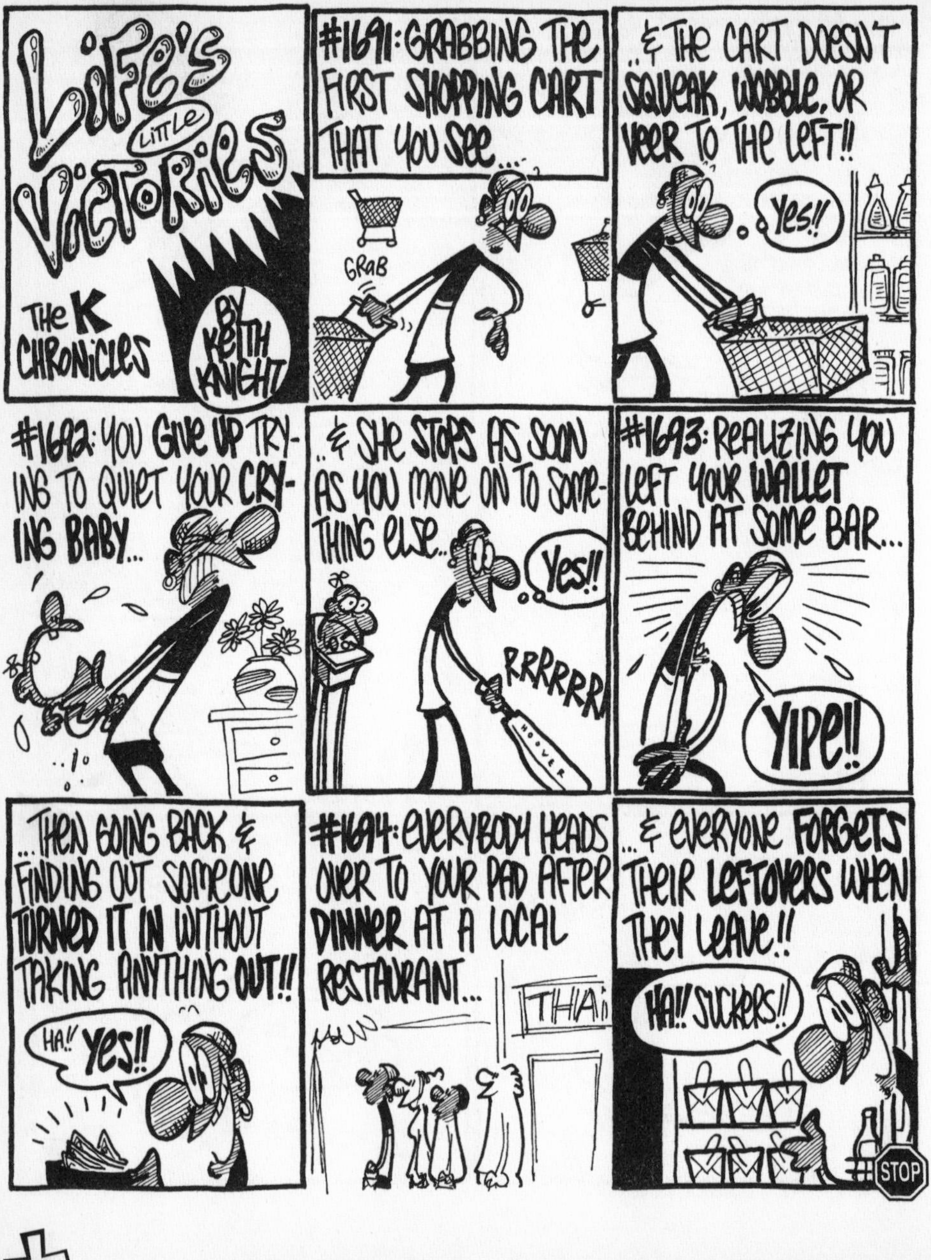
Life's Little Victories
The K Chronicles
By Keith Knight
#1691: Grabbing the first shopping cart that you see...
GRAB
...& the cart doesn't squeak, wobble, or veer to the left!!
Yes!!
#1692: You give up trying to quiet your crying baby...
...& she stops as soon as you move on to something else...
Yes!!
RRRRRRR
HOOVER
#1693: Realizing you left your wallet behind at some bar...
YIPE!!
...then going back & finding out someone turned it in without taking anything out!!
HA!! YES!!
#1694: Everybody heads over to your pad after dinner at a local restaurant...
THAI
...& everyone forgets their leftovers when they leave!!
HA!! SUCKERS!!
STOP

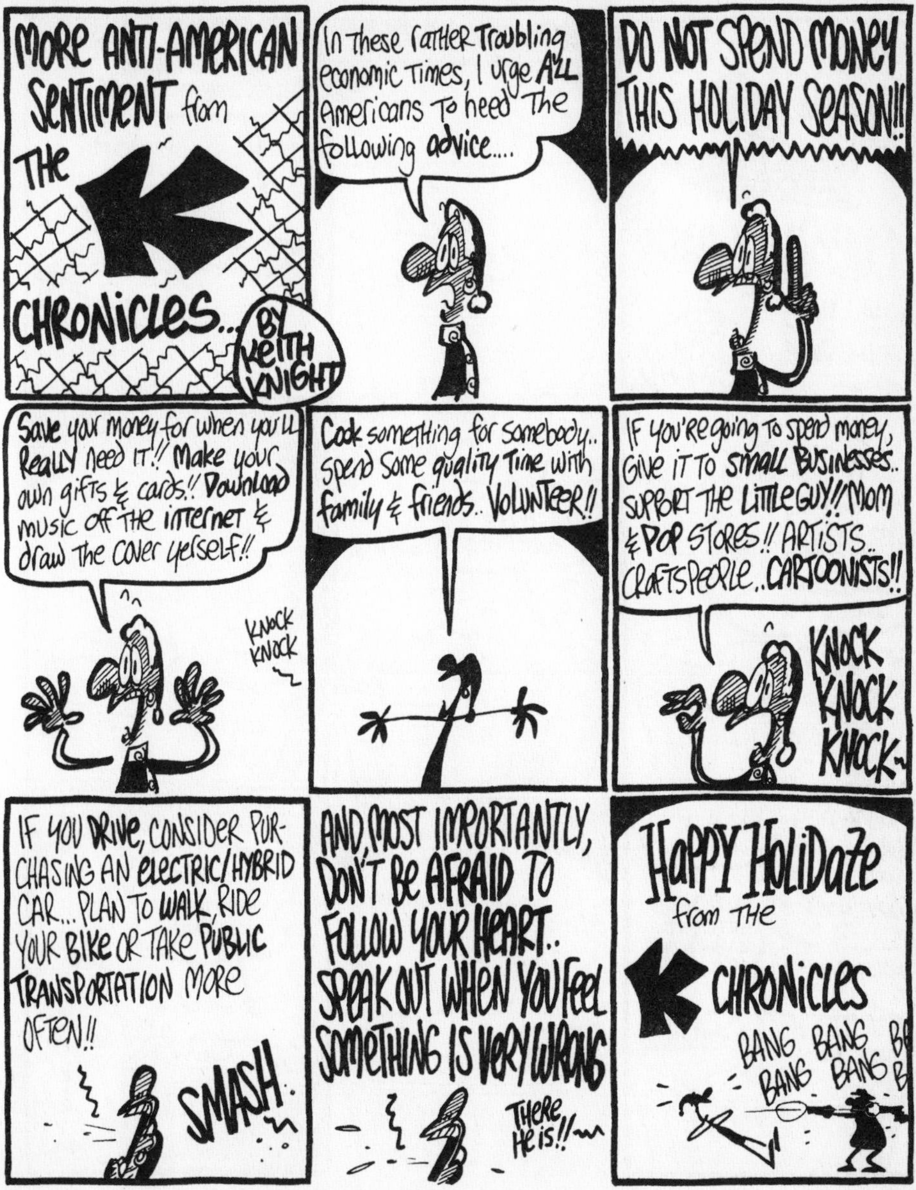

MORE ANTI-AMERICAN SENTIMENT from THE **K** CHRONICLES...

BY KEITH KNIGHT

In these rather troubling economic times, I urge ALL Americans to heed the following advice....

DO NOT SPEND MONEY THIS HOLIDAY SEASON!!

Save your money for when you'll REALLY need it!! Make your own gifts & cards!! Download music off the internet & draw the cover yerself!!

KNOCK KNOCK

Cook something for somebody.. spend some quality time with family & friends.. VOLUNTEER!!

IF you're going to spend money, give it to small businesses.. support the LITTLE GUY!! MOM & POP STORES!! ARTISTS.. CRAFTSPEOPLE.. CARTOONISTS!!

KNOCK KNOCK KNOCK~

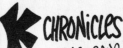

IF YOU DRIVE, CONSIDER PURCHASING AN ELECTRIC/HYBRID CAR... PLAN TO WALK, RIDE YOUR BIKE OR TAKE PUBLIC TRANSPORTATION MORE OFTEN!!

SMASH!

AND, MOST IMPORTANTLY, DON'T BE AFRAID TO FOLLOW YOUR HEART.. SPEAK OUT WHEN YOU FEEL SOMETHING IS VERY WRONG

THERE HE IS!!

HAPPY HOLIDAZE from THE **K** CHRONICLES

BANG BANG BANG BANG B

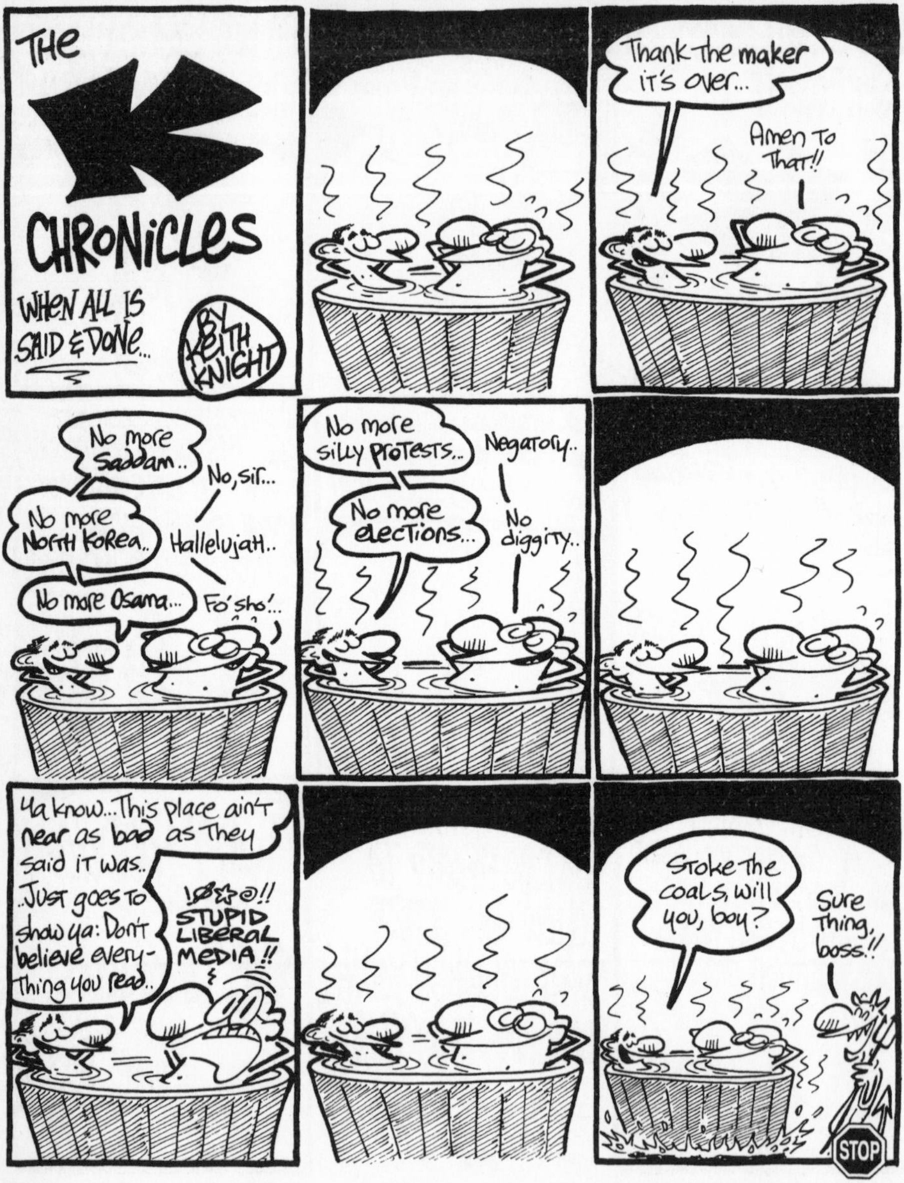
THE K CHRONICLES
WHEN ALL IS SAID & DONE...
BY KEITH KNIGHT
Thank the maker it's over...
Amen To That!!
No more Saddam..
No, sir...
No more North Korea..
Hallelujah..
No more Osama...
Fo'sho'!...
No more silly protests...
Negatory..
No more elections...
No diggity..
Ya know...This place ain't near as bad as They said it was.. ..Just goes to show ya: Don't believe every-thing you read..
STUPID LIBERAL MEDIA!!
Stoke the coals, will you, boy?
Sure Thing, boss!!
STOP